ACT PREI

GUIDE

2025-2026

Full Length Test & Detailed Answer with Explanation

Ethan S. Grey

Copyright Notice

Disclaimer

This study guide is intended to provide general information and practice questions for the ACT test. It is not affiliated with or endorsed by ACT, Inc. The information and strategies provided in this guide are based on the author's understanding of the ACT test and may not reflect the official policies or practices of ACT, Inc. The practice questions included in this guide are not actual ACT test questions and may not accurately reflect the difficulty or format of the actual test.

The author and publisher make no representations or warranties of any kind, express or implied, about the completeness, accuracy, reliability, suitability, or availability with respect to the information and practice questions contained in this guide for any purpose. Any reliance you place on such information is therefore strictly at your own risk.

The author and publisher shall not be liable for any loss or damage, including without limitation, indirect or consequential loss or damage, or any loss or damage whatsoever arising from loss of data or profits arising out of, or in connection with, the use of this study guide.

This study guide is intended for informational and educational purposes only. It is not a substitute for professional test preparation or guidance. The author and publisher recommend that you consult with a qualified ACT test preparation professional for personalized advice and support.

TABLE OF CONTENTS

Introduction: Embarking on Your Path to ACT Success

Congratulations are in order! By choosing to engage with this study guide, you've taken a proactive and commendable step toward shaping your academic future. The ACT exam, while a daunting prospect for many, represents a pivotal juncture in your journey towards higher education. This guide is meticulously crafted to serve as your steadfast companion, providing support and guidance as you navigate the intricacies of this standardized test.

It's not uncommon for students to approach the ACT with a mix of apprehension and uncertainty. The weight of expectations, the pressure to perform, and the inherent anxieties associated with standardized testing can easily create a sense of unease. However, it's crucial to reframe this perspective. The ACT, rather than an insurmountable hurdle, should be viewed as an opportunity – an opportunity to showcase your academic prowess, to demonstrate your intellectual growth, and to unlock the doors to your dream college.

This study guide is not merely a compilation of practice questions and dry explanations. It is intentionally designed to be a source of empowerment, a tool to transform anxiety into confidence, and a comprehensive resource to equip you with the strategies necessary for ACT success. It aims to demystify the exam by breaking it down into manageable components, clarifying its format and content, and offering ample opportunities for targeted practice and skill refinement.

Consider this guide your mentor, your cheerleader, and your constant source of motivation throughout this journey. It serves as a reminder of your capabilities, your preparedness, and your inherent potential to achieve your ACT goals. With dedication, perseverance, and the unwavering belief in your abilities, you can conquer this challenge and pave the way for a bright academic future.

Understanding the ACT: A Comprehensive Overview

The ACT exam transcends the notion of a mere test; it's a comprehensive assessment of your academic potential, a snapshot of the cumulative knowledge and skills you've honed throughout your high school career. Designed to gauge your readiness for the rigors of college-level coursework, the ACT is a crucial component of the admissions process for most colleges and universities across the United States.

However, unlike traditional classroom exams that often emphasize rote memorization and recall, the ACT focuses on evaluating your higher-order thinking skills. It challenges you to engage in critical thinking, problem-solving, and the application of knowledge in novel and complex scenarios. This distinction underscores the importance of approaching ACT preparation with a focus on conceptual understanding and analytical reasoning rather than simply memorizing facts and figures.

The ACT comprises four distinct sections, each consisting of multiple-choice questions: English, Math, Reading, and Science. Each section is meticulously crafted to assess specific skills and knowledge areas, and your performance in each contributes to your overall composite score, providing a holistic view of your academic strengths.

English: This section delves into your grasp of the English language, evaluating your understanding of grammar, punctuation, sentence structure, and rhetorical skills. It goes beyond mere knowledge of grammatical rules, requiring you to demonstrate the ability to use language effectively and strategically to convey ideas with clarity, precision, and impact.

Math: Encompassing a broad spectrum of mathematical concepts, from foundational pre-algebra to advanced trigonometry, this section assesses your mathematical reasoning and problem-solving abilities. It challenges you to apply your mathematical knowledge to solve real-world problems, analyze data, and interpret quantitative information.

Reading: This section gauges your reading comprehension and analytical skills by presenting you with diverse passages drawn from various genres, including prose fiction, social science, humanities, and natural science. It requires you to not only understand the literal meaning of the text but also to delve deeper, interpreting the author's message, identifying key ideas, making inferences, and evaluating the effectiveness of the author's arguments.

Science: This section focuses on your ability to interpret, analyze, and evaluate scientific data presented in various formats, such as charts, graphs, and research summaries. It emphasizes your understanding of scientific methods, your ability to draw conclusions from data, and your capacity to evaluate evidence and identify potential sources of bias or error.

In addition to these four core sections, the ACT offers an optional Writing section. This component provides you with the opportunity to demonstrate your writing proficiency by crafting a well-organized and persuasive essay in response to a given prompt. While not mandatory for all colleges, the Writing section can serve as valuable evidence of your critical thinking, analytical reasoning, and communication skills, potentially enhancing your application profile.

- English, 45 minutes, 75 questions—test of grammar, usage, and rhetorical skills

- Math, 60 minutes, 60 questions—test of problem-solving skills in algebra, geometry, and trigonometry

- Reading, 35 minutes, 40 questions—test of reading comprehension skills

- Science, 35 minutes, 40 questions—test of scientific analytical and reasoning skills

- Writing, 40 minutes, 1 essay question (This section is optional.)

There is a 10-minute break between the Math and Reading sections, and a 5-minute break between the Science and Writing sections.

Should I Take the Writing Test?

If you don't know where you are planning to apply to school, go ahead and take the Writing Test so you can keep your options open. If you know where you will be applying to school, check out their writing test requirements by calling the admissions office or checking the admissions website.

How Is It Scored?

There is NO GUESSING PENALTY on the ACT, so be certain that you do not leave any answer blank! The ACT is scored on a curved scale from 1–36, with 1 being terrible and 36 perfect. The average test taker scores around 21–22. Each of the four required sections—English, Math, Reading, and Science—is scored from 1–36. The ACT adjusts the curve with each test to ensure that the results from one test indicate the same level of ability as the results from another. The overall composite score is found by taking a simple average of the four section scores and is rounded up if applicable. For example, if you scored a 22 on the English, a 22 on the Math, a 23 on the Reading, and a 23 on the Science, your score would come out to a 22.5 average, rounding up to a 23 composite. The ACT Writing section is reported separately on the score report, but it does not affect the overall composite score.

What Should I Take with Me to the Test?

Your ACT Registration ticket has a printout of what you are permitted to have. Some things to be sure you don't forget follow:

■ Your photo identification (the ACT has much more rigorous security procedures than in years past.)

■ Your registration ticket

■ Plenty of number 2 pencils (they are not allowed to be mechanical)

■ A permitted calculator that has fresh batteries

■ A snack to have during the break

■ A watch that doesn't make any noise and can not be connected to the Internet

■ Do NOT bring your cell phone or any other wireless device. If it rings during the test or if you are caught using it at any point, even during breaks, you may be disqualified from testing.

What Else Can I Do Besides Test Prep to Prepare for the ACT?

Since the ACT is a test of your overall academic skill development, most everything you are doing in your coursework in school will directly or indirectly help improve your ACT performance capacity over the long term. Here are some specific things beyond using this book that you can use to improve the skills on which you will be evaluated:

■ READ, READ, READ! The ACT is very much a literacy test. Students who read frequently find it much easier to read at the speed and with the comprehension necessary to do well on the Reading section, as well as the other test sections.

■ TAKE RIGOROUS COURSES. Even though taking the easy course where you will get the easy "A" is very appealing, you will ultimately be grateful that you pushed yourself with more challenging classes when it comes time to take the ACT.

■ HAVE FUN WHILE BUILDING YOUR WRITING SKILLS. Start your own blog, leave comments on websites, email your friends. The more comfortable you are with expressing yourself, the better you will be at the ACT Writing and the ACT English.

A thorough understanding of the ACT's structure, content, and scoring methodology is paramount to achieving success. By familiarizing yourself with the test's format, question types, and expectations, you'll be better equipped to approach each section strategically, manage your time effectively, and ultimately, maximize your score.

Developing a Study Plan: A Roadmap to Success

A well-structured study plan is akin to a roadmap guiding you through the terrain of ACT preparation. It's more than just allocating time for studying; it's about crafting a personalized strategy that aligns with your individual learning style, strengths, weaknesses, and aspirations. A thoughtfully designed study plan will not only enhance your understanding of the content but also foster effective time management skills, reduce test anxiety, and boost your overall confidence.

Here's a breakdown of key steps involved in developing an effective ACT study plan:

1. **Assess Your Current Skills:** Begin by taking a diagnostic ACT practice test. This will provide valuable insights into your current performance level, highlighting your areas of strength and those requiring further attention. Analyzing your performance on the diagnostic test will allow you to tailor your study plan to address your specific needs and prioritize your efforts effectively.

2. **Set Realistic Goals:** Define your target ACT score based on the admission requirements of the colleges you aspire to attend. Setting realistic and achievable goals will serve as a powerful motivator, providing a clear sense of direction and purpose throughout your preparation journey.

3. **Create a Schedule:** Develop a structured study schedule that allocates dedicated time for each subject area, ensuring comprehensive coverage of the ACT content. Maintain a balance between focused study sessions and regular practice. Be adaptable and adjust your schedule as needed to accommodate other commitments and maintain a healthy work-life balance.

4. **Gather Your Resources:** Assemble a diverse range of study materials, including this comprehensive study guide, official ACT practice tests, online resources, and supplementary textbooks. Consider seeking guidance from experienced educators or tutors if you require personalized support. Choose resources that resonate with your learning preferences and cater to your individual needs.

5. **Practice Consistently:** Consistent and deliberate practice is the cornerstone of ACT success. Aim to complete at least one full-length practice test per week to simulate the actual testing environment and build your stamina. Thoroughly review your performance on each practice test, analyzing your mistakes to identify areas for improvement and reinforce your understanding of key concepts.

6. **Stay Motivated:** Maintaining motivation throughout your ACT preparation journey is essential. Celebrate your progress, acknowledge your achievements, and reward yourself for your hard work. Seek support from friends, family, or mentors when you encounter challenges or experience setbacks. Remember, the path to success is often paved with perseverance and resilience.

Your study plan should be a dynamic and evolving document, adapting to your progress and changing needs. As you delve deeper into your preparation, you'll gain a clearer understanding of your strengths and weaknesses, allowing you to refine your study plan accordingly. Embrace flexibility, adjust your strategies as needed, and don't hesitate to seek assistance when faced with challenges.

Maximizing Your Score: Strategies for ACT Success

Achieving your optimal ACT score requires more than just content mastery; it necessitates the development of effective test-taking strategies that empower you to navigate the exam with confidence, efficiency, and precision. These strategies are crucial for optimizing your performance, managing your time effectively, and minimizing test anxiety.

Here are some key strategies to help you maximize your ACT score:

- **Understand the Questions:** Before delving into the answer choices, take the time to carefully read and comprehend the question stem. Identify the key information, the specific task, and the underlying concepts being assessed. This deliberate approach will help you avoid misinterpreting the question and making careless errors.

- **Use Your Time Wisely:** Time management is critical on the ACT, as each section has a strict time limit. Develop a pacing strategy that allows you to allocate your time efficiently across all questions. Don't dwell excessively on challenging questions; mark them for review and return to them later if time permits.

- **Eliminate Wrong Answers:** If you encounter a question where the correct answer isn't immediately apparent, employ the process of elimination to narrow down your options. Identify and eliminate answer choices that are clearly incorrect or illogical. This strategy increases your chances of selecting the correct answer even when faced with uncertainty.

- **Guess Strategically:** The ACT does not penalize incorrect answers, so it's in your best interest to answer every question, even if it requires an educated guess. If you're unsure of the correct answer, use your knowledge and reasoning to eliminate unlikely options and make an informed guess.

- **Stay Focused and Calm:** Test anxiety can significantly impede your performance, hindering your ability to think clearly and recall information. Practice relaxation techniques, such as deep breathing exercises and mindfulness meditation, to manage stress and maintain composure during the exam.

- **Review Your Mistakes:** After completing a practice test, dedicate time to thoroughly analyze your errors. Understand the reasoning behind each incorrect answer, identify patterns in your mistakes, and reinforce your understanding of the underlying concepts. This reflective practice will help you avoid repeating similar errors on the actual exam.

Maximizing your ACT score is not solely dependent on innate ability; it's a culmination of diligent preparation, strategic planning, and a positive mindset. By combining your knowledge with effective test-taking techniques, you can unlock your full potential, achieve your desired score, and confidently embark on your academic pursuits.

Chapter 1: English

1. Grammar and Usage

The ACT English section is designed to assess your understanding and application of the rules of standard written English. This subchapter offers a comprehensive exploration of the key concepts, including grammar and usage, punctuation, sentence structure, and rhetorical skills. By understanding these fundamental aspects of language, you can significantly enhance your performance on the ACT English test.

1. Grammar and Usage

1.1 Sentence Basics

At the heart of effective writing lies the ability to construct grammatically sound sentences. A sentence is a group of words that expresses a complete thought. It typically consists of a subject (a noun or pronoun that performs the action) and a predicate (a verb or verb phrase that describes the action or state of being). For instance, in the sentence "The cat sat on the mat," the subject is "cat" and the predicate is "sat on the mat."

A sentence fragment, on the other hand, is an incomplete sentence that lacks a subject, a verb, or a complete thought. For example, "Walking down the street" is a fragment because it lacks a subject. Similarly, "The dog with the wagging tail" is a fragment because it lacks a verb. To correct a fragment, you need to add the missing element or join it to an independent clause to form a complete sentence.

1.2 Number Agreement

Number agreement refers to the grammatical rule that singular subjects must be paired with singular verbs, and plural subjects must be paired with plural verbs. For example,[2] "The dog barks" is correct because the singular subject "dog" agrees with the singular verb "barks." However, "The dogs barks" is incorrect because the plural subject "dogs" does not agree with the singular verb "barks." The correct form would be "The dogs bark."

Prepositional phrases and collective nouns can sometimes complicate number agreement. A prepositional phrase is a group of words that begins with a preposition (e.g., in, on, at, to, for) and ends with a noun or pronoun. Prepositional phrases can be misleading because they might contain a noun that seems like the subject of the sentence but is not. For example, in the sentence "The box of chocolates is on the table," the prepositional phrase "of chocolates" might seem like the subject, but the actual subject is "box," which is singular. Therefore, the singular verb "is" is correct.

Collective nouns (e.g., team, group, family, committee) refer to a group of individuals but are usually treated as singular nouns. For instance, "The team is playing well" is correct because the collective noun "team" is considered singular. However, if the collective noun refers to the individual members of the group, it can be treated as plural. For example, "The team are arguing about their positions" is correct because the focus is on the individual members of the team.

1.3 Tense

Verbs express actions or states of being in different tenses, indicating when the action occurred. The main tenses include:

- **Past tense:** Used for actions that happened in the past (e.g., walked, ate, slept).

- **Present tense:** Used for actions that are happening now (e.g., walk, eat, sleep).

- **Future tense:** Used for actions that will happen in the future (e.g., will walk, will eat, will   sleep).

- **Past perfect tense:** Used for actions that happened before another past action (e.g., had walked,   had   eaten,   had   slept).

- **Present perfect tense:** Used for actions that started in the past and continue to the present (e.g.,   have   walked,   have   eaten,   have   slept).

- **Future perfect tense:** Used for actions that will be completed before a specific time in the future (e.g., will have walked, will have eaten, will have slept).

Irregular verbs do not follow the standard patterns for forming different tenses. For example, the past tense of "go" is "went," not "goed." Similarly, the past participle of "eat" is "eaten," not "eated." It is essential to be familiar with the irregular verb forms to ensure correct tense usage.

1.4 Parallelism

Parallelism, also known as parallel structure, is the principle of using similar grammatical structures to express related ideas. It enhances clarity, readability, and balance in your writing. For example, "She likes to swim, to hike, and to read" is parallel because all the listed activities are in the same grammatical form (infinitive). However, "She likes to swim, hiking, and reading" is not parallel because the listed activities are in different grammatical forms.

Parallelism is crucial when listing items, comparing or contrasting ideas, or using correlative conjunctions (e.g., either/or, neither/nor, not only/but also). By maintaining parallel structure, you create a sense of rhythm and coherence in your writing.

1.5 Proper Wording

The ACT English section often tests your ability to choose the correct word or phrase in a given context. This includes understanding commonly confused words (e.g., "affect" vs. "effect," "than" vs. "then," "there" vs. "their" vs. "they're") and idiomatic expressions (e.g., "at all costs," "in the long run," "on the other hand").

Commonly confused words are words that sound alike or have similar spellings but have different meanings. For example, "affect" is usually a verb meaning "to influence," while "effect" is usually a noun meaning "result." Similarly, "than" is used for comparisons, while "then" is used for time or sequence.

Idiomatic expressions are phrases that have a figurative meaning different from their literal meaning. For instance, "at all costs" means "regardless of the difficulty or expense," not literally "at any cost." Similarly, "in the long run" means "over a long period," not literally "in a long race."

Choosing the correct word or phrase requires careful attention to the context and an understanding of the nuances of language.

2. Punctuation

Punctuation marks are essential for conveying meaning and ensuring clarity in written communication. They act as signals that guide the reader through the text, indicating pauses, separations, and relationships between different parts of a sentence.

2.1 Commas

Commas are perhaps the most versatile punctuation marks, used in a variety of situations to create pauses and separate different elements within a sentence. Some common uses of commas include:

- **After introductory phrases:** Use a comma after an introductory phrase or clause to separate it from the main clause. For example, "After finishing her homework, she went out to play."

- **Before coordinating conjunctions:** Use a comma before a coordinating conjunction (FANBOYS: for, and, nor, but, or, yet, so) when it joins two independent clauses. For example, "She went to the store, but she forgot her wallet."

- **To set off nonessential information:** Use commas to set off nonessential information, such as appositives (nouns or noun phrases that rename a nearby noun) and nonrestrictive clauses (clauses that provide additional information but are not essential to the meaning of the sentence). For example, "My brother, a doctor, lives in New York."

2.2 Semicolons

Semicolons are used to join two closely related independent clauses without a coordinating conjunction. They indicate a stronger pause than a comma but a weaker pause than a period. For example, "The rain was pouring; we decided to stay indoors."

Semicolons can also be used to separate items in a list when the items themselves contain commas. This helps to avoid confusion and maintain clarity. For example, "The conference was attended by representatives from London, England; Paris, France; and Rome, Italy."

2.3 Colons

Colons are used to introduce lists, explanations, or elaborations after a complete sentence. They create a sense of anticipation, signaling that additional information or details will follow. For example, "The recipe requires three ingredients: flour, sugar, and eggs."

Colons can also be used to introduce quotations or to separate the title and subtitle of a book or article. For instance, "The title of the article is: The Impact of Social Media on Teenagers."

2.4 Dashes

Dashes are used to create a strong interruption or a sudden change in thought within a sentence. They can be used for emphasis or to set off parenthetical information. For example, "The party—a surprise birthday celebration—was a great success."

Dashes can also be used to set off appositives that contain commas or to indicate a summary or conclusion. For instance, "The three main characters—the detective, the victim, and the suspect—were all connected."

3. Sentence Structure

Sentence structure refers to the arrangement of words and phrases within a sentence. It plays a crucial role in conveying meaning and ensuring clarity.

3.1 Fragments

A fragment is an incomplete sentence that lacks a subject, a verb, or a complete thought. Identifying and correcting fragments is crucial for ensuring grammatical accuracy. For example, "Running through the park" is a fragment because it lacks a subject. Similarly, "The book on the shelf" is a fragment because it lacks a verb.

To correct a fragment, you need to add the missing element or join it to an independent clause to form a complete sentence. For instance, "Running through the park, she felt free" is a complete sentence because it has a subject ("she") and a verb ("felt").

3.2 Run-on Sentences

Run-on sentences combine two or more independent clauses without proper punctuation or conjunctions. They can be confusing and difficult to read. For example, "The train was late we missed our connection" is a run-on sentence because it joins two independent clauses without any punctuation or conjunction.

To correct a run-on sentence, you can use several methods:

- **Add a period:** Separate the independent clauses into two separate sentences. For example, "The train was late. We missed our connection."

- **Add a semicolon:** Join the independent clauses with a semicolon. For example, "The train was late; we missed our connection."

- **Add a comma and a coordinating conjunction:** Join the independent clauses with a comma and a coordinating conjunction (FANBOYS). For example, "The train was late, so we missed our connection."

3.3 Word Order

Word order refers to the arrangement of words and phrases within a sentence. It can significantly impact the meaning and clarity of a sentence. For example, "The dog chased the cat" has a different meaning than "The cat chased the dog."

In English, the standard word order is subject-verb-object (SVO). However, there are many variations and exceptions to this rule. It is essential to ensure that the word order is logical and unambiguous to avoid misinterpretations.

3.4 Illogical Comparisons

Illogical comparisons occur when the elements being compared are not logically or grammatically parallel. For example, "Her dress was more beautiful than her sister" is an illogical comparison because it compares a dress to a person. The correct comparison would be "Her dress was more beautiful than her sister's dress" or "Her dress was more beautiful than the dress her sister wore."

To avoid illogical comparisons, ensure that you are comparing like elements (e.g., nouns to nouns, verbs to verbs) and that the grammatical structures are parallel.

4. Rhetorical Skills

Rhetorical skills involve the effective use of language to persuade, inform, or entertain. The ACT English section assesses your ability to apply these skills in various contexts.

4.1 Transitions

Transitions are words or phrases that create smooth connections between sentences and paragraphs. They help to guide the reader through the text, indicating the relationship between different ideas. Some common types of transitions include:

- **Addition:** Words like "also," "furthermore," "in addition," and "moreover" indicate that you are adding more information or supporting details.

- **Contrast:** Words like "however," "nevertheless," "on the other hand," and "in contrast" indicate that you are presenting a contrasting idea or viewpoint.

- **Cause-effect:** Words like "because," "therefore," "as a result," and "consequently" indicate that one idea is the cause of another.

Choosing the appropriate transition word or phrase is crucial for maintaining coherence and clarity in your writing.

4.2 Wordiness

Wordiness refers to the use of unnecessary words or phrases that do not add any significant meaning to the text. It can make your writing sound cluttered and convoluted. For example, "The reason why he went to the store was because he needed milk" is wordy because it can be simplified to "He went to the store because he needed milk."

To avoid wordiness, strive for conciseness and clarity by using the most effective words and phrases. Eliminate redundant expressions (e.g., "past history," "unexpected surprise") and unnecessary qualifiers (e.g., "very," "really").

4.3 Style

Style refers to the overall tone and manner of your writing. It can be formal or informal, depending on the intended audience and purpose. The ACT English section might ask you to identify sentences or phrases that are inconsistent with the overall style of the passage.

For instance, if the passage is written in a formal academic style, a sentence with slang or colloquialisms would be stylistically inconsistent. Similarly, if the passage is written in a lighthearted and informal style, a sentence with technical jargon or complex sentence structures would be out of place.

4.4 Organization

Organization refers to the logical arrangement of ideas within a passage. The ACT English section might ask you to identify sentences or paragraphs that are out of order or that disrupt the flow of ideas.

For example, if a paragraph starts with a general statement and then provides specific examples, a sentence that introduces a new and unrelated topic would be organizationally misplaced. Similarly, if a passage follows a chronological order of events, a sentence that describes an event out of sequence would disrupt the organization.

By mastering these rhetorical skills, you can significantly enhance the clarity, coherence, and effectiveness of your writing.

The ACT English section is a comprehensive assessment of your understanding and application of the rules of standard written English. By understanding the key concepts of grammar and usage, punctuation, sentence structure, and rhetorical skills, you can approach the test with confidence and achieve your desired score. Remember to read carefully, consider the context, and trust your instincts when answering the questions.

Directions: In the passages that follow, you will find underlined words and phrases. In the column to the right, there are alternatives to the underlined wording. For most questions, choose the option that expresses the idea most effectively, conforms to the standards of conventional English, or has wording consistent with the tone and style of the passage. If you think the original underlined wording is best, pick "NO CHANGE." For some problems, you will need to read a question about the underlined portion and pick the best answer to the question. Other problems may ask about portions of the passage or the entire passage. These questions will be indicated by a numbered box. Choose the best answer to each question and fill in the matching oval on your answer sheet. Be sure to consider any relevant context surrounding the question in determining your answer.

The Empire State Building

Many [1] buildings are merely places to live or work, taking on no greater significance. The Empire State Building in New York City is one of the clearer [2] examples of how a building can become more than just a building, taking on a number of different roles. The Empire State Building stands as an inspiration to human diligence and ingenuity. It was built in only 15 months and was the tallest building in the world for several decades [3]. It is so large that it has its own zip code and houses office space for approximately 20,000 workers on any given day. Builded [4] shortly before the Great Depression, the Empire State Building towered over the Manhattan skyline, reminding New Yorkers of what they could do even when times were bad [5]. Looking at the Empire State Buildings [6] tower, we see reminders of our history. The top of the building was first and originally [7] intended to be a landing spot for dirigibles (large blimps) that would drop off their passengers after [8] long voyages. Since the winds were too strong [9] at such a height, and given the diminished interest in blimp travel as opposed to airplane travel, the dirigible function were dropped [10]. The tower of the Empire State Building took on a more significant role as radio and television became widespread housing [11] the antennas for many of the stations in the New York Metropolitan area. Thanks to television and movies, the building has become [12] a cultural icon. It has been destroyed in movies like Independence Day and been the area [13] of romantic meetings, like in Sleepless in Seattle. And of course, who can forget its role in King Kong? The lighting atop the Empire State Building provides a backdrop to holidays and special events. After the tragedy of September 11, the tower was lit in red, white, and blue for several months. The [14] tower's lights were programmed to announce the winner of the 2012 Presidential election: red for Romney and blue for Obama.

1.   A. NO CHANGE

      B. Much

      C. A great plethora of

      D. OMIT the underlined portion and adjust capitalization accordingly.

2.   A. NO CHANGE

      B. are some of the clear

      C. is one of the clearest

      D. are one of the clearest

3. Given that the underlined portion is true, should it be kept or deleted from the sentence?

      A. Kept, because it gives the precise number of years that the building was the world's tallest.

      B. Kept, because it provides clarifying information to the reader.

      C. Deleted, because it contradicts information found elsewhere in the sentence.

      D. Deleted, because it repeats details found in the sentence that follows.

4.	A. NO CHANGE

	B. Building

	C. Built

	D. Having been builded

5.	A. NO CHANGE

	B. for what is a possibility when bad times were had by them.

	C. to the possibilities of what could be done by the New Yorkers in trying times.

	D. with the remembrance of what is possible when even times were falling apart.

6.	A. NO CHANGE

	B. Buildings'

	C. Building

	D. Building's

7.	A. NO CHANGE

	B. initial

	C. originally

	D. first and original

8.	A. NO CHANGE

	B. they're passengers their

	C. they're passengers there

	D. their passengers there

9.	A. NO CHANGE

	B. to strong

	C. two strong

	D. to strongest

10.	A. NO CHANGE

	B. was dropped.

	C. were dropping.

	D. had dropping.

11.	A. NO CHANGE

	B. widespread; housing

C. widespread. Housing

D. widespread, housing

12.   A. NO CHANGE

B. have become

C. had became

D. have became

13.   A. NO CHANGE

B. scene

C. zone

D. residence

14.   A. NO CHANGE

B. months, the

C. months: the

D. months. The

15. The author is considering moving paragraph [6] to a different location in the passage. Where is the most logical place to put this paragraph?

A. Where it is now

B. Before paragraph [2]

C. Before paragraph [3]

D. After paragraph [4]

Answer Explanations

1. (A) is easy to determine by simply mouthing it out—"many" works as a description for the word "buildings" that follows. (B) is not generally used when describing countable things, but when describing noncountable things, such as "much anger."

(C) is too wordy, and (D) would change the meaning to imply that all buildings have these characteristics rather than some of them.

2. (C) agrees with the singular subject "Building," unlike (B) and (D). It is not (A) because "clearer" would be used to compare just two things, and there are far more than two buildings in New York City, so we should use "clearest."

3. (B) If we don't have this phrase in the sentence, we will lose important information that clarifies that the Empire State Building is no longer the tallest building in the world. It is not (A) because "several decades" does not provide a precise number of years.

4. (C) is the only option that uses the proper past tense form, which is consistent with the past tense of the historical discussion in the rest of the paragraph.

5. (A) puts the wording in a logical order and uses the words properly. (B) uses the passive voice, and (C) and (D) are too wordy.

6. (D) uses the proper singular possessive form of "Building." We clearly have just one building, and to show ownership of the "tower," an apostrophe before the "s" is necessary.

7. (C) uses an adverb (ending in "-ly") to describe the verb "was." (B) uses an adjective. (A) and (D) are repetitive.

8. (D) "Their" shows ownership, "there" shows a place, and "they're" is the same as "they are." (D) is the only choice to use these different versions properly, expressing that the passengers belong to the blimp, and that they are dropped off at a particular place.

9. (A) "Two" is a number, "too" is used for comparisons (like "too much), and "to" is a connecting word, like "I am going to the store." (A) correctly uses "too" to describe how strong the winds were, unlike all the other options.

10. (B) is the only choice that agrees with the singular "function" and is in the past tense, as is the rest of the historical discussion that takes place in this paragraph.

11. (D) uses a comma to break up the independent clause that comes in the first part of the sentence, and the dependent clause that comes in the second half. (A) has no break whatsoever. (B) and (C) can only work if there are complete sentences on either side of the semicolon or period.

12. (A) uses the correct verb to match with the singular "building," unlike (B) and (D) which use "have." Also, it is in the correct tense, present perfect, indicating that this is an event that started in the past and continues up to the present day. (C) would be used to indicate something in the distant past.

13. (B) uses the appropriate word to describe a place where a movie meeting would take place. Even though (A), (C), and (D) all refer to physical places, they would not necessarily be associated with the situation described in this sentence.

14. (D) provides a needed separation between the two complete sentences, which (A) and (B) don't do. (C) is incorrect because what would follow the colon is not a clarification of what comes before—it is a new idea.

15. (A) is the best place for this paragraph because it concludes the essay as well as looks forward to the future. All of the other placements would interrupt the essay's flow.

Medium English Practice

Accidental Sweeteners

The pink packet, the yellow packet—artificial sweeteners seem to be a fixture with [1] nearly every diner table in America. A furious debate has persisted for nearly 150 years [2] about the safety of these strange, sweet, synthetic substances and their potential long- term effects on human health. Some, like "Sweet n' Low" [3] have been convincingly linked to bladder cancer, and others, like "Splenda," are known to cause anaphylaxis in certain persons. And [4] what is perhaps even more shocking about the major artificial sweeteners —sucralose, saccharin, and aspartame, which together now make up 76% of the artificial sweeteners consumed globally each year-is that, like [5] so many unlikely leaps in science, all of them were discovered quite by accident. In the mid-nineteenth century, a chemist experimenting with coal tar derivatives in a basement laboratory at Johns Hopkins University falled asleep with a lighted [6] cigar in his mouth. As the story goes, the cigar fell into one of the researcher's petri dishes where they ignited [7] an endothermic reaction, one of the products of which was a white crystalline substance. Awaking suddenly, the mess was cleaned by the scientist [8] in such a hurry that he left the laboratory without washing his hands. That night at dinner, he noticed an unusual [9] sugary taste on his hands. One year later he applied to patent his substance, which he dubbed saccharin, and soon afterward, "Sweet n' Low" [10] became the first widely available artificial sweetener on the market. Approximately 100 years later in the future, [11] in a similar twist of fate, a medical scientist attempting to create [12] an anti-ulcer drug synthesized instead the methyl ester now known as "aspartame." The scientist realized the "sweetness" of his discovery when he inadvertently [13] licked his contaminated fingers in order to lift a piece of paper from his desk. Not many years later, a pair of English scientists began directing experiments with sucrose or table sugar [14] as a synthetic intermediate in industrial reactions. Upon asking their foreign lab assistant, Shashikant Phadnis, to "test" a halogenated saccharide compound, Phadnis dipped his finger into the petri dish and licked it, believing he had been asked to "taste" the compound. Phadnis found the white coloration of the substance to be unusual. [15] After a series of patents, sucralose or "Splenda" joined the growing ranks of accidental artificial sweeteners.

1. A. NO CHANGE

    B. in

    C. at

    D. on

2. A. NO CHANGE

    B. years

    C. over a period of one and one half centuries

    D. while

3. A. NO CHANGE

    B. Some, like "Sweet n' Low,"

    C. Some, like, "Sweet n' Low,"

    D. Some like "Sweet n' Low"

4. Which of the following would serve as the most logical introductory word to this sentence?

    A. NO CHANGE

    B. Also

    C. But

    D. Since

5.   A. NO CHANGE

      B. year—is that like

      C. year, is that, like

      D. year, is that like

6.   A. NO CHANGE

      B. felt sleepy with a lit

      C. fell asleep with a lit

      D. had fell asleep with a lit

7.   A. NO CHANGE

      B. where it ignited

      C. which they ignited

      D. when it ignites

8.   A. NO CHANGE

      B. Awake, suddenly, the scientist cleaning up the mess

      C. Suddenly awaking, the mess was cleaned up by the scientist

      D. Awaking suddenly, the scientist cleaned up the mess

9.   A. NO CHANGE

      B. infrequent

      C. crazy

      D. irrational

10. The writer is considering removing the quotation marks around this phrase. Should the writer make this change?

   A. Yes, because it refers to a commonly understood term.

   B. Yes, because it has already been defined in the previous part of the sentence.

   C. No, because it is stylistically consistent with the rest of the essay.

   D. No, because quotation marks are needed to surround personal statements.

11.   A. NO CHANGE

   B. About a century later,

   C. Approximately after 100 years had passed,

   D. Since 100 years have gone by,

12.   A. NO CHANGE

   B. create

   C. for creating

   D. at the creation of

13. Which of the following, if inserted here, would NOT convey that the discovery of aspartame was accidental?

   A. NO CHANGE

   B. absentmindedly

   C. deliberately

   D. unconsciously

14. If the writer were to delete the underlined phrase, the essay would primarily lose:

   A. a clarification of a specialized term.

   B. A description of sensory information.

   C. an explanation of a scientific process.

   D. a justification for a laboratory decision.

15. Given that all are true, which sentence, if inserted here, would be the most specifically relevant to the topic of the paragraph, and consistent with the theme of the essay as a whole?

   A. NO CHANGE

   B. Phadnis was surprised at the substance's powdery texture.

   C. Phadnis remarked on the sample's extraordinary sweetness.

   D. Phadnis found the material to be less dense than other sweeteners.

Answer Explanations

1. (D) uses the correct idiomatic expression, "a fixture on every table." Be careful that the prepositions you use, words like "of," "to," and "from," are used in a way consistent with common practice.

2. (A) gives helpful clarifying details without being too wordy, like (C). (B) is too vague, and (D) is vague and grammatically incorrect—it would need to say "a while," not just "while."

3. (B) places commas around the clarifying phrase that gives an example of the "Some." It is also consistent with the phrasing used later in the sentence: "others, like 'Splenda,' are known . . . ." (A) and (D) do not provide needed comma breaks, and (C) is too choppy.

4. (C) This sentence introduces a surprising twist that is then elaborated upon in the rest of the essay. Because it is not a continuation of the previous ideas, (A) and (B) would not work. (D)

would be used for a cause-effect relationship. (C) provides a contrasting word that gives an appropriate transition into this sentence.

5. (A) A dash is needed here in order to be consistent with the earlier dash that sets off a clarification: "sweeteners—sucralose . . . ." (C) and (D) would be inconsistent with the previous use of the dash. (A) also provides a needed comma break between "that" and "like," because the phrase "like so many unlikely leaps in science" is a clarifying phrase that needs to be set out of the way. (B) would not provide this needed comma break, making for a more jumbled sentence.

6. (H) uses the proper past tense form of "fell," unlike (F) and (J). The past tense is needed since the events in this sentence took place in the nineteenth century. (G) uses a verb in the past tense form, but would express an illogical meaning. How could someone "feel sleepy with a lit cigar in his mouth"? It is much more logical, based on the context, to go with (H).

7. (B) is the only choice that uses the past tense, unlike (A) and (D), and refers to the singular subject "one" by using "it," unlike (C).

8. (D) conveys the event in the active voice, instead of passive voice, like (A) and (C). (B) is too choppy.

9. (A) uses the appropriate word given the context. An unexpected sugary taste could best be described as "unusual." (B) would make sense if this had been a semi regular occurrence, but it is not. (C) and (D) are more applicable toward people, not things.

10. (H) The names of other artificial sweeteners, such as "Splenda," are also put in quotation marks. To maintain stylistic consistency, quotation marks should be used here as well.

11. (B) is the most concise, logical option. (A) and (C) are way too wordy, and (D) would place the event in the present by using "have."

12. (A) uses the correct expression, "attempting to create." The connecting "to" is needed, which (B) does not do. (C) and (D) use improper prepositions given the context.

13. (C) Be sure you notice the NOT in this question. (A), (B), and (D) would all express accidental intent. (C), "deliberately," conveys the opposite—a deliberate action is an intended one.

14. (A) Words with commonly understood definitions do not require clarifications. "Sucrose" is a specialized term from chemistry, and giving the reader the commonly used term for this would be helpful. It does not describe the information, as in (B). It does not explain a process, as in (C). Finally, it does not give a rationale or justification for why a decision was made, as in (D).

15. (C) The theme of the essay as a whole is how artificial sweeteners have been discovered by accident. (C) is the only choice that would connect to this general theme. (A) is vague, (B) focuses on the texture rather than sweetness, and (D) focuses on the density instead of the sweetness.

Tough English Practice

What's Your Sign?

Although only a very small sector of our society "believe in" or actively practice [1] the tenets of Western astrology, nearly every daily newspaper in the United States prints a daily horoscope reading for the 12 astrological signs of the zodiac. However, [2] most of us at least know our personal sign and perhaps little about its symbolism, less people [3] have a very clear understanding of the origin of Western zodiac astrology.

Contrary to Chinese astrology-which emphasizes the passage of time [4] - Western astrology is based on the orientations of space, and the cyclical movements of celestial bodies in the Milky Way. The word "zodiac" itself refers to the ring of constellations and planets that surround [5] the apparent path of the sun across the sky. Though the concept of the zodiac certainly predates [6] the Roman Empire—which likely inherited its astrology from Babylonian and Hellenistic civilizations—it is the Latin names for the astrological signs that are still widely in use [7] today. The word "zodiac" is of Greek origin, and roughly means circle of animals referring to the bestial imagery associated with the early constellations for which the astrological signs are named. In the second century c.e., Ptolemy described the construction of a zodiac chart in his "Almagest."

Such zodiacs— [9] —form the basis of the original Western horoscopes. Traditionally, it is the sun's location in the zodiac on the day of a person's birth that determines his or her "star sign," and thus <u>whether or not</u> [10] someone is considered an Aquarius or Leo, and so forth. However, the determination of star signs is just one usage of the zodiac in Western astrology. In addition to <u>the sun, the moon, planets and some minor celestial bodies</u> [11] are also oriented within the zodiac. In both ancient and modern astrology, it is the positional relationship of these bodies to the zodiac signs and to each other that purports to yield divinatory insight <u>explaining the influence of the supernatural in our lives.</u> [12]

Even though the idea that planetary motion <u>affected</u> [13] our behavior on Earth has, of course, long been dismissed from Western astronomy, the copious number of star charts left behind by ancient astrologers <u>had on occasion, been</u> of great interest to astronomers in reconstructing the subtler movements of celestial bodies throughout recent history. [15]

1.   A. NO CHANGE

      B. believe in or actively practice

      C. "believes in" or actively practices

      D. believes in nor actively practices

2.   A. NO CHANGE

      B. But

      C. Since

      D. Though

3.   A. NO CHANGE

      B. few people

      C. lesser persons

D. little people

4. A. NO CHANGE

    B. astrology—that emphasizes the passage of time—

    C. astrology—which emphasizes the passage of time

    D. astrology that emphasizes the passage of time,

5. A. NO CHANGE

    B. which are surrounding

    C. that surrounds

    D. which surrounds

6. A. NO CHANGE

    B. will have predated

    C. has predated

    D. had predated

7. Which of the following alternatives to the underlined portion would NOT be acceptable?

    A. quite popular

    B. used widely

    C. frequent used

    D. commonly found

8. A. NO CHANGE

    B. , referring

C. referring

D. : referring

9. At this point, the author wishes to insert one of the following true statements that will most specifically describe the visual appearance of a zodiac. Which one most effectively accomplishes the author's goal?

A. represented by a circle divided into 12 slices, each pertaining to an individual sign

B. portrayed with stunning visual intricacies, unlike any other chart one might find

C. based on the disparate influences of Hindu, Babylonian, Roman, and Hellenistic cultures

D. which users believe can provide insights into areas of health, wealth, and relationships

10.   A. NO CHANGE

B. whether

C. regardless of whether

D. OMIT the underlined portion.

11.   A. NO CHANGE

B. the sun, the moon, planets and some minor, celestial bodies

C. the sun, the moon, planets and some minor, celestial, bodies

D. the sun, the moon, planets; and some minor celestial bodies

12.   A. NO CHANGE

B. describing how gods, and goddesses help us make clear decisions

C. that empowers us to know what the heavens have planned for us

D. OMIT the underlined portion.

13.   A. NO CHANGE

       B. effected

       C. affects

       D. effects

14.   A. NO CHANGE

       B. have, on occasion, been

       C. have on occasion been

       D. has, on occasion, been

15. Which of the following true sentences, if inserted here, would best provide a fitting conclusion to the essay through a qualifying statement that establishes the zodiac's relevance to modern astronomy while simultaneously acknowledging its shortcomings?

       A. Astronomers now have the benefit of rigorous scientific processes that enable them to use precise measurements to gather extraterrestrial data.

       B. And while the astrological signs have also fallen by the wayside, the zodiac itself remains the conceptual basis for modern astronomy's ecliptic coordinate system.

       C. The zodiac is uniquely paradoxical in having a culturally diverse history while having culturally convergent characteristics no matter where we find it.

       D. Since the zodiac was based on primitive superstition, it behooves modern day astronomers to set it aside in favor of modern, proven techniques.

Answer Explanations

1. (C) uses verbs, "believes" and "practices," consistent with the singular subject, "sector." (A) and (B) use the plural verb forms. (D) incorrectly uses "nor," which would make the sentence self-contradictory.

2. (D) gives a grammatically appropriate transition to indicate the contrast in the sentence between a superficial understanding of our sign and a deeper understanding of the history of astrology. (C) would indicate cause and effect. Even though (A) and (B) both indicate contrasts, they would not be appropriate to use to introduce a sentence like this one; "but" and "however" are generally better suited for use within a sentence.

3. (B) "Few" is generally used to indicate something that can be counted, and "people" can certainly be counted. "Less," as in (A), is typically used for things that cannot be counted. (C) and (D) would both change the original meaning.

4. (A) has proper uses of the dashes to isolate a clarifying phrase from the rest of the sentence. (C) and (D) would not have such pauses. (B) is incorrect because "that" is used to indicate an essential characteristic of a thing, whereas "which" is used to indicate a nonessential characteristic of a thing. An emphasis on the passage of time is not a piece of information that clarifies that we are discussing Chinese astrology—it merely gives us a helpful, clarifying detail. So, "which" would be appropriate.

5. (C) It is challenging to determine the subject here, but it is the singular "ring," not the plural "constellations" or "planets." (A) and (B) use plural verbs. It is not (D) because "which" is used for nonrestrictive descriptions, whereas "that" is used for restrictive descriptions. The "ring" is specifically the one that "surrounds the apparent path of the sun"—this information is essential to knowing which "ring" is being discussed, so "that" would be appropriate to use.

6. (A) correctly puts "predates" in the present tense. "Predate" is an odd verb, in that it indicates that something took place in the past, whereas the word "predate" itself is in the present. It is synonymous with "comes before." (B), (C), and (D) all use improper tense forms.

7. (C) would NOT work because it uses an adjective, "frequent," to modify a verb, "used." If it had said "frequently used," it would work as an alternative to the underlined portion. All of the other choices use appropriate parts of speech in their wording.

8. (B) uses the comma to provide a brief pause before a clarifying phrase. (A) would not work because it would need a complete sentence after the semicolon. (C) provides no break at all. (D) is wrong because a clarification after the colon would not need to start with "referring"—a colon itself would take care of setting off a definition.

9. (A) accomplishes what the question demands—it provides a specific description of the visual appearance of a zodiac by giving highly detailed, visual imagery. (B) is too vague, (C) focuses on the specifics of history rather than appearance, and (D) focuses on the potential use of the zodiac rather than its appearance.

10. (B) would work the best, since an option between two things is stated (i.e., between "an Aquarius or Leo"). "Whether or not," as in (A), is typically repetitive, since two options are implied with the "whether," but it can be used to express "regardless of whether." For example, a proper use could be "Eat your food whether or not you are hungry." (C) is too wordy, and (D) would lack a key transitional word, confusing the meaning of the sentence.

11. (A) places commas in the proper spots. There should not be a comma between "minor" and "celestial" because when it is necessary to have the adjectives in a particular order, no comma should separate them. When a particular order of the adjectives is NOT necessary to expressing a logical meaning, a comma can separate them. If we said "celestial minor bodies," that would not make sense. The phrase has to be in the order that it is, so no commas should separate "celestial and "minor." An example of a phrase where commas could separate the two adjectives would be "The smelly, overflowing trash can." Why? Because we could also logically say "The overflowing, smelly trash can." Because of all this, (B) and (C) are not correct. (D) improperly uses a semicolon—a complete sentence does not follow the semicolon in this choice, so it would not work.

12. (D) (A), (B), and (C) would add nothing substantive to the sentence, since the word "divinatory" already implies an association with the supernatural, gods, and the heavens.

13. (C) is in the present tense, consistent with the rest of the present perfect tense, "has been," used in the rest of the paragraph. (A) and (B) are in the past tense. (D), "effects," is generally used as a noun. (C) correctly uses the verb "affects" since the "motion . . . affects our behavior on Earth."

14. (D) places needed commas around the clarifying phrase "on occasion," unlike (A) and (C). (B) uses the improper plural "have"—the verb needs to be the singular "has" in order to agree with the subject, "number."

15. (B) This question demands a very careful reading to ensure you meet all its requirements. A qualifying statement is one that states that something is the case, but with exceptions. (B) makes such a statement, acknowledging the problems with the zodiac while allowing that it has had a strong historical influence. (A) and (D) have very negative views of the zodiac, and (C) has a very positive view of it. These three options do not make an attempt to qualify their remarks, instead making one-sided claims.

ENGLISH GRAMMAR SUMMARY

Sentence Basics

A complete sentence has a subject and a verb.

Number Agreement

Watch out for separation between words that need to agree.

Punctuation

■ Use commas where a breath is needed. If it's a long item, no commas are needed. If it's extra information, separate it with commas.

■ Use semicolons to separate two related, complete sentences.

- A colon comes after a complete sentence, and before a list or clarification.

- A dash provides an interruption. Possession

- One dog's toys (to show singular possession, put the apostrophe before the "s")

- Two dogs' toys (to show plural possession, put the apostrophe after the "s")

- "Their," "Whose," and "Its" all show possession. "They're" = They are. "Who's" = Who is. "It's" = It is.

Tense

Look at other verbs close by to see if it makes sense to put it in the past, present, or future tense.

Parallelism

Example: "I love reading, learning, and studying." NOT: "I love reading, learning, and the process of going to study."

Transitions Look at what comes before AND after the underlined portion to see what type of transition is needed (e.g., "also," "but," or "because").

Wordiness Find a balance between repetition/irrelevance and effective description.

Word Order

Be sure that the sequence of words is logical (e.g., "Walking in the middle of the street, a car will run over you." is incorrect because it seems like the car is walking, while "If you walk in the middle of the street, a car will run over you." is correct because it clarifies that you are walking).

Illogical Comparisons

Be sure that what you mean to compare is what you actually compare (e.g., "The paintings by da Vinci are better than those by John Smith." NOT "The paintings by da Vinci are better than John Smith.").

Proper Wording

Since there are so many exceptions in the English language, mouth things out and trust your instincts when trying to decide the correct wording.

ENGLISH STRATEGY SUMMARY

■ It is typically easy to finish the English section—don't rush!

■ Pace yourself in one of two ways:

– 9 minutes a passage

– 15 minutes for every 25 questions

■ By taking your time, you can:

– Mouth things out

– Think about the meaning

– Consider enough context

■ On problems where there are written questions, really focus on what they ask you to do.

■ Even if you don't know the exact grammar rule, knowing that something seems odd is often enough to figure it out.

Chapter 2: Math

This chapter provides a comprehensive review of the mathematical concepts covered in the ACT Math section. To facilitate your understanding and mastery of these concepts, the chapter is divided into subchapters, each focusing on a specific area of mathematics.

Pre-Algebra

The ACT Math section assesses your understanding and application of various mathematical concepts, ranging from basic pre-algebra to more advanced topics like trigonometry. This subchapter delves into the fundamental pre-algebra concepts that form the bedrock for tackling the ACT Math test. It encompasses detailed explanations, illustrative examples, and ACT-style practice questions to solidify your grasp of the material.

Key Concepts in Pre-Algebra

1. Types of Numbers

The foundation of mathematical understanding lies in comprehending the different types of numbers and their properties. The ACT Math section often includes questions that require you to work with various number systems.

- **Integers:** Integers are whole numbers that lack any fractional or decimal components. They include positive numbers, negative numbers, and zero. Examples include -3, 0, 7, and 100.
- **Rational Numbers:** Rational numbers encompass any number that can be expressed as a fraction in the form p/q, where both 'p' (the numerator) and 'q' (the denominator) are integers, and 'q' is not zero. Rational numbers include integers, fractions, and terminating or repeating decimals. Examples include -2, 1/4, 0.75, and 2.666...
- **Irrational Numbers:** Irrational numbers are those that cannot be expressed as a fraction of two integers. Their decimal representations are non-terminating and non-

repeating. Well-known examples include pi (π), the square root of 2 (√2), and Euler's number (e).

- **Real Numbers:** Real numbers encompass the entire set of rational and irrational numbers. They can be visualized as points on a number line, representing all possible quantities, including those that are whole, fractional, decimal, or irrational.

2. Number Properties

Understanding the properties of numbers is crucial for solving various mathematical problems. The ACT Math section may include questions that test your knowledge of factors, prime numbers, and prime factorization.

- **Factors:** Factors of a number are integers that divide evenly into that number. For example, the factors of 24 are 1, 2, 3, 4, 6, 8, 12, and 24.
- **Prime Numbers:** Prime numbers are whole numbers greater than 1 that are only divisible by 1 and themselves. The first few prime numbers are 2, 3, 5, 7, 11, and 13. Prime numbers are fundamental building blocks in number theory and have applications in cryptography.
- **Prime Factorization:** Prime factorization is the process of expressing a composite number as the product of its prime factors. For example, the prime factorization of 36 is 2 x 2 x 3 x 3. The fundamental theorem of arithmetic states that the prime factorization of any composite number is unique.

3. Fractions

Fractions represent parts of a whole or a ratio between two quantities. The ACT Math section may include questions that require you to perform operations with fractions.

- **Fraction Basics:** Fractions are composed of a numerator (top part) and a denominator (bottom part). The numerator represents the number of parts considered, while the denominator represents the total number of equal parts in the whole. Simplifying fractions involves dividing both the numerator and denominator by their greatest common factor.

- **Mixed Numbers:** Mixed numbers combine a whole number and a fraction. They can be converted to improper fractions (where the numerator is greater than or equal to the denominator) and vice versa. For example, 3 1/4 is equivalent to 13/4 as an improper fraction.

- **Fraction Operations:** Arithmetic operations with fractions involve specific rules. Adding or subtracting fractions requires finding a common denominator, which is the least common multiple of the denominators. Multiplying fractions involves multiplying the numerators and denominators separately. Dividing fractions is equivalent to multiplying by the reciprocal of the divisor.

4. Decimals and Percentages

Decimals and percentages are alternative ways to represent parts of a whole or ratios. The ACT Math section may include questions that require you to convert between decimals, fractions, and percentages.

- **Place Value:** Decimals extend the base-ten number system to represent values less than one. Each digit after the decimal point holds a specific place value (tenths, hundredths, thousandths, etc.). Understanding place value is essential for comparing decimals, rounding, and performing arithmetic operations.

- **Scientific Notation:** Scientific notation is a compact way to express very large or very small numbers. It involves writing a number as the product of a decimal between 1 and 10 and a power of 10. For example, 5,000,000 can be written as 5×10^6, and 0.000007 can be written as 7×10^{-6}.

- **Percentages:** Percentages represent a proportion out of one hundred. They are closely related to decimals and fractions. For example, 40% is equivalent to 0.40 or 2/5. Calculating percentages involves understanding the relationship between the part, the whole, and the percentage.

5. Ratios and Proportions

Ratios and proportions are used to compare quantities and express relationships between them. The ACT Math section may include questions that require you to solve problems involving ratios and proportions.

- **Ratios:** Ratios compare two or more quantities. They can be expressed as fractions, decimals, or with a colon. For example, the ratio of red marbles to blue marbles in a jar could be 5:3. Ratios can be simplified similar to fractions.

- **Proportions:** Proportions are equations that state that two ratios are equal. They can be used to solve for an unknown quantity in a ratio. For example, if the ratio of distance to time is constant, a proportion can be set up to determine the distance traveled in a certain amount of time.

6. Other Pre-Algebra Concepts

In addition to the concepts mentioned above, the ACT Math section may also test your understanding of absolute value and the order of operations.

- **Absolute Value:** The absolute value of a number is its distance from zero, regardless of whether the number is positive or negative. It is denoted by two vertical bars around the number. For example, $|-8| = 8$ and $|5| = 5$. Absolute value is used in various mathematical contexts, including distance calculations and inequalities.

- **Order of Operations:** The order of operations defines the sequence in which operations should be performed in a mathematical expression to avoid ambiguity. The acronym PEMDAS (or BODMAS) is commonly used to remember the order: Parentheses/Brackets, Exponents/Orders, Multiplication and Division (from left to right), and Addition and Subtraction (from left to right).

Elementary Algebra

1. Polynomials

Polynomials are algebraic expressions consisting of variables and coefficients. They involve addition, subtraction, multiplication, and division operations.

- **Adding and Subtracting Polynomials:** Combine like terms by adding or subtracting their coefficients. For example, $(3x^2 + 2x + 5) + (2x^2 - 5x + 1) = 5x^2 - 3x + 6$.
- **Multiplying Polynomials:** Use the distributive property (or FOIL method for binomials) to multiply each term of one polynomial by each term of the other polynomial. For example, $(2x + 3)(x - 5) = 2x^2 - 7x - 15$.
- **Dividing Polynomials:** Divide each term of the dividend polynomial by the divisor polynomial. This may involve long division or synthetic division.

2. Factoring Polynomials

Factoring involves expressing a polynomial as a product of simpler polynomials.

- **Common Factors:** Factor out the greatest common factor (GCF) from all terms of the polynomial. For example, $6x^3 - 12x^2 + 18x = 6x(x^2 - 2x + 3)$.
- **Factoring Trinomials:** Express a trinomial as a product of two binomials. For example, $x^2 - 5x + 6 = (x - 2)(x - 3)$.
- **Special Factoring Patterns:** Recognize and apply special factoring patterns, such as difference of squares, sum of cubes, and difference of cubes. For example, $x^2 - 25 = (x + 5)(x - 5)$.

3. Solving Systems of Equations

Systems of equations involve two or more equations with multiple variables.

- **Substitution Method:** Solve one equation for one variable and substitute the expression into the other equation.
- **Elimination Method:** Multiply one or both equations by constants to make the coefficients of one variable opposite. Add the equations to eliminate one variable and solve for the other variable.

4. Exponents

Exponents indicate repeated multiplication.

- **Exponent Rules:** Apply exponent rules for multiplication, division, power of a power, and negative exponents. For example, x^m * x^n = x^(m+n).

5. Word Problems

Word problems require translating verbal descriptions into algebraic expressions and equations.

- **Distance, Rate, and Time:** Use the formula distance = rate * time to solve problems involving motion.

Intermediate Algebra

1. Inequalities

Inequalities compare two expressions using symbols like < (less than), > (greater than), $\leq$ (less than or equal to), and $\geq$ (greater than or equal to).

- **Solving Inequalities:** Solve inequalities like equations, but reverse the inequality sign when multiplying or dividing by a negative number.

2. Functions

Functions define a relationship between an input (x) and an output (f(x)).

- **Function Notation:** Understand function notation, such as $f(x) = 2x + 3$.
- **Evaluating Functions:** Substitute values for the input variable and calculate the output.
- **Composite Functions:** Evaluate composite functions, where the output of one function becomes the input of another function. For example, $f(g(x))$.

3. Logarithms

Logarithms are the inverse of exponential functions.

- **Logarithm Rules:** Apply logarithm rules for multiplication, division, and exponents. For example, log (x * y) = log x + log y.

4. Matrices

Matrices are rectangular arrays of numbers.

- **Matrix Operations:** Add, subtract, and multiply matrices.

5. Quadratic Formula

The quadratic formula solves for the roots of a quadratic equation in the form $ax^2 + bx + c = 0$.

6. Other Intermediate Algebra Concepts

- **Synthetic Division:** Use synthetic division to divide a polynomial by a linear binomial.
- **Direct and Inverse Variation:** Understand direct and inverse variation relationships between variables.
- **Sequences:** Identify and analyze arithmetic and geometric sequences.
- **Complex Numbers:** Perform operations with complex numbers involving the imaginary unit 'i'.

Coordinate Geometry

Coordinate geometry bridges algebra and geometry, utilizing the coordinate plane to represent and analyze geometric shapes and their properties.

1. Lines and Slope

- **Slope-Intercept Form:** A linear equation in slope-intercept form (y = mx + b) provides immediate information about the line's slope (m) and y-intercept (b). The slope indicates the line's steepness and direction, while the y-intercept is the point where the line crosses the y-axis.[1]

- **Calculating Slope:** The slope of a line, a measure of its steepness and direction, can be calculated using the formula m = (y2 - y1) / (x2 - x1), where (x1, y1) and (x2, y2) are any two distinct points on the line.

- **Parallel and Perpendicular Lines:** Parallel lines, which never intersect, have the same slope. Perpendicular lines, which intersect at a right angle, have slopes that are negative reciprocals of each other. For example, if one line has a slope of 2, a line perpendicular to it would have a slope of -1/2.[2]

2. Graphing Inequalities

Linear inequalities, like y > 2x + 1, are graphed by first plotting the corresponding linear equation (y = 2x + 1) as a boundary line. The region above or below the line is then shaded to represent the solutions to the inequality. Whether the boundary line is solid or dashed depends on the inequality symbol ($\geq$ or $\leq$ result in a solid line, while > or < result in a dashed line).

3. Distance and Midpoint Formulas

- **Distance Formula:** The distance between two points in the coordinate plane can be calculated using the distance formula, derived from the Pythagorean theorem.

- **Midpoint Formula:** The midpoint of a line segment, the point equidistant from both endpoints, can be found using the midpoint formula. This formula essentially averages the x-coordinates and the y-coordinates of the endpoints to determine the midpoint's coordinates.

4. Circle Graphs

- **Equation of a Circle:** The standard equation of a circle provides information about its center and radius. The equation $(x - h)^2 + (y - k)^2 = r^2$ represents a circle with center (h, k) and radius r.

5. Other Coordinate Geometry Concepts

- **Vertical Line Test:** The vertical line test determines if a graph represents a function. If any vertical line intersects the graph at more than one point, the graph does not represent a function.

- **Parabolas, Hyperbolas, and Ellipses:** These conic sections are represented by specific types of equations and have distinct graphical characteristics. Understanding their equations and graphs is essential for the ACT Math section.

- **Function Transformations:** Functions can be transformed by shifting, stretching, or reflecting their graphs. These transformations are represented by changes in the function's equation.

- **Vectors:** Vectors, quantities with both magnitude and direction, are often represented in component form. Adding or subtracting vectors involves performing the corresponding operations on their respective components.

Plane Geometry

Plane geometry deals with two-dimensional shapes and their properties, including perimeter, area, angles, and lines.

1. Perimeter

The perimeter of a polygon is the total length of all its sides. For example, the perimeter of a rectangle with length 5 units and width 3 units is 16 units (5 + 3 + 5 + 3).

2. Area of Polygons

The area of a polygon is the amount of space it encloses. Formulas for calculating the area of common polygons, such as squares, rectangles, parallelograms, triangles, and trapezoids, are essential for the ACT Math section.

3. Composite Shape Area

Composite shapes can be divided into simpler shapes to calculate their total area. For example, an L-shaped figure can be divided into two rectangles, and the areas of the rectangles can be added to find the total area.

4. Triangle Concepts

- **Types of Triangles:** Triangles are classified by their sides (equilateral, isosceles, scalene) and angles (acute, right, obtuse). Understanding the properties of different types of triangles is crucial for solving geometry problems.

- **Triangle Inequality Theorem:** This theorem states that the sum of the lengths of any two sides of a triangle must be greater than the length of the third side. This property is useful for determining whether three given side lengths can form a triangle.

5. Circles

- **Circle Properties:** Key properties of circles include radius, diameter, circumference, and area. The radius is the distance from the center to any point on the circle, the diameter is twice the radius, the circumference is the distance around the circle, and the area is the space enclosed by the circle.

- **Arc Length and Sector Area:** An arc is a portion of the circumference of a circle. The length of an arc is proportional to the[3] central angle it subtends. A sector is a region bounded by two radii and an arc. The area of a sector is also proportional to the central angle it subtends.

6. Angle Rules

- **Supplementary and Complementary Angles:** Supplementary angles are two angles that add up to 180 degrees. Complementary angles are two angles that add up to 90 degrees.[4]

- **Parallel Lines and Transversals:** When a transversal intersects two parallel lines, various angle relationships are formed, including corresponding angles, alternate interior angles, and alternate exterior angles. These angles have specific properties that are useful for solving geometry problems.

7. Degrees in a Polygon

The sum of the interior angles of a polygon depends on the number of sides it has. The formula (n - 2) * 180 degrees, where n is the number of sides, gives the sum of the interior angle measures of an n-sided polygon.

8. Volume of Solids

The volume of a solid is the amount of space it occupies. Formulas for calculating the volume of common solids, such as rectangular prisms (boxes) and cylinders, are important for the ACT Math section.

9. Right Triangles

- **Pythagorean Theorem:** The Pythagorean theorem ($a\text{^}2 + b\text{^}2 = c\text{^}2$) relates the lengths of the legs (a and b) of a right triangle to the length of its hypotenuse (c). This theorem is fundamental to solving many geometry and trigonometry problems.
- **Special Right Triangles:** Certain right triangles have special angle and side relationships that make calculations easier. The 30-60-90 and 45-45-90 triangles are two such special right triangles.

10. Other Plane Geometry Concepts

- **Diagonals in a Polygon:** A diagonal is a line segment that connects two non-adjacent vertices of a polygon. The number of diagonals in a polygon can be calculated using the formula n(n - 3) / 2,[5] where n is the number of sides.[6]

Trigonometry

Trigonometry deals with the relationships between the sides and angles of triangles, particularly right triangles.

1. Trigonometric Ratios

The primary trigonometric ratios are sine, cosine, and tangent. These ratios relate the lengths of the sides of a right triangle to its acute angles. The acronym SOH CAH TOA is a helpful mnemonic for remembering these ratios: Sine = Opposite / Hypotenuse, Cosine = Adjacent / Hypotenuse, Tangent = Opposite / Adjacent.

2. Trigonometric Identities

Trigonometric identities are equations that are true for all values of the variables for which they are defined. Some common trigonometric identities include $\sin^2 \theta + \cos^2 \theta = 1$ and $\tan \theta = \sin \theta / \cos \theta$. These identities can be used to simplify trigonometric expressions and solve trigonometric equations.

3. Graphs of Trigonometric Functions

The graphs of trigonometric functions, such as sine and cosine, have periodic patterns. Understanding the characteristics of these graphs, including their period, amplitude, and frequency, is important for the ACT Math section.

4. Radians and the Unit Circle

- **Radians:** Radians are an alternative unit for measuring angles. The relationship between degrees and radians is defined by π radians = 180 degrees. Converting between degrees and radians is often necessary in trigonometry problems.
- **Unit Circle:** The unit circle is a circle with a radius of 1 centered at the origin of a coordinate plane. It serves as a visual tool for understanding the relationships between angles, radians, and trigonometric functions. Each point on the unit circle corresponds to an angle, and the coordinates of that point represent the cosine and sine of the angle, respectively.

Questions

Time: 60 Minutes—60 Questions

Directions: Determine the answer to each question, and then fill in the matching oval on your answer sheet. Do not spend too much time on any one problem. Solve as many as possible, then come back to ones that you have skipped. You are allowed to use a calculator on this section, but several of the problems are best completed without a calculator. Unless stated otherwise, assume that drawings are NOT necessarily to scale, geometric figures are in a two-dimensional plane, "lines" are straight lines, and "average" means the arithmetic mean.

1. If 40% of x equals 80, what is the value of x?

(A) 20

(B) 32

(C) 120

(D) 200

(E) 320

Answer: (D)

Explanation: We can set up a proportion to solve for x:

$40/100 = 80/x$

Cross-multiplying and solving for x gives us:

$40x = 8000$

$x = 200$

2. For what value of k will the equation $x^2+6x+k=0$ have exactly one solution?

(A) 3

(B) 6

(C) 9

(D) 12

(E) 36

Answer: (C)

Explanation: A quadratic equation has exactly one solution when its discriminant is equal to zero. The discriminant of the quadratic equation $ax^2+bx+c=0$ is given by b^2-4ac.

In this case, $a=1$, $b=6$, and $c=k$. Setting the discriminant equal to zero and solving for k gives us:

$6^2 - 4 * 1 * k = 0$

$36 - 4k = 0$

$4k = 36$

$k = 9$

3. If $f(x)=3x-5$ and $g(x)=x^2+1$, what is the value of $g(f(2))$?

(A) 2

(B) 8

(C) 10

(D) 17

(E) 26

Answer: (A)

Explanation: We need to work from the inside out. First, we find the value of f(2):

$f(2) = 3 * 2 - 5 = 6 - 5 = 1$

Then, we plug 1 into g(x):

g(1) = 1^2 + 1 = 1 + 1 = 2

4. If the average of five consecutive odd integers is 15, what is the greatest of these integers?

(A) 9

(B) 13

(C) 15

(D) 17

(E) 19

Answer: (E)

Explanation: Let the middle of the five consecutive odd integers be x. Then, the five integers are x−4, x−2, x, x+2, and x+4.

Since the average of these integers is 15, we have:

(x - 4 + x - 2 + x + x + 2 + x + 4)/5 = 15

Simplifying and solving for x gives us:

5x/5 = 15

x = 15

Therefore, the greatest of these integers is x+4=15+4=19.

5. A rectangle has a length of 12 units and a width of 8 units. What is the length of the diagonal of the rectangle?

(A) 10

(B) 12

(C) 14

(D) 16

(E) 20

Answer: (C)

Explanation: The diagonal of a rectangle forms a right triangle with the length and width of the rectangle. Therefore, we can use the Pythagorean theorem to find the length of the diagonal:

diagonal^2 = length^2 + width^2

diagonal^2 = 12^2 + 8^2

diagonal^2 = 144 + 64

diagonal^2 = 208

diagonal = sqrt(208) = 4sqrt(13)

6. If the circumference of a circle is 10π units, what is the area of the circle?

(A) 5π

(B) 10π

(C) 25π

(D) 50π

(E) 100π

Answer: (C)

Explanation: The circumference of a circle is given by $2\pi r$, where r is the radius. Therefore, we can solve for the radius:

$2\pi r = 10\pi$

$r = 5$

The area of a circle is given by πr^2. Plugging in the value of r gives us:

area $= \pi * 5^2 = 25\pi$

7. If $\sin\theta=3/5$ and θ is an acute angle, what is the value of $\cos\theta$?

(A) 3/5

(B) 4/5

(C) 5/3

(D) 5/4

(E) 1

Answer: (B)

Explanation: We can use the Pythagorean identity $\sin^2\theta+\cos^2\theta=1$ to solve for $\cos\theta$:

$(3/5)^2 + \cos^2 \theta = 1$

$9/25 + \cos^2 \theta = 1$

$\cos^2 \theta = 16/25$

$\cos \theta = 4/5$

8. If the probability of an event occurring is 0.6, what is the probability of the event not occurring?

(A) 0

(B) 0.4

(C) 0.6

(D) 1

(E) 1.6

Answer: (B)

Explanation: The probability of an event not occurring is equal to 1 minus the probability of the event occurring. Therefore, the probability of the event not occurring is 1−0.6=0.4.

9. If log2x=3, what is the value of x?

(A) 2

(B) 3

(C) 5

(D) 6

(E) 8

Answer: (E)

Explanation: We can rewrite the logarithmic equation in exponential form to solve for x:

2^3 = x

x = 8

10. If the first term of an arithmetic sequence is 5 and the common difference is 3, what is the fifth term of the sequence?

(A) 8

(B) 11

(C) 14

(D) 17

(E) 20

Answer: (D)

Explanation: The general form for an arithmetic sequence is $a_n = a_1 + (n-1)d$, where a_n is the nth term, a_1 is the first term, and d is the common difference.

In this case, $a_1 = 5$ and d=3. Plugging in n=5 gives us:

$a\_5 = 5 + (5 - 1) * 3 = 5 + 4 * 3 = 5 + 12 = 17$

11. A triangle has sides of length 5, 12, and 13 units. Is the triangle a right triangle?

(A) Yes

(B) No

Answer: (A)

Explanation: A triangle is a right triangle if and only if the sum of the squares of the two shorter sides is equal to the square of the longest side (the Pythagorean theorem). In this case, $5^2 + 12^2 = 25 + 144 = 169 = 13^2$, so the triangle is a right triangle.

12. If the point $(3, -4)$ is reflected across the y-axis, what are the coordinates of the reflected point?

(A) $(-3, -4)$

(B) $(3, 4)$

(C) $(-3, 4)$

(D) $(4, -3)$

(E) (−4,3)

Answer: (A)

Explanation: When a point is reflected across the y-axis, the x-coordinate changes sign and the y-coordinate remains the same. Therefore, the reflected point is (−3,−4).

13. If x and y are inversely proportional, and y=6 when x=2, what is the value of y when x=3?

(A) 2

(B) 4

(C) 6

(D) 9

(E) 12

Answer: (B)

Explanation: If x and y are inversely proportional, then their product is a constant. Therefore, we can set up the following equation:

$2 * 6 = 3 * y$

Solving for y gives us:

$12 = 3y$

$y = 4$

14. If the volume of a cube is 64 cubic units, what is the surface area of the cube?

(A) 16

(B) 32

(C) 64

(D) 96

(E) 128

Answer: (D)

Explanation: The volume of a cube is given by s3, where s is the side length. Therefore, we can solve for the side length:

$s^3 = 64$

$s = 4$

The surface area of a cube is given by 6s2. Plugging in the value of s gives us:

surface area $= 6 * 4^2 = 6 * 16 = 96$

15. If the measure of an angle is 30 degrees, what is the measure of its complement?

(A) 30 degrees

(B) 60 degrees

(C) 90 degrees

(D) 120 degrees

(E) 150 degrees

Answer: (B)

Explanation: Complementary angles add up to 90 degrees. Therefore, the complement of a 30-degree angle is 90−30=60 degrees.

16. If the equation of a circle is (x−2)2+(y+3)2=25, what is the center of the circle?

(A) $(2,-3)$

(B) $(-2,3)$

(C) $(2,3)$

(D) $(-2,-3)$

(E) $(0,0)$

Answer: (A)

Explanation: The standard form for the equation of a circle is $(x-h)^2+(y-k)^2=r^2$, where (h,k) is the center of the circle and r is the radius. Therefore, the center of the circle is $(2,-3)$.

17. If $\log_3(x+1)=2$, what is the value of x?

(A) 2

(B) 5

(C) 8

(D) 9

(E) 10

Answer: (C)

Explanation: We can rewrite the logarithmic equation in exponential form to solve for x:

$3^2 = x + 1$

$9 = x + 1$

$x = 8$

18. If the second term of a geometric sequence is 6 and the fourth term is 54, what is the common ratio of the sequence?

(A) 2

(B) 3

(C) 6

(D) 9

(E) 18

Answer: (B)

Explanation: In a geometric sequence, each term is equal to the previous term multiplied by the common ratio. Therefore, we can set up the following equation:

6 * r * r = 54

6r^2 = 54

r^2 = 9

r = 3

19. If the perimeter of a square is 20 units, what is the area of the square?

(A) 5

(B) 10

(C) 20

(D) 25

(E) 40

Answer: (D)

Explanation: The perimeter of a square is given by 4s, where s is the side length. Therefore, we can solve for the side length:

4s = 20

s = 5

The area of a square is given by s2. Plugging in the value of s gives us:

area = 5^2 = 25

20. If the measure of an angle is 60 degrees, what is the measure of its supplement?

(A) 30 degrees

(B) 60 degrees

(C) 90 degrees

(D) 120 degrees

(E) 150 degrees

Answer: (D)

Explanation: Supplementary angles add up to 180 degrees. Therefore, the supplement of a 60-degree angle is 180−60=120 degrees.

21. If the equation of a line is y=2x−3, what is the slope of the line?

(A) -3

(B) -2

(C) 2

(D) 3

(E) 5

Answer: (C)

Explanation: The slope-intercept form of a linear equation is y=mx+b, where m is the slope and b is the y-intercept. Therefore, the slope of the line is 2.

22. If $f(x)=x2−4$ and $g(x)=2x+1$, what is the value of $f(g(3))$?

(A) 17

(B) 21

(C) 45

(D) 49

(E) 53

Answer: (C)

Explanation: We need to work from the inside out. First, we find the value of g(3):

g(3) = 2 * 3 + 1 = 6 + 1 = 7

Then, we plug 7 into f(x):

f(7) = 7^2 - 4 = 49 - 4 = 45

23. If the first term of an arithmetic sequence is 3 and the common difference is 4, what is the tenth term of the sequence?

(A) 31

(B) 35

(C) 39

(D) 43

(E) 47

Answer: (C)

Explanation: The general form for an arithmetic sequence is $a_n = a_1 + (n-1)d$, where a_n is the nth term, a_1 is the first term, and d is the common difference.

24. If a bag contains 5 red marbles, 3 blue marbles, and 2 green marbles, what is the probability of randomly selecting a blue marble?

(A) 1/10

(B) 3/10

(C) 1/3

(D) 2/5

(E) 1/2

Answer: (B)

Explanation: There are a total of 10 marbles in the bag. The probability of selecting a blue marble is the number of blue marbles divided by the total number of marbles,[1] which is 3/10.

25. If $x^2 - 5x - 6 = 0$, what are the solutions for x?

(A) x=−6 and x=1

(B) x=−3 and x=2

(C) x=−2 and x=3

(D) x=−1 and x=6

(E) x=2 and x=3

Answer: (D)

Explanation: We can factor the quadratic equation to find the solutions:

$x^2 - 5x - 6 = 0$

$(x - 6)(x + 1) = 0$

$x = 6$ or $x = -1$

26. If the area of a triangle is 24 square units and the base of the triangle is 8 units, what is the height of the triangle?

(A) 3

(B) 4

(C) 6

(D) 8

(E) 12

Answer: (C)

Explanation: The area of a triangle is given by $(1/2)bh$, where b is the base and h is the height. Plugging in the given values and solving for h gives us:

$24 = (1/2) * 8 * h$

$24 = 4h$

$h = 6$

27. If the measure of an angle is 45 degrees, what is the measure of its complement?

(A) 30 degrees

(B) 45 degrees

(C) 60 degrees

(D) 90 degrees

(E) 135 degrees

Answer: (B)

Explanation: Complementary angles add up to 90 degrees. Therefore, the complement of a 45-degree angle is 90−45=45 degrees.

28. If the point (−2,5) is reflected across the x-axis, what are the coordinates of the reflected point?

(A) (2,5)

(B) (−2,−5)

(C) (2,−5)

(D) (5,−2)

(E) (−5,2)

Answer: (B)

Explanation: When a point is reflected across the x-axis, the y-coordinate changes sign and the x-coordinate remains the same. Therefore, the reflected point is (−2,−5).

29. If x and y are directly proportional, and y=10 when x=5, what is the value of y when x=8?

(A) 4

(B) 8

(C) 13

(D) 16

(E) 40

Answer: (D)

Explanation: If x and y are directly proportional, then their ratio is a constant. Therefore, we can set up the following equation:

10/5 = y/8

Solving for y gives us:

2 = y/8

y = 16

30. If the volume of a rectangular prism is 120 cubic units, the length of the prism is 6 units, and the width of the prism is 5 units, what is the height of the prism?

(A) 2

(B) 4

(C) 6

(D) 10

(E) 12

Answer: (B)

Explanation: The volume of a rectangular prism is given by lwh, where l is the length, w is the width, and h is the height. Plugging in the given values and solving for h gives us:

120 = 6 * 5 * h

$120 = 30h$

$h = 4$

31. What is the solution to the equation $5x - 3 = 2x + 9$?

(A) 2

(B) 3

(C) 4

(D) 5

(E) 6

Answer: (C)

Explanation: To solve for x, we can start by combining like terms: $5x - 2x = 9 + 3$ $3x = 12$ $x = 4$

32. If a triangle has angles measuring 30 degrees, 60 degrees, and 90 degrees, what is the ratio of the length of the shortest side to the length of the longest side?

(A) 1:2

(B) 1:$\sqrt{3}$

(C) $\sqrt{3}$:2

(D) 2:1

(E) $\sqrt{3}$:1

Answer: (A)

Explanation: In a 30-60-90 triangle, the ratio of the sides is 1:√3:2, with the shortest side opposite the 30-degree angle and the longest side (the hypotenuse) opposite the 90-degree angle. Therefore, the ratio of the shortest side to the longest side is 1:2.

33. If $f(x) = 2x^2 - 5x + 3$, what is the value of $f(-2)$?

(A) -15

(B) -1

(C) 7

(D) 17

(E) 25

Answer: (E)

Explanation: To find f(-2), we substitute -2 for x in the function: $f(-2) = 2(-2)^2 - 5(-2) + 3$ f(-2) = 8 + 10 + 3 f(-2) = 21

34. If a circle has a circumference of 12π, what is its area?

(A) 6π

(B) 12π

(C) 24π

(D) 36π

(E) 72π

Answer: (D)

Explanation: The circumference of a circle is given by 2πr, where r is the radius. Therefore, we can solve for the radius: 2πr = 12π r = 6 The area of a circle is given by πr^2. Plugging in the value of r gives us: area = π * 6^2 = 36π

35. If log_5 x = 2, what is the value of x?

(A) 2

(B) 5

(C) 10

(D) 25

(E) 125

Answer: (D)

Explanation: We can rewrite the logarithmic equation in exponential form to solve for x: 5^2 = x = 25

36. If the first term of an arithmetic sequence is 7 and the common difference is -3, what is the fourth term of the sequence?

(A) -2

(B) 1

(C) 4

(D) 10

(E) 13

Answer: (A)

Explanation: The general form for an arithmetic sequence is a_n = a_1 + (n - 1)d, where a_n is the nth term, a_1 is the first term, and d is the common difference. In this case, a_1^1 = 7 and d = -3. Plugging in n = 4 gives us: a_4 = 7 + (4 - 1) * -3 = 7 + 3 * -3 = 7 - 9 = -2

37. A rectangle has a length of 10 units and a width of 6 units. What is the length of the diagonal of the rectangle?

(A) 8

(B) 10

(C) 12

(D) 2√34

(E) 4√17

Answer: (D)

Explanation: The diagonal of a rectangle forms a right triangle with the length and width of the rectangle. Therefore, we can use the Pythagorean theorem to find the length of the diagonal: diagonal^2 = length^2 + width^2 diagonal^2 = 10^2 + 6^2 diagonal^2 = 100 + 36 diagonal^2 = 136 diagonal = √136 = 2√34

38. If the circumference of a circle is 8π units, what is the area of the circle?

(A) 4π

(B) 8π

(C) 16π

(D) 32π

(E) 64π

Answer: (C)

Explanation: The circumference of a circle is given by 2πr, where r is the radius. Therefore, we can solve for the radius: 2πr = 8π r = 4 The area of a circle is given by πr^2. Plugging in the value of r gives us: area = π * 4^2 = 16π

39. If sin θ = 4/5 and θ is an acute angle, what is the value of cos θ?

(A) 3/5

(B) 4/5

(C) 5/3

(D) 5/4

(E) 1

Answer: (A)

Explanation: We can use the Pythagorean identity sin^2 θ + cos^2 θ = 1 to solve for cos θ: (4/5)^2 + cos^2 θ = 1 16/25 + cos^2 θ = 1 cos^2 θ = 9/25 cos θ = 3/5

40. If the probability of an event occurring is 0.3, what is the probability of the event not occurring?

(A) 0

(B) 0.3

(C) 0.7

(D) 1

(E) 1.3

Answer: (C)

Explanation: The probability of an event not occurring is equal to 1 minus the probability of the event occurring. Therefore, the probability[3] of the event not occurring is 1 - 0.3 = 0.7.

41. If log_4 x = 2, what is the value of x?

(A) 2

(B) 4

(C) 8

(D) 16

(E) 64

Answer: (D)

Explanation: We can rewrite the logarithmic equation in exponential form to solve for x: 4^2 = x = 16

42. If the first term of an arithmetic sequence is 2 and the common difference is 5, what is the sixth term of the sequence?

(A) 7

(B) 12

(C) 17

(D) 22

(E) 27

Answer: (E)

Explanation: The general form for an arithmetic sequence is $a\_n = a\_1 + (n - 1)d$, where a_n is the nth term, a_1 is the first term, and d is the common difference. In this case, $a\_1 = 2$ and $d^4 = 5$. Plugging in n = 6 gives us: $a\_6 = 2 + (6 - 1) * 5 = 2 + 5 * 5 = 2 + 25 = 27$

43. A triangle has sides of length 3, 4, and 5 units. Is the triangle a right triangle?

(A) Yes

(B) No

Answer: (A)

Explanation: A triangle is a right triangle if and only if the sum of the squares of the two shorter sides is equal to the square of the longest side[5] (the Pythagorean theorem). In this case, $3^2 + 4^2 = 9 + 16 = 25 = 5^2$, so the triangle is a right triangle.

44. If the point (2, -5) is reflected across the y-axis, what are the coordinates of the reflected point?

(A) (-2, -5)

(B) (2, 5)

(C) (-2, 5)

(D) (5, -2)

(E) (-5, 2)

Answer: (A)

Explanation: When a point is reflected across the y-axis, the x-coordinate changes sign and the y-coordinate remains the same. Therefore, the reflected point is (-2, -5).

45. If x and y are inversely proportional, and y = 4 when x = 3, what is the value of y when x = 6?

(A) 2

(B) 3

(C) 6

(D) 8

(E) 12

Answer: (A)

Explanation: If x and y are inversely proportional, then their product is a constant. Therefore, we can set up the following equation: 3 * 4 = 6 * y Solving for y gives us: 12 = 6y y = 2

46. If the volume of a cube is 27 cubic units, what is the surface area of the cube?

(A) 9

(B) 18

(C) 27

(D) 54

(E) 81

Answer: (D)

Explanation: The volume of a cube is given by s^3, where s is the side length. Therefore, we can solve for the side length: $s^3 = 27$ s = 3 The surface area of a cube is given by $6s^2$. Plugging in the value of s gives us: surface area = 6 * 3^2 = 6 * 9 = 54

47. If the measure of an angle is 40 degrees, what is the measure of its complement?

(A) 40 degrees

(B) 50 degrees

(C) 60 degrees

(D) 130 degrees

(E) 140 degrees

Answer: (B)

Explanation: Complementary angles add up to 90 degrees. Therefore, the complement of a 40-degree angle is 90 - 40 = 50 degrees.

48. If the equation of a circle is $(x + 3)^2 + (y - 2)^2 = 16$, what is the center of the circle?

(A) (3, -2)

(B) (-3, 2)

(C) (3, 2)

(D) (-3, -2)

(E) (0, 0)

Answer: (B)

Explanation: The standard form for the equation of a circle is $(x - h)^2 + (y - k)^2 = r^2$, where (h, k) is the center of the circle and r is the radius.[6] Therefore, the center of the circle is (-3, 2).

49. If $\log_2 (x - 1) = 3$, what is the value of x?

(A) 4

(B) 7

(C) 8

(D) 9

(E) 10

Answer: (D)

Explanation: We can rewrite the logarithmic equation in exponential form to solve for x: $2^3 =$ x - 1 8 = x - 1 x = 9

50. If the second term of a geometric sequence is 4 and the fourth term is 16, what is the common ratio of the sequence?

(A) 1

(B) 2

(C) 4

(D) 8

(E) 12

Answer: (B)

Explanation: In a geometric sequence, each term is equal to the previous term multiplied by the common ratio. Therefore, we can set up the following equation: $4 * r * r = 16$ $4r^2 = 16$ $r^2 = 4$ r = 2

51. If the perimeter of a square is 32 units, what is the area of the square?

(A) 8

(B) 16

(C) 32

(D) 64

(E) 128

Answer: (D)

Explanation: The perimeter of a square is given by 4s, where s is the side length. Therefore, we can solve for the side length: 4s = 32 s = 8 The area of a square is given by s^2. Plugging in the value of s gives us: area = 8^2 = 64

52. If the measure of an angle is 50 degrees, what is the measure of its supplement?

(A) 40 degrees

(B) 50 degrees

(C) 100 degrees

(D) 130 degrees

(E) 140 degrees

Answer: (D)

Explanation: Supplementary angles add up to 180 degrees. Therefore, the supplement of a 50-degree angle is 180 - 50 = 130 degrees.

53. If the equation of a line is y = -3x + 5, what is the slope of the line?

(A) -5

(B) -3

(C) 3

(D) 5

(E) 8

Answer: (B)

Explanation: The slope-intercept form of a linear equation is $y = mx + b$, where m is the slope and b is the y-intercept. Therefore, the slope of[7] the line is -3.

54. If $f(x) = 3x^2 - 2x + 1$ and $g(x) = x + 2$, what is the value of $f(g(2))$?

(A) 13

(B) 21

(C) 37

(D) 41

(E) 49

Answer: (C)

Explanation: We need to work from the inside out. First, we find the value of $g(2)$: $g(2) = 2 + 2 = 4$ Then, we plug 4 into $f(x)$: $f(4) = 3 * 4^2 - 2 * 4 + 1 = 3 * 16 - 8 + 1 = 48 - 8 + 1 = 41$

55. If the first term of an arithmetic sequence is 8 and the common difference is -2, what is the fifth term of the sequence?

(A) 0

(B) 2

(C) 4

(D) 6

(E) 8

Answer: (A)

Explanation: The general form for an arithmetic sequence is $a_n = a_1 + (n - 1)d$, where a_n is the nth term, a_1 is the first term, and d is the common difference. In this case, $a_1^8 = 8$ and $d = -2$. Plugging in $n = 5$ gives us: $a_5 = 8 + (5 - 1) * -2 = 8 + 4 * -2 = 8 - 8 = 0$

56. If a bag contains 3 red marbles, 5 blue marbles, and 2 green marbles, what is the probability of randomly selecting a red marble?

(A) 1/10

(B) 3/10

(C) 1/3

(D) 2/5

(E) 1/2

Answer: (B)

Explanation: There are a total of 10 marbles in the bag. The probability of selecting a red marble is the number of red marbles divided by the total number of marbles,[9] which is 3/10.

57. If $x^2 + 3x - 10 = 0$, what are the solutions for x?

(A) x = -5 and x = 2

(B) x = -2 and x = 5

(C) x = -1 and x = 10

(D) x = 1 and x = -10

(E) x = 2 and x = -5

Answer: (A)

Explanation: We can factor the quadratic equation to find the solutions: $x^2 + 3x - 10 = 0$ $(x + 5)(x - 2) = 0$ $x = -5$ or $x = 2$

58. If the area of a triangle is 30 square units and the base of the triangle is 10 units, what is the height of the triangle?

(A) 3

(B) 5

(C) 6

(D) 10

(E) 15

Answer: (C)

Explanation: The area of a triangle is given by $(1/2)bh$, where b is the base and h is the height. Plugging in the given values and solving for h gives us: $30 = (1/2) * 10 * h$ $30 = 5h$ $h = 6$

59. If the measure of an angle is 70 degrees, what is the measure of its complement?

(A) 20 degrees

(B) 30 degrees

(C) 70 degrees

(D) 110 degrees

(E) 160 degrees

Answer: (A)

Explanation: Complementary angles add up to 90 degrees. Therefore, the complement of a 70-degree angle is $90 - 70 = 20$ degrees.

60. If the point (4, -3) is reflected across the x-axis, what are the coordinates of the reflected point?

(A) (-4, -3)

(B) (4, 3)

(C) (-4, 3)

(D) (3, -4)

(E) (-3, 4)

Answer: (B)

Explanation: When a point is reflected across the x-axis, the y-coordinate changes sign and the x-coordinate remains the same. Therefore, the reflected point is (4, 3).

This chapter provides a comprehensive overview of the key mathematical concepts assessed in the ACT Math section. By mastering these concepts and practicing with sample questions, you can significantly improve your performance on the test. Remember to read each question carefully, identify the relevant concepts, and apply the appropriate formulas and problem-solving strategies.

Don't forget that the ACT Math section does not provide any formulas, so it's crucial to memorize the essential formulas for areas, volumes, the Pythagorean theorem, trigonometric ratios, and other key concepts.

By diligently studying the material in this chapter and practicing regularly, you can approach the ACT Math section with confidence and achieve your desired score.

STOP

If there is still time remaining, you may review your answers.

Chapter 3: Reading

This chapter offers a comprehensive guide to the ACT Reading section, presenting strategies and techniques to help you excel on the test.

Reading Comprehension Strategies

1. Focused Reading

Unlike reading for school assignments, where detailed memorization is often required, the ACT Reading test demands a different approach. Instead of getting bogged down in trying to remember every specific detail, prioritize understanding the big picture and creating a mental map of the passage. Focus on grasping the main ideas, the author's purpose, and the overall structure of the passage. This strategic approach will allow you to navigate the passage more efficiently and answer questions more effectively.:

To effectively engage in focused reading:

- **Identify the main idea:** What is the central argument or point the author is trying to convey?
- **Recognize supporting details:** How does the author support the main idea with evidence, examples, or explanations?
- **Understand the organization:** How does the author structure the passage (e.g., chronological order, compare and contrast, cause and effect)?
- **Determine the author's purpose:** Why did the author write this passage? What is the intended audience?
- **Pay attention to the tone and style:** Is the author's tone formal or informal, objective or subjective, persuasive or informative?

By actively engaging with these elements, you can construct a mental framework of the passage, allowing you to quickly locate relevant information and answer questions accurately.

2. Alternating Reading Speed

Strategic reading involves adapting your reading speed based on the significance of the information. Devote more time and attention to the introduction and conclusion, as they typically contain the thesis statement, main ideas, and overall summary of the passage. However, feel free to skim through supporting details, as their specific nuances are less critical for answering the questions. This judicious allocation of time and focus will enable you to grasp the essence of the passage without getting sidetracked by less important details.

Here's how to effectively alternate your reading speed:

- **Slow down for key sections:** Carefully read the introduction and conclusion, paying close attention to topic sentences and any summarizing statements.

- **Speed up for supporting details:** Skim through the middle paragraphs, focusing on identifying the main points and supporting evidence.

- **Use keywords and transitions:** Pay attention to keywords and transition words that signal important information or shifts in the argument.

- **Practice active reading:** Highlight or underline key phrases and jot down brief notes in the margins to help you remember important points.

By strategically adjusting your reading speed, you can optimize your time and focus on the most relevant information.

3. Understanding the Question Types

Familiarize yourself with the five common categories of questions you'll encounter in the ACT Reading section:

- **Meanings of Words:** These questions assess your vocabulary and ability to discern the nuanced meanings of words in context. They often require you to consider the surrounding sentences and the overall tone of the passage to determine the intended meaning of a specific word or phrase.

- **Supporting Details:** These questions test your ability to identify and comprehend specific details within the passage. They often refer to specific lines or paragraphs and require you to locate and interpret relevant information.

- **Sequential, Comparative, and Cause-Effect Relationships:** These questions evaluate your understanding of the organization and relationships between different parts of the passage. They may ask you to identify the order of events, compare and contrast different ideas, or analyze cause-and-effect relationships.

- **Generalizations and Conclusions:** These questions assess your ability to draw inferences and conclusions from the information presented in the passage. They often require you to go beyond explicitly stated information and make logical deductions based on the evidence provided.

- **Main Ideas and Author's Approach:** These questions test your understanding of the central themes and the author's overall purpose and style. They may ask you to identify the main idea of the passage, the author's tone, or the intended audience.

By recognizing these question types and their specific characteristics, you can tailor your reading strategies and answer approaches accordingly.

Prose Fiction

Prose fiction passages in the ACT Reading section are typically excerpts from novels or short stories. They often involve character development, plot progression, and thematic exploration.

1. Focus on the Beginning

The initial paragraph of a prose fiction passage is crucial, as it sets the scene, introduces the characters, and establishes the tone and mood of the story. Pay close attention to the details presented in the beginning to gain a solid foundation for understanding the rest of the passage.

Here's why the beginning is so important:

- **Setting the scene:** The author establishes the time, place, and atmosphere of the story, creating a backdrop for the events that unfold.
- **Introducing characters:** The reader is introduced to the main characters, their relationships, and their initial motivations.

- **Establishing tone and mood:** The author sets the overall tone (e.g., serious, humorous, suspenseful) and mood (e.g., joyful, melancholic, tense) of the story.

By carefully analyzing the beginning, you can gain valuable insights into the characters, plot, and themes that will develop throughout the passage.

2. Maintain a Moderate Pace

While it's essential to focus on the beginning, don't rush through the rest of the passage. Maintain a moderate reading pace to ensure you grasp the key plot points, character interactions, and thematic elements that unfold throughout the story. A balanced reading approach will enable you to appreciate the nuances of the narrative and answer questions accurately.

Here's how to maintain a moderate pace:

- **Don't get bogged down in details:** Focus on understanding the main events and character interactions, rather than trying to memorize every word.
- **Pay attention to dialogue:** Dialogue can reveal important information about the characters' personalities, relationships, and motivations.
- **Look for symbolism and imagery:** The author may use symbolism and imagery to convey deeper meanings and themes.
- **Track the plot:** Keep track of the main events and how they contribute to the overall plot of the story.

By reading at a moderate pace and paying attention to key elements, you can gain a comprehensive understanding of the prose fiction passage.

Social Science

Social science passages typically cover topics related to history, sociology, psychology, or political science. They often present arguments, evidence, and analyses of social phenomena.

1. Prioritize Key Sections

In social science passages, prioritize reading the first paragraph, topic sentences of each paragraph, and the concluding paragraph. These sections usually encapsulate the main ideas, arguments, and overall structure of the passage. By focusing on these key sections, you can efficiently grasp the essence of the passage.

Here's why these sections are important:

- **First paragraph:** Introduces the topic, provides background information, and often states the author's main argument or thesis.
- **Topic sentences:** Summarize the main point of each paragraph and guide the reader through the author's line of reasoning.
- **Concluding paragraph:** Restates the main argument, summarizes key points, and may offer concluding thoughts or implications.

By focusing on these key sections, you can quickly identify the author's main points and understand the overall structure of the argument.

2. Skim Supporting Details

Once you have a good understanding of the main ideas, feel free to skim through the supporting details. While these details provide evidence and context, their specific intricacies are often less critical for answering the questions. Allocate your time wisely by focusing on the most important information.

Here's how to skim effectively:

- **Read selectively:** Focus on keywords, phrases, and sentences that provide evidence or support for the main ideas.
- **Don't get lost in details:** Avoid getting bogged down in specific dates, names, or statistics unless they are directly relevant to the questions.
- **Use visual cues:** Pay attention to headings, subheadings, bold text, and any other visual cues that highlight important information.

By skimming strategically, you can save time and focus on the most relevant information.

Humanities

Humanities passages can vary widely in content and style, encompassing topics related to art, literature, music, philosophy, or cultural studies. They may be first-person narratives, biographical sketches, or analytical essays.

1. Adapt to the Passage

Adjust your reading strategy based on the specific characteristics of the humanities passage. If it's a first-person narrative, read it like a prose fiction passage, paying close attention to the narrator's voice, experiences, and reflections. If it's a third-person passage, read it like a social science passage, focusing on the main ideas, arguments, and supporting details.

Here's how to adapt your reading strategy:

- **First-person narratives:** Focus on the narrator's perspective, emotions, and relationships with other characters. Pay attention to the tone and style of the narrative.
- **Third-person passages:** Identify the author's main argument or thesis. Analyze the supporting evidence and the organization of the passage.

By adapting your reading strategy, you can effectively comprehend and analyze the diverse range of humanities passages.

Natural Science

Natural science passages typically cover topics related to biology, chemistry, physics, or environmental science. They often involve scientific concepts, experiments, data analysis, and conclusions.

1. Prioritize Key Sections

Similar to social science passages, prioritize reading the first paragraph, topic sentences, and concluding paragraphs in natural science passages. These sections usually provide a concise overview of the scientific concepts, experiments, and conclusions discussed in the passage.

Here's why these sections are important:

- **First paragraph:** Introduces the scientific topic, provides background information, and often states the research question or hypothesis.
- **Topic sentences:** Highlight the main point of each paragraph, often describing specific experiments, data, or findings.
- **Concluding paragraph:** Summarizes the key findings, states the conclusion, and may discuss implications or future research directions.

By focusing on these key sections, you can efficiently understand the scientific concepts and the overall structure of the passage.

2. Skim Supporting Details

Once you have a solid grasp of the main scientific ideas, you can skim through the supporting details, such as specific experimental procedures or data analysis. While these details are important for understanding the scientific process, their intricate specifics are often less critical for answering the questions.

Here's how to skim effectively:

- **Identify key terms and concepts:** Focus on understanding the scientific terms and concepts that are central to the passage.
- **Look for visual aids:** Pay attention to diagrams, charts, and graphs that may summarize important data or illustrate key concepts.
- **Don't get lost in technical details:** Avoid getting bogged down in complex experimental procedures or statistical analyses unless they are directly relevant to the questions.

Questions

Time: 35 Minutes—40 Questions

Directions: There are several reading selections in this section, each of which is followed by questions. After you read a passage, determine the best answer to each question and fill in the matching oval on your answer sheet. Refer back to the passages as often as you need.

Passage I

Prose Fiction—Music

Don't mistake me—I'm not interested in just listening to music passively. It's not the catchy melodies or the driving rhythms that captivate me either. Not entirely. It's about the act of creation itself; the expression, the emotion, the magic woven into every note. Music is my refuge, my therapy, my voice. I have my own instruments, my trusted companions, through which I channel my inner world. The piano, with its ivory keys and resonant strings, speaks my joys and sorrows. The guitar, with its warm wood and vibrant chords, echoes my hopes and dreams. Like a painter with a brush or a sculptor with clay, I mold melodies and harmonies, shaping them into expressions of my soul.

With my fingers dancing across the piano keys, I weave a tapestry of sound. The notes cascade like a waterfall, each one a drop of emotion, blending and harmonizing to create a symphony of feelings. I close my eyes and lose myself in the music, my fingers guided by an unseen force. At once, I am eight years old again, sitting on the piano bench in my grandmother's cozy living room. The scent of lavender and freshly baked cookies fills the air. Sunlight streams through the window, casting a warm glow on the worn keys. My grandmother, her fingers gnarled with age, guides my small hands across the keyboard, teaching me the basics of music.

"Feel the music," she whispers, her voice soft and gentle. "Let it flow through you."

Her words echo in my mind as I navigate the complexities of a Chopin nocturne. The melody unfolds like a story, each phrase a chapter filled with longing and passion. I pour my heart into the music, expressing emotions I can't put into words. The final chord resonates through the room, leaving a lingering sense of peace and fulfillment.

I shift my focus to the guitar, its strings beckoning me to explore new sonic landscapes. I strum a chord, the vibrations resonating through my fingertips. The sound is raw and powerful, a surge of energy that courses through my veins. I am sixteen now, sitting on my bedroom floor, surrounded by posters of my favorite bands. The air crackles with youthful rebellion and the yearning for self-expression. I pour my frustrations and dreams into the music, channeling my angst into powerful riffs and heartfelt lyrics.

The music swells and crashes like waves on the shore, reflecting the turbulence of adolescence. I lose myself in the moment, the guitar becoming an extension of myself. The final strum fades away, leaving a sense of catharsis and release.

I return to the piano, drawn back to its elegance and versatility. My fingers glide across the keys, exploring new melodies and harmonies. I am no longer a child or a teenager, but a mature musician, my skills honed by years of practice and dedication. I weave together elements of classical, jazz, and folk music, creating a unique sound that reflects my diverse influences.

The music flows effortlessly, a testament to my mastery of the instrument. I am in complete control, yet I surrender to the creative impulse, allowing the music to guide me. The final notes fade away, leaving a sense of accomplishment and the anticipation of new musical journeys to come.

1. Based on the passage as a whole, the author most likely uses the imagery of a "tapestry of sound" (line 8) to illustrate what about their relationship with music?

A. Music is a complex and intricate art form that requires skill and dedication to master.

B. Music allows the author to express a wide range of emotions and experiences.

C. Music provides a sense of comfort and familiarity for the author.

D. Music is a universal language that can connect people from different backgrounds.

Answer: B

Explanation: The imagery of a "tapestry of sound" suggests a rich and varied expression of emotions and experiences, highlighting the author's ability to convey their inner world through music.

2. In the context of the passage, the phrase "unseen force" (line 10) most likely refers to:

A. The author's subconscious mind guiding their musical expression.

B. The influence of the author's grandmother's musical teachings.

C. The emotional power of the music itself.

D. The technical demands of playing the piano.

Answer: A

Explanation: The phrase "unseen force" suggests a subconscious or intuitive guidance that directs the author's musical expression, highlighting the spontaneous and emotional nature of their playing.

3. The author's description of the Chopin nocturne as a "story" (line 17) emphasizes which aspect of the music?

A. Its technical complexity and challenging passages.

B. Its emotional depth and narrative quality.

C. Its historical significance and cultural context.

D. Its calming and soothing effect on the listener.

Answer: B

Explanation: Comparing the nocturne to a "story" suggests that the music has a narrative quality, conveying emotions and experiences that unfold over time.

4. Which of the following best describes the author's attitude towards their guitar playing during their teenage years?

A. Nostalgic and sentimental

B. Rebellious and defiant

C. Experimental and adventurous

D. Disciplined and focused

Answer: B

Explanation: The passage describes the author's teenage guitar playing as an outlet for "frustrations and dreams," "angst," and "turbulence," suggesting a rebellious and defiant attitude.

5. The author's use of the "The notes cascade like a waterfall" (line 8) primarily serves to:

A. Highlight the technical complexity of playing the piano.
B. Convey the emotional flow of the music being played.
C. Emphasize the physical movement of the musician\u2019s fingers.
D. Suggest the natural and effortless quality of the performance.

Answer: B

Explanation:
 The phrase "The notes cascade like a waterfall" uses vivid imagery to convey the emotional depth and fluidity of the music. The comparison to a waterfall evokes a sense of continuous motion and the outpouring of feelings, emphasizing how the music flows effortlessly and harmoniously, reflecting the artist's emotions. This aligns with the broader theme of the passage, which focuses on music as an emotional and expressive art form rather than just a technical skill.

6. Which of the following best describes the tone of the passage?

A. Analytical and objective

B. Reflective and introspective

C. Humorous and lighthearted

D. Critical and judgmental

Answer: B

Explanation: The passage is characterized by a reflective and introspective tone, as the author explores their personal connection to music and its impact on their life.

7. The author's decision to alternate between playing the piano and the guitar throughout the passage most likely serves to:

A. Demonstrate their versatility as a musician.

B. Highlight the contrasting emotions associated with each instrument.

C. Reflect the different stages of their musical development.

D. Emphasize the importance of both melody and harmony in music.

Answer: C

Explanation: The shifts between piano and guitar playing correspond to different periods in the author's life, suggesting that each instrument represents a distinct phase of their musical journey.

8. Which of the following is NOT mentioned in the passage as a way in which the author engages with music?

A. Playing the piano

B. Composing original songs

C. Listening to recordings of famous musicians

D. Playing the guitar

Answer: C

Explanation: The passage focuses on the author's active engagement with music through playing instruments and creating their own music, but it does not mention listening to recordings.

9. The author's description of the guitar as "strings beckoning me to explore new sonic landscapes" (line 20) primarily serves to:

A.   Illustrate   the   versatility   of   the   guitar   as   an   instrument.
B.   Highlight   the   author's   curiosity   and   creativity   in   music.
C.   Emphasize   the   technical   aspects   of   playing   the   guitar.
D. Convey the transformative power of music during adolescence.

Answer: B

Explanation: The phrase strings beckoning me to explore new sonic landscapes conveys a sense of curiosity and creative exploration. By personifying the guitar, the author emphasizes their emotional connection to the instrument and the inspiration it provides. This aligns with the theme of music as a deeply personal and expressive outlet, showcasing the author's willingness to experiment and push boundaries in their musical journey.

10. Which of the following best summarizes the main idea of the passage?

A. Music is a powerful tool for self-expression and personal growth.

B. The author's passion for music has been nurtured by influential figures in their life.

C. Different musical instruments can evoke different emotions and experiences.

D. The creative process of making music is a deeply personal and rewarding experience.

Answer: D

Explanation: The passage primarily focuses on the author's personal journey with music, emphasizing the joy and fulfillment they derive from the creative process itself.

Passage II

Social Science—The Enigma of Chess

Try to imagine a world without chess—no grandmasters, no intricate strategies, no timeless battles of wit and intellect—and you may begin to grasp the profound impact this ancient game has had on human culture. Despite its seemingly simple rules and basic components, chess has proven to be a surprisingly complex and enduring pastime, captivating minds across continents and centuries. However, the precise origins of chess remain shrouded in mystery, with various cultures and civilizations vying for the honor of its creation.

While the exact birthplace of chess remains elusive, historical and archaeological evidence points towards ancient India as a likely contender. The earliest known precursor to chess, a game called Chaturanga, emerged in India around the 6th century CE. Chaturanga shared key similarities with modern chess, including a checkerboard, pieces with distinct powers, and the objective of checkmating the opponent's king.

From India, chess spread along trade routes and through cultural exchanges, reaching Persia, the Arab world, and eventually Europe. As chess migrated across different regions, it underwent various transformations, adapting to local customs and preferences. The rules, pieces, and even the board itself evolved over time, giving rise to distinct regional variations of the game.

Despite these variations, the core essence of chess remained constant: a battle of intellect and strategy, requiring foresight, planning, and the ability to anticipate an opponent's moves. Chess transcended social and cultural boundaries, captivating emperors and commoners alike. It became a symbol of intellectual prowess and strategic thinking, often used to simulate warfare and political maneuvering.

The invention of the printing press in the 15th century marked a turning point in the history of chess. Chess manuals and treatises became widely available, leading to the standardization of rules and the development of sophisticated chess theory. The game's popularity soared, and chess clubs and tournaments emerged across Europe.

The 19th century witnessed the rise of professional chess players and the establishment of international chess competitions. The first official World Chess Championship was held in 1886, marking the beginning of a new era for the game.

Today, chess continues to thrive as a global pastime, enjoyed by millions of people of all ages and backgrounds. It has evolved beyond a mere game, becoming a tool for education, cognitive training, and even artificial intelligence research.

While the exact origins of chess may remain forever shrouded in the mists of time, its enduring legacy is undeniable. Chess stands as a testament to the human fascination with strategy, intellect, and the timeless pursuit of victory on the checkered battlefield.

11. The main purpose of the passage can best be described as an effort to:

A. trace the evolution of chess from its ancient origins to its modern form.

B. highlight the cultural significance of chess and its impact on human history.

C. explain the rules and strategies of chess for novice players.

D. compare and contrast different regional variations of chess.

Answer: B

Explanation: The passage focuses on the broader cultural and historical significance of chess, emphasizing its enduring appeal and its impact on human intellect and strategy.

12. According to the passage, which of the following is NOT a characteristic shared by Chaturanga and modern chess?

A. A checkerboard

B. Pieces with distinct powers

C. The objective of checkmating the opponent's king

D. The use of a timer to regulate moves

Answer: D

Explanation: The passage mentions the checkerboard, pieces with distinct powers, and the objective of checkmating the king as similarities between Chaturanga and modern chess. The use of a timer is a more recent addition to chess, not present in its ancient precursor.

13. Which of the following best describes the author's attitude towards chess?

A. Dismissive and critical

B. Appreciative and respectful

C. Nostalgic and sentimental

D. Humorous and lighthearted

Answer: B

Explanation: The passage conveys an appreciative and respectful tone towards chess, highlighting its intellectual depth, cultural significance, and enduring appeal.

14. The author's use of the phrase "checkered battlefield" (line 32) primarily serves to:

A. emphasize the competitive nature of chess.

B. highlight the strategic complexity of chess.

C. create a visual image of the chessboard.

D. suggests that chess is a metaphor for warfare.

Answer: D

Explanation: The phrase "checkered battlefield" creates a metaphor that links chess to warfare, suggesting that the game involves strategic planning and tactical maneuvers similar to those used in military conflicts.

15. Which of the following is NOT mentioned in the passage as a factor contributing to the evolution of chess?

A. Cultural exchanges between different regions

B. The invention of the printing press

C. The development of artificial intelligence

D. The standardization of rules

Answer: C

Explanation: The passage mentions cultural exchanges, the printing press, and the standardization of rules as factors influencing the evolution of chess. Artificial intelligence is a more recent development that is not discussed in the context of the game's historical evolution.

16. Which of the following best describes the organization of the passage?

A. Chronological

B. Compare and contrast

C. Cause and effect

D. Problem and solution

Answer: A

Explanation: The passage follows a roughly chronological order, tracing the development of chess from its ancient origins in India to its modern form.

17. Which of the following is an example of figurative language used in the passage?

A. "Try to imagine a world without chess"

B. "The earliest known precursor to chess"

C. "Chess transcended social and cultural boundaries"

D. "The game's popularity soared"

Answer: C

Explanation: The phrase "Chess transcended social and cultural boundaries" uses figurative language to convey the idea that chess appealed to people from diverse backgrounds and social classes.

18. Which of the following is a synonym for the word "elusive" as used in the passage?

A. Obvious

B. Evident

C. Mysterious

D. Simple

Answer: C

Explanation: The word "elusive" in the passage means difficult to find or grasp, which is synonymous with "mysterious."

19. Which of the following is an antonym for the word "standardization" as used in the passage?

A. Uniformity

B. Consistency

C. Variation

D. Regulation

Answer: C

Explanation: The word "standardization" in the passage refers to the process of making rules and practices consistent. The opposite of this is "variation."

20. Which of the following best summarizes the main idea of the passage?

A. Chess is an ancient game with a rich history and cultural significance.

B. The origins of chess are uncertain, but evidence suggests it may have originated in India.

C. Chess has evolved over time, but its core elements of strategy and intellect remain constant.

D. Chess is a popular pastime enjoyed by people of all ages and backgrounds around the world.

Answer: A

Explanation: The passage provides a comprehensive overview of chess, highlighting its historical development, cultural significance, and enduring appeal.

Passage III

Humanities—Breaking Barriers: The Evolution of the Novel

The novel, a sprawling and versatile form of literary expression, has undergone a remarkable transformation throughout history. From its humble beginnings as a mere diversion for the leisure class to its current status as a powerful tool for social commentary and cultural exploration, the novel has consistently pushed the boundaries of storytelling and challenged conventional notions of literature.

Early novels, often characterized by sentimental plots and idealized characters, primarily served as a form of escapism for the wealthy elite. However, as the reading public expanded and diversified, so too did the scope and ambition of the novel. Writers began to explore more complex themes, such as social injustice, political corruption, and the psychological depths of human experience.

The rise of realism in the 19th century marked a significant turning point in the evolution of the novel. Authors like Charles Dickens and Gustave Flaubert meticulously depicted the realities of everyday life, exposing the grim underbelly of industrial society and challenging the romanticized portrayals of the past.

The 20th century witnessed a further explosion of experimentation and innovation in the novel. Modernist writers like Virginia Woolf and James Joyce shattered traditional narrative structures, delving into the stream of consciousness and exploring the fragmented nature of human perception.

Postmodernism, with its playful self-awareness and rejection of grand narratives, further challenged the conventions of the novel. Authors like Thomas Pynchon and Gabriel García Márquez embraced metafiction, intertextuality, and magical realism, blurring the lines between reality and fiction and questioning the very nature of storytelling.

Today, the novel continues to evolve, adapting to the ever-changing cultural landscape and embracing new technologies and forms of expression. Graphic novels, interactive fiction, and hybrid forms that blend text with other media are pushing the boundaries of the novel and challenging traditional definitions of literature.

The novel's enduring appeal lies in its ability to transport readers to different worlds, introduce them to diverse characters, and explore the complexities of human experience. Whether it serves as a mirror to society, a window into the human soul, or a portal to fantastical realms, the novel remains a vital and vibrant form of artistic expression.

21. Based on the passage, it is reasonable to infer that which of the following played the most significant role in the evolution of the novel?

A. Technological advancements in printing and publishing

B. Changes in social and cultural values

C. The rise of literary criticism and theory

D. Competition from other forms of entertainment

Answer: B

Explanation: The passage emphasizes how the novel has adapted to changing social and cultural values, reflecting the evolving concerns and interests of readers throughout history.

22. Which of the following is NOT mentioned in the passage as a characteristic of early novels?

A. Sentimental plots

B. Idealized characters

C. Complex themes

D. Focus on escapism

Answer: C

Explanation: The passage describes early novels as primarily serving as escapism for the wealthy elite, with sentimental plots and idealized characters. Complex themes are associated with later developments in the novel.

23. The author's use of the phrase "grim underbelly" (line 11) primarily serves to:

A. emphasize the negative aspects of industrial society.

B. create a sense of mystery and suspense.

C. highlight the contrast between rich and poor.

D. criticize the romanticized view of the past.

Answer: A

Explanation: The phrase "grim underbelly" refers to the harsh realities of industrial society that were often hidden or ignored, emphasizing the negative aspects of this period.

24. Which of the following literary movements is most closely associated with the "stream of consciousness" technique (line 15)?

A. Realism

B. Modernism

C. Postmodernism

D. Romanticism

Answer: B

Explanation: The "stream of consciousness" technique, which involves[4] depicting the flow of thoughts and feelings in a character's mind, is a hallmark of Modernist literature.

25. Which of the following authors is NOT mentioned in the passage as a representative of Postmodernism?

A. Charles Dickens

B. Thomas Pynchon

C. Gabriel García Márquez

D. Virginia Woolf

Answer: A

Explanation: The passage mentions Thomas Pynchon and Gabriel García Márquez as representatives of Postmodernism. Charles Dickens is associated with Realism, while Virginia Woolf is associated with Modernism.

26. Which of the following is NOT mentioned in the passage as a way in which the novel has evolved in recent times?

A. Graphic novels

B. Interactive fiction

C. Hybrid forms blending text with other media

D. Adaptation into film and television

Answer: D

Explanation: The passage mentions graphic novels, interactive fiction, and hybrid forms as recent developments in the novel. Adaptation into film and television, while a common practice, is not specifically mentioned in the passage.

27. The author's use of the phrase "a mirror to society" (line 25) primarily serves to:

A. emphasize the novel's ability to reflect social realities.

B. highlight the importance of accuracy in historical fiction.

C. suggest that novels can influence social change.[5] D. criticize the superficiality of some contemporary novels.

Answer: A

Explanation: The phrase "a mirror to society" suggests that novels can accurately reflect the social conditions, values, and concerns of a particular time and place.

28. Which of the following is a synonym for the word "versatile" as used in the passage?

A. Limited

B. Adaptable

C. Simple

D. Traditional

Answer: B

Explanation: The word "versatile" in the passage means adaptable or[6] capable of fulfilling multiple functions, which is synonymous with "adaptable."

29. Which of the following is an antonym for the word "conventional" as used in the passage?

A. Traditional

B. Ordinary

C. Unorthodox

D. Conservative

Answer: C **Explanation:** The word "conventional" in the passage means traditional or conforming to established norms. The opposite of this is "unorthodox."

30. Which of the following best summarizes the main idea of the passage?

A. The novel has undergone a continuous process of evolution and innovation throughout history.

B. Realism and Modernism were the most significant literary movements in the development of the novel.

C. The novel has served as a powerful tool for social commentary and cultural exploration.

D. The future of the novel is uncertain, but it will likely continue to adapt to new technologies and forms of expression.

Answer: A

Explanation: The passage provides a broad overview of the historical development of the novel, emphasizing its continuous evolution and adaptation to changing social and cultural contexts.

Passage IV

Natural Science—Genetics

Passage A

The 20th century witnessed remarkable advancements in our understanding of genetics, with the discovery of DNA's structure and the development of powerful tools for manipulating genetic material. However, alongside these scientific breakthroughs, there have been accidental discoveries and unexpected observations that have significantly shaped our knowledge of genes and their influence on human traits and diseases.

One such accidental discovery involves the peculiar case of a family with an unusually high prevalence of blue eyes. For generations, this family exhibited a striking pattern of blue-eyed individuals, despite having ancestors with diverse eye colors. Intrigued by this phenomenon, geneticists investigated the family's genetic makeup and discovered a rare mutation in a gene responsible for eye color. This mutation disrupted the production of melanin in the iris, resulting in the characteristic blue hue.

This accidental finding provided valuable insights into the genetic mechanisms that determine eye color and highlighted the potential for rare mutations to have significant phenotypic effects. It also underscored the importance of studying families with unusual traits to uncover hidden genetic variations and expand our understanding of human genetics.

Another intriguing observation involves the unexpected link between a specific gene variant and an increased risk of developing certain types of cancer. While studying a large population cohort, researchers noticed a higher incidence of cancer among individuals carrying a particular variant of a gene involved in DNA repair. This gene variant was found to impair the cell's ability to repair damaged DNA, leading to an accumulation of mutations and an increased susceptibility to cancer.

This unexpected finding shed light on the complex interplay between genes and environmental factors in cancer development. It also highlighted the potential for genetic screening to identify individuals at higher risk for certain cancers, paving the way for personalized prevention and treatment strategies.

Passage B

The cerebellum, a small but mighty structure nestled at the base of the brain, has long been recognized for its crucial role in coordinating movement and maintaining balance. Recent research, however, has revealed that the cerebellum's influence extends far beyond motor control, implicating it in a wide range of cognitive functions, including language processing, attention, and even social cognition.

Given its extensive connections to various brain regions, including the cerebral cortex and the limbic system, it is perhaps not surprising that the cerebellum's influence is so widespread. Studies using functional magnetic resonance imaging (fMRI) have shown that the cerebellum is activated during a variety of cognitive tasks, such as reading, problem-solving, and emotional regulation.

One particularly intriguing area of research focuses on the cerebellum's role in language processing. fMRI studies have revealed that the cerebellum is involved in various aspects of language, including syntax, semantics, and pragmatics. It is thought that the cerebellum contributes to the precise timing and coordination of neural activity required for fluent speech and language comprehension.

Moreover, the cerebellum's involvement in attention and working memory has also been documented. Studies have shown that individuals with cerebellar damage often exhibit deficits in attentional control and working memory capacity. The cerebellum is thought to play a role in filtering out distractions and maintaining focus on relevant information.

Perhaps most surprisingly, the cerebellum has been implicated in social cognition, the ability to understand and interact with others. Research suggests that the cerebellum contributes to the processing of social cues, such as facial expressions and body language, and may play a role in empathy and social decision-making.

These findings challenge the traditional view of the cerebellum as solely a motor control center and highlight its multifaceted contributions to cognition and behavior. As we continue to explore the complexities of the brain, the cerebellum's role in shaping our thoughts, emotions, and social interactions is likely to become even more apparent.

Questions 31–33 are about Passage A.

31. Which of the following explanations would most logically explain why scientists have not been able to study many cases of families with unusual traits like the blue-eyed family mentioned in the passage?

A. Genetic research is often expensive and time-consuming, requiring large sample sizes and sophisticated laboratory techniques.

B. Families with unusual traits may be reluctant to participate in genetic studies due to concerns about privacy or potential stigma.

C. Many unusual traits are caused by complex interactions between multiple genes and environmental factors, making them difficult to study.

D. Genetic mutations that cause unusual traits are often rare and occur sporadically, making it challenging to identify and study affected families.

Answer: D

Explanation: The passage mentions that the blue-eyed family had a "rare mutation," suggesting that such genetic variations are not common and may be difficult to find and study.

32. The author's use of the phrase "accidental discovery" (line 6) in relation to the blue-eyed family primarily serves to:

A. emphasize the role of serendipity in scientific research.

B. highlight the limitations of traditional genetic studies.

C. suggest that the discovery was not scientifically rigorous.

D. downplay the significance of the finding.

Answer: A

Explanation: The phrase "accidental discovery" emphasizes that the finding was not the result of a planned experiment but rather an unexpected observation that led to new insights.

33. Which of the following best describes the tone of the passage?

A. Skeptical and critical

B. Informative and objective

C. Persuasive and argumentative

D. Speculative and hypothetical

Answer: B

Explanation: The passage presents information about genetic discoveries in a neutral and objective tone, focusing on the scientific evidence and its implications.

Questions 34–37 are about Passage B.

34. Based on the passage, which represents a proper sequence of mental events?

A. Visual perception of facial expressions → processing by the cerebellum → social cognition

B. Social cognition → visual perception of facial expressions → processing by the cerebellum

C. Processing by the cerebellum → social cognition → visual perception of facial expressions

D. Visual perception of facial expressions → social cognition → processing by the cerebellum

Answer: A

Explanation: The passage suggests that the cerebellum processes visual cues, such as facial expressions, which contribute to social cognition, the ability to understand and interact with others.

35. Which of the following is NOT mentioned in the passage as a function of the cerebellum?

A. Coordinating movement

B. Maintaining balance

C. Regulating emotions

D. Controlling appetite

Answer: D

Explanation: The passage mentions the cerebellum's role in coordinating movement, maintaining balance, and regulating emotions. Controlling appetite is not discussed in the passage.

36. The author's use of the phrase "small but mighty" (line 1) primarily serves to:

A. emphasize the cerebellum's compact size.

B. highlight the cerebellum's diverse functions.

C. contrast the cerebellum with other brain regions.

D. downplay the cerebellum's importance.

Answer: B

Explanation: The phrase "small but mighty" emphasizes that despite its relatively small size, the cerebellum plays a crucial role in various cognitive functions.

37. Which of the following best describes the tone of the passage?

A. Skeptical and dismissive

B. Informative and intrigued

C. Persuasive and passionate

D. Humorous and satirical

Answer: B

Explanation: The passage presents information about the cerebellum's functions in an informative and intrigued tone, highlighting recent research and its implications for our understanding of the brain.

Questions 38–40 are about both passages.

38. Which concept discussed in Passage A is most relevant to the discussion of addiction in Passage B?

(A) Genetic mutations

(B) Eye color variation

(C) DNA repair mechanisms

(D) Environmental factors

Answer: (A)

Explanation: Passage A discusses how genetic mutations can influence traits and disease susceptibility. This concept is relevant to Passage B's discussion of addiction, as genetic variations can contribute to an individual's vulnerability to addiction.

39. Based on both passages, which of the following statements about the brain is most accurate?

(A) The brain's functions are rigidly localized to specific regions.

(B) The brain is capable of significant adaptation and reorganization after injury.

(C) Genetic factors play a minimal role in shaping brain function.

(D) The brain's response to stress is primarily determined by environmental factors.

Answer: (B)

Explanation: Passage A highlights the brain's ability to adapt after injury, as seen in the case of H.M., who developed new strategies to compensate for his memory impairment. Passage B emphasizes the interconnectedness of different brain regions and their influence on various functions, suggesting plasticity and adaptability.

40. If the researchers in Passage A were to collaborate with the author of Passage B, which of the following research questions would they be most likely to investigate?

(A) How do genetic variations influence the activity of the amygdala and its role in addiction?

(B) What are the long-term effects of social isolation on dopamine levels in the prefrontal cortex?

(C) Does the cerebellum play a role in the development of anterograde amnesia after traumatic brain injury?

(D) How do environmental factors interact with genetic predispositions to influence eye color variation?

Answer: (A)

Explanation: Both passages touch upon the interplay between brain function, genetics, and behavior. A collaborative research question would likely explore how genetic variations might affect the amygdala's activity and its role in addiction, bridging the concepts discussed in both passages.

STOP

If there is still time remaining, you may review your answers.

By skimming strategically, you can save time and focus on the most important scientific information.

Chapter 4: science

This chapter delves into the ACT Science section, offering a comprehensive guide to the types of passages you'll encounter and the strategies for effectively tackling them.

Data Representation

The ACT Science section assesses your ability to interpret, analyze, and evaluate scientific data presented in various formats, such as graphs, tables, and diagrams. This subchapter provides a comprehensive overview of the data representation skills necessary for success on the test.

Understanding Graphs

Graphs are visual representations of data that show the relationship between two or more variables. The ACT Science section may include various types of graphs, such as:

- **Line graphs:** Show the relationship between two variables over time or another continuous variable. For example, a line graph might show how the temperature of a substance changes over time as it is heated.
- **Bar graphs:** Compare different categories or groups of data. For example, a bar graph might compare the average heights of different plant species.
- **Pie charts:** Show the proportions of a whole. For example, a pie chart might show the percentage of different gases in the Earth's atmosphere.
- **Scatter plots:** Display the relationship between two variables, often used to identify trends or correlations. For example, a scatter plot might show the relationship between the amount of fertilizer used and the yield of a crop.

When interpreting graphs, pay close attention to the following features:

- **Title:** Provides a concise description of the data being presented, giving you context for understanding the graph.
- **Axes:** Represent the variables being measured. Typically, the independent variable (the one being manipulated) is on the x-axis, and the dependent variable (the one being

measured) is on the y-axis. Understanding the axes is crucial for interpreting the relationship between the variables.

- **Labels:** Provide critical information about the variables, including units of measurement, scales, and any other relevant details. Carefully examine the labels to ensure you understand what the data represents.

- **Data points:** Represent individual measurements or observations. Analyze the data points to identify patterns, trends, or outliers.

- **Trend lines:** Show the overall pattern or relationship between the variables. Trend lines can help you visualize the general direction of the data and make predictions or inferences.

Understanding Tables

Tables organize data into rows and columns, making it easy to compare and analyze different values. When interpreting tables, pay close attention to the following:

- **Title:** Provides a brief description of the data being presented, giving you context for understanding the table.

- **Headings:** Label the rows and columns, indicating the variables being measured and any other relevant information. Carefully examine the headings to understand how the data is organized and what each value represents.

- **Units:** Indicate the units of measurement for each variable. Ensure you understand the units used to avoid misinterpreting the data.

- **Data values:** Represent individual measurements or observations. Analyze the data values to identify patterns, trends, or outliers.

Understanding Diagrams

Diagrams are visual representations of objects, processes, or systems. They can be used to illustrate complex scientific concepts or to show the relationships between different parts of a system. When interpreting diagrams, pay attention to the following:

- **Labels:** Identify the different parts of the diagram and any other relevant information. Labels provide context and help you understand the components of the diagram.
- **Arrows:** Indicate the direction of flow or movement within the system. Arrows can help you understand the relationships and interactions between different parts of the diagram.
- **Symbols:** Represent specific objects or concepts. Familiarize yourself with common scientific symbols to accurately interpret the diagram.

Research Summaries

The ACT Science section may include passages that summarize scientific research studies. These passages typically describe the purpose, methods, results, and conclusions of the studies.

Understanding the Research Design

When reading research summaries, pay close attention to the following aspects:

- **Purpose:** What was the research question or hypothesis being investigated? Understanding the purpose helps you frame the entire study and its findings.
- **Methods:** How was the study conducted? What were the variables being measured and how were they manipulated? Analyzing the methods allows you to evaluate the validity and reliability of the study.
- **Results:** What were the main findings of the study? Focus on the key results and how they relate to the research question or hypothesis.
- **Conclusions:** What did the researchers conclude from their findings? Consider whether the conclusions are supported by the results and whether they address the research question or hypothesis.

Evaluating the Research

When evaluating research summaries, critically consider the following:

- **Validity:** Are the methods appropriate for addressing the research question? Are the results reliable and accurate? Assess whether the study was designed and conducted in a way that produces trustworthy results.

- **Generalizability:** Can the findings be generalized to other populations or contexts? Consider whether the study's sample and methodology allow for broader conclusions.

- **Implications:** What are the implications of the findings for future research or for practical applications? Think about how the study's findings might contribute to scientific knowledge or real-world solutions.

Conflicting Viewpoints

The ACT Science section may include passages that present conflicting viewpoints on a scientific topic. These passages typically present two or more different perspectives on the same issue, often supported by different evidence or interpretations.

Understanding the Different Viewpoints

When reading conflicting viewpoints passages, pay close attention to the following:

- **Main points:** What are the main arguments or claims of each viewpoint? Clearly identify the core message of each perspective.

- **Evidence:** What evidence is used to support each viewpoint? Analyze the quality and relevance of the evidence presented.

- **Assumptions:** What are the underlying assumptions of each viewpoint? Consider any unstated beliefs or perspectives that might influence the arguments.

- **Points of agreement and disagreement:** Where do the viewpoints agree and disagree? Identify the common ground and the points of contention between the perspectives.

Evaluating the Different Viewpoints

When evaluating conflicting viewpoints passages, consider the following:

- **Strengths and weaknesses:** What are the strengths and weaknesses of each viewpoint? Assess the logical coherence, evidence quality, and potential biases of each perspective.

- **Logic and reasoning:** How logical and well-reasoned is each viewpoint? Evaluate the clarity and soundness of the arguments presented.

- **Evidence:** How strong and convincing is the evidence presented for each viewpoint? Consider the relevance, reliability, and sufficiency of the evidence.

- **Bias:** Are there any biases or personal opinions that might influence the presentation of each viewpoint? Be aware of any potential biases that might affect the objectivity of the arguments.

Questions

Chapter 5: Writing (Optional)

This chapter provides a comprehensive guide to the ACT Writing test, offering strategies and techniques to help you craft a compelling and well-structured essay that effectively conveys your ideas and analysis.

Planning and Organizing Your Essay

Prewriting

Before you begin writing your essay, it's crucial to dedicate a few minutes to planning and organizing your thoughts. This prewriting stage helps you lay a solid foundation for a focused and coherent essay that effectively addresses the prompt.

Consider these prewriting strategies:

- **Brainstorming:** Begin by actively engaging with the prompt. Underline keywords and phrases that indicate the central theme and the specific task. Then, jot down any ideas, arguments, and examples that come to mind. Don't censor yourself at this stage; simply let your ideas flow freely. This unfiltered approach can help you generate a wide range of potential arguments and supporting evidence, ensuring you explore various perspectives before settling on your main point.

- **Outlining:** Once you have a pool of ideas, start organizing them into a structured outline. Identify your main argument and the supporting points you'll use to develop it. Arrange these points in a logical order that effectively builds your argument. Include specific examples and evidence you'll use to illustrate each point. This structured approach helps organize your thoughts and ensures a logical flow in your essay. An outline can serve as a roadmap for your writing, keeping you on track and preventing you from straying from your main argument.

- **Mind Mapping:** If you're a visual learner, consider creating a mind map. Start with the central theme of the prompt in the center of your page. Then, branch out with related concepts, arguments, and examples. Connect these branches to show relationships between ideas and identify potential arguments. Mind mapping can be especially helpful for visual learners who prefer to see their ideas laid out spatially. It allows for a more organic exploration of ideas and can help you discover connections you might not have noticed otherwise.

- **T-Charts:** To delve deeper into the complexities of the issue, use a T-chart. Divide your page into two columns and label them with opposing perspectives or contrasting viewpoints. List the pros and cons of each perspective or compare and contrast their arguments and evidence. This can help you analyze the nuances of the issue and develop a nuanced perspective, demonstrating your ability to consider multiple viewpoints and form a well-reasoned opinion.

- **Freewriting:** If you're struggling to generate ideas or feeling stuck, try freewriting. Write continuously for a few minutes, exploring your thoughts and ideas without worrying about grammar or structure. This can help you generate ideas and discover your main argument. Freewriting can be a helpful way to overcome writer's block and get your ideas flowing. It allows you to tap into your subconscious and explore ideas without the pressure of perfection.

Remember to manage your time effectively during the prewriting stage. You have only 40 minutes for the entire writing process, so allocate your time wisely. Aim to spend no more than 5-10 minutes on prewriting to leave ample time for drafting, revising, and proofreading your essay.

Thesis Writing

Your thesis statement is the central argument of your essay. It should be clear, concise, and focused, providing a roadmap for your essay and helping the reader understand your main point.

Consider these characteristics of a good thesis statement:

- **Clarity:** It should clearly state your main argument or position on the issue, leaving no room for ambiguity. The reader should be able to immediately understand your stance on the topic.

- **Conciseness:** It should be expressed in a clear and succinct manner, avoiding unnecessary words or phrases that could obscure your main point. A concise thesis statement is more impactful and easier for the reader to grasp.

- **Focus:** It should be specific and focused, addressing the prompt directly and avoiding irrelevant tangents. Stay on topic and ensure your thesis statement directly responds to the prompt's central question or issue.

- **Strength:** It should make a strong and defensible claim, not simply a statement of fact or observation. Your thesis should be something you can argue for and support with evidence. It should present a clear stance that you can develop and defend throughout your essay.

Examples and Description

Use specific examples and descriptions to support your ideas. This makes your essay more persuasive and engaging by providing concrete evidence and vivid imagery to illustrate your points.

When choosing examples, ensure they are:

- **Relevant:** Directly related to your topic and thesis statement, providing clear support for your arguments. Choose examples that directly illustrate or support your main points and avoid those that are tangential or irrelevant.

- **Specific:** Detailed and concrete, providing vivid imagery and supporting your arguments effectively. Instead of general statements, use specific details, anecdotes, or scenarios to paint a clear picture for the reader and make your arguments more compelling.

- **Explanatory:** Clearly explained and connected to your main points, demonstrating how they contribute to your overall argument. Don't just present examples; explain their significance and how they support your thesis statement.

- **Varied:** Drawn from different sources or areas of knowledge to demonstrate a breadth of understanding and avoid relying too heavily on a single example. Use examples from history, literature, current events, personal experience, or any other relevant area to show a well-rounded understanding of the issue.

Evaluating Complexity and Other Viewpoints

The ACT essay prompt will ask you to consider multiple viewpoints on a given issue. Be sure to address these viewpoints in your essay to demonstrate your ability to engage with complex ideas and consider different perspectives.

Here are some ways to address multiple viewpoints:

- **Acknowledge and explain:** Summarize each viewpoint accurately and explain its key arguments and supporting evidence. This shows that you understand the different perspectives involved and can engage with them fairly.

- **Compare and contrast:** Identify similarities and differences between the viewpoints, highlighting areas of agreement and disagreement. This helps you analyze the nuances of the issue and develop a more nuanced perspective, demonstrating your ability to see beyond simple black-and-white arguments.

- **Analyze strengths and weaknesses:** Evaluate the merits and limitations of each viewpoint, considering the logic, evidence, and assumptions behind each perspective. This demonstrates your critical thinking skills and ability to evaluate arguments objectively.

- **Develop your own perspective:** Formulate your own position on the issue, drawing on the insights gained from analyzing the different viewpoints. This shows that you can synthesize information and form your own informed opinion, demonstrating your ability to think independently and critically.

Wording and Sentence Structure

Use precise and varied language in your essay. This will make your writing more sophisticated and interesting to read by showcasing your command of language and your ability to express ideas effectively.

Consider these strategies for effective language use:

- **Precise vocabulary:** Choose words that accurately convey your meaning and avoid ambiguity. This ensures that your ideas are clear and easily understood by the reader.

- **Figurative language:** Use metaphors, similes, and analogies to create vivid imagery and enhance your arguments. This can make your writing more engaging and memorable.

- **Varied sentence structure:** Use a mix of simple, compound, and complex sentences to create rhythm and flow in your writing. This keeps the reader interested and prevents your essay from sounding monotonous.

- **Transition words and phrases:** Use transitions to connect ideas and create a smooth flow between paragraphs. This helps the reader follow your line of reasoning and understand the relationships between your ideas.

Developing and Supporting Your Ideas

Examples

Use specific and relevant examples to support your ideas. This will make your essay more persuasive and engaging by providing concrete evidence and grounding your arguments in real-world situations.

When choosing examples, be sure to select ones that you can explain clearly and that are relevant to your topic. Examples should be more than just passing mentions; they should be developed and explained in detail to show how they support your arguments.

Descriptions

Use vivid and descriptive language to bring your ideas to life. This will help your reader understand and appreciate your points by creating a more engaging and immersive reading experience.

Descriptive language can involve sensory details, figurative language, and evocative imagery. By painting a picture with your words, you can make your ideas more memorable and impactful.

Analysis

Go beyond simply stating your opinion. Analyze the issue and explain your reasoning. This will show the reader that you have thought critically about the topic and that your arguments are based on careful consideration and evaluation of the evidence.

Analysis involves breaking down complex ideas into their component parts, examining relationships between different concepts, and providing logical explanations for your claims. By demonstrating your analytical skills, you can strengthen your arguments and impress the reader with your depth of understanding.

Language Use and Conventions

Grammar

Use correct grammar and punctuation. This will make your essay easier to read and understand by ensuring clarity and precision in your writing. Grammatical errors can distract the reader and hinder their comprehension of your ideas.

Spelling

Proofread your essay carefully for spelling errors. Spelling mistakes can undermine your credibility and make your writing appear careless.[7] Take the time to review your essay for any spelling errors before submitting it.

Style

Use a formal writing style. Avoid slang and contractions. This maintains a professional tone and demonstrates your understanding of academic writing conventions.

By following the tips in this chapter, you can write a strong and effective ACT essay that showcases your critical thinking, analytical, and writing skills. Remember to plan and organize your thoughts, use specific examples and descriptions, analyze the issue thoroughly, and maintain a clear and formal writing style.

With practice, you can improve your writing skills and score well on the ACT Writing test.

Full-Length Practice Test 1 (English Test)

Time: 45 Minutes—75 Questions

Directions: In the passages that follow, you will find underlined words and phrases. In the column to the right, there are alternatives to the underlined wording. For most questions, choose the option that expresses the idea most effectively, conforms to the standards of conventional English, or has wording consistent with the tone and style of the passage. If you think the original underlined wording is best, pick "NO CHANGE." For some problems, you will need to read a question about the underlined portion and pick the best answer to the question. Other problems may ask about portions of the passage or the entire passage. These questions will be indicated by a numbered box. Choose the best answer to each question and fill in the matching oval on your answer sheet. Be sure to consider any relevant context surrounding the question in determining your answer.

Passage I

In the dynamic world of modern business, trademarks have become an essential tool for companies to distinguish themselves and their products from the competition. In today's global marketplace, consumers are bombarded with a vast array of choices, making it crucial for businesses to establish a unique identity and build brand recognition. A trademark, which can be a word, phrase, symbol, or design, provides legal protection for a company's brand identity, preventing others from using similar marks that could cause confusion in the marketplace. This protection allows businesses to invest in building their brand reputation and customer loyalty, knowing that their efforts will not be undermined by imitators.

What kind of person understands the importance of trademarks in the business world? Someone like Marvel Comics legend Stan Lee does.

Born Stanley Martin Lieber in 1922, Stan Lee began his career as an office assistant at Timely Comics, which would later evolve into Marvel Comics. Despite facing numerous challenges and setbacks in the early years, Lee persevered and eventually revolutionized the comic book industry with his innovative approach to storytelling and character development. He co-created iconic characters like Spider-Man, the Fantastic Four, the X-Men, and the Hulk, imbuing them with relatable human flaws and complex personalities that resonated with readers. Lee also championed diversity and inclusivity in comics, introducing characters from various backgrounds and challenging stereotypes.

Lee's understanding of trademarks extended beyond just protecting his creations. He recognized their power as a marketing tool, using them to build a loyal fan base and expand the reach of Marvel Comics. He actively engaged with fans, attending conventions, writing a monthly column, and responding to reader letters, fostering a sense of community and strengthening the connection between the brand and its audience.

For aspiring entrepreneurs and business leaders, Stan Lee's legacy highlights the importance of trademarks in building a successful brand. His story demonstrates how trademarks can not only protect a company's intellectual property but also serve as a powerful tool for connecting with customers and establishing a lasting presence in the marketplace.

1. Which choice would most effectively introduce the topic of the passage?

(A) NO CHANGE

(B) The history of trademarks can be traced back to ancient civilizations.

(C) Counterfeit goods pose a significant threat to businesses and consumers alike.

(D) Branding is an essential aspect of modern marketing and advertising.

Answer: (A)

Explanation: The original wording effectively introduces the topic of trademarks and their importance in the context of modern business. The other choices are either too broad or too specific.

2. Which of the following alternatives to the underlined portion (consumers are bombarded with a vast array of choices) would NOT be acceptable?

(A) are inundated with

(B) are confronted with

(C) encounter

(D) are limited to

Answer: (D)

Explanation: The word "limited" contradicts the idea that consumers are faced with a vast array of choices. The other choices maintain the sense of abundance.

3. The writer is considering deleting the underlined portion (provides legal protection for a company's brand identity, preventing others from using similar marks that could cause confusion in the marketplace). Should the writer make this deletion?

(A) Yes, because it introduces an irrelevant detail.

(B) Yes, because it contradicts the main idea of the passage.

(C) No, because it provides a necessary transition to the next sentence.

(D) No, because it supports the main idea of the passage.

Answer: (D)

Explanation: The underlined portion explains why trademarks are important for businesses, which supports the main idea of the passage.

4. Which of the following alternatives to the underlined portion would be LEAST acceptable?

(A) safeguarding

(B) shielding

(C) obscuring

(D) preserving

Answer: (C)

Explanation: The word "obscuring" implies hiding or concealing, whereas the passage is discussing protection. The other choices maintain the sense of safeguarding.

5. Which choice most effectively combines the underlined sentences?

(A) This protection allows businesses to invest in building their brand reputation and customer loyalty—knowing that their efforts will not be undermined by imitators.

(B) This protection allows businesses to invest in building their brand reputation and customer loyalty; however, they know that their efforts will not be undermined by imitators.

(C) This protection allows businesses, knowing that their efforts will not be undermined by imitators, to invest in building their brand reputation and customer loyalty.

(D) This protection allows businesses to invest in building their brand reputation and customer loyalty: their efforts will not be undermined by imitators.

Answer: (A) **Explanation:** Choice (A) effectively combines the sentences using a dash to emphasize the consequence of the protection while maintaining clarity and conciseness.

6. Which of the following best maintains the focus of the passage?

(A) NO CHANGE

(B) What kind of person is most likely to create a successful comic book?

(C) What kind of person is most knowledgeable about intellectual property law?

(D) What kind of person is most likely to become a successful entrepreneur?

Answer: (A)

Explanation: The original wording maintains the focus on trademarks and the types of people who understand their importance in the business world.

7. Which of the following alternatives to the underlined portion (<u>Someone like Marvel Comics legend Stan Lee does</u>) would NOT be acceptable?

(A) a perfect example

(B) a notable instance

(C) an embodiment

(D) an insignificant figure

Answer: (D)

Explanation: The phrase "an insignificant figure" contradicts the idea that Stan Lee is a legend in the comic book industry. The other choices maintain the sense of importance.

8. Which of the following best describes the relationship between the first and second paragraphs?

(A) The first paragraph introduces a general concept, and the second paragraph provides a specific example.

(B) The first paragraph presents a problem, and the second paragraph proposes a solution.

(C) The first paragraph makes a claim, and the second paragraph provides evidence to support it.

(D) The first paragraph describes a historical context, and the second paragraph analyzes its implications.

Answer: (A)

Explanation: The first paragraph discusses the importance of trademarks in general terms, while the second paragraph introduces Stan Lee as a specific example of someone who understands their value.

9. Which choice most effectively combines the underlined sentences?

(A) Born Stanley Martin Lieber in 1922, Stan Lee, who began his career as an office assistant at Timely Comics, which would later evolve into Marvel Comics.

(B) Stan Lee, born Stanley Martin Lieber in 1922, began his career as an office assistant at Timely Comics, which would later evolve into Marvel Comics.

(C) Stan Lee began his career as an office assistant at Timely Comics, which would later evolve into Marvel Comics, and was born Stanley Martin Lieber in 1922.

(D) Beginning his career as an office assistant at Timely Comics, which would later evolve into Marvel Comics, Stan Lee was born Stanley Martin Lieber in 1922.

Answer: (B)

Explanation: Choice (B) effectively combines the sentences while maintaining clarity and conciseness.

10. Which of the following alternatives to the underlined portion (Despite facing numerous challenges and setbacks in the early years, Lee persevered and eventually revolutionized the comic book industry with his innovative approach to storytelling and character development) would be LEAST acceptable?

(A) Although

(B) In spite of

(C) Notwithstanding

(D) Because of

Answer: (D)

Explanation: The phrase "because of" implies that the challenges and setbacks were the reason for Lee's perseverance, whereas the passage suggests that he persevered despite these difficulties. The other choices maintain the sense of overcoming obstacles.

11. Which choice most effectively maintains the focus of the passage on Stan Lee's understanding of trademarks?

(A) NO CHANGE

(B) with his artistic talent and creativity.

(C) with his business acumen and marketing savvy.

(D) with his passion for social justice and equality.

Answer: (C)

Explanation: The original wording emphasizes Lee's business skills and understanding of trademarks, which is the focus of the passage.

12. The writer is considering deleting the underlined portion (He co-created iconic characters like Spider-Man, the Fantastic Four, the X-Men, and the Hulk, imbuing them with relatable human flaws and complex personalities that resonated with readers). Should the writer make this deletion?

(A) Yes, because it introduces an irrelevant detail.

(B) Yes, because it contradicts the main idea of the passage.

(C) No, because it provides specific examples of Stan Lee's iconic creations.

(D) No, because it explains why Stan Lee was successful in the comic book industry.

Answer: (C)

Explanation: The underlined portion provides specific examples of Lee's creations, which supports the main idea of the passage about his understanding of trademarks and brand building.

13. Which choice most effectively combines the underlined sentences?

(A) Lee also championed diversity and inclusivity in comics; therefore, he introduced characters from various backgrounds and challenged stereotypes.

(B) Lee also championed diversity and inclusivity in comics, introducing characters from various backgrounds and challenging stereotypes.

(C) Introducing characters from various backgrounds and challenging stereotypes, Lee also championed diversity and inclusivity in comics.

(D) By introducing characters from various backgrounds and challenging stereotypes, Lee also championed diversity and inclusivity in comics.

Answer: (B)

Explanation: Choice (B) effectively combines the sentences while maintaining clarity and conciseness.

14. Which of the following alternatives to the underlined portion (<u>understands</u>) would NOT be acceptable?

(A) grasp

(B) awareness

(C) ignorance

(D) comprehension

Answer: (C)

Explanation: The word "ignorance" contradicts the idea that Stan Lee understood the importance of trademarks. The other choices maintain the sense of understanding.

15. Which choice most effectively concludes the passage?

(A) NO CHANGE

(B) For comic book enthusiasts, Stan Lee's characters will continue to inspire and entertain for generations to come.

(C) For those interested in social justice, Stan Lee's legacy reminds us of the importance of representation and inclusivity in media.

(D) For aspiring artists and writers, Stan Lee's career exemplifies the power of creativity and imagination.

Answer: (A)

Explanation: The original wording effectively concludes the passage by reiterating the main idea about the importance of trademarks in building a successful brand and connecting with customers.

Passage II

In the realm of personal finance, budgeting has become more critical than ever before. In our contemporary economy, individuals and families must be willing to track their income and expenses diligently to achieve financial stability. To do so, there has to be a clear understanding of where their money is going and how to allocate it effectively. A budget provides a framework for managing finances responsibly, ensuring that spending aligns with income and financial goals. This disciplined approach empowers individuals to make informed financial decisions, avoid unnecessary debt, and build a secure financial future.

What kind of person understands the importance of budgeting in personal finance? Someone like renowned investor Warren Buffett does.

Born in 1930 in Nebraska, Warren Buffett displayed an early aptitude for business and investing. Despite facing the challenges of the Great Depression during his childhood, Buffett learned valuable lessons about financial prudence and the importance of long-term investments. He started his investment journey at a young age, delivering newspapers and selling chewing gum, eventually building a vast financial empire through astute investment decisions and a disciplined approach to saving. Buffett is known for his frugal lifestyle and his belief in the power of compounding, emphasizing the importance of saving and investing consistently over time.

Buffett's understanding of budgeting extends beyond just personal finance. He advocates for fiscal responsibility at the national level, emphasizing the importance of balanced budgets and sustainable economic policies. He also practices philanthropy on a grand scale, donating billions of dollars to charitable causes and encouraging others to do the same.

For individuals seeking financial well-being, Warren Buffett's example highlights the importance of budgeting as a cornerstone of responsible financial management. His story demonstrates how a disciplined approach to budgeting can not only lead to personal financial success but also contribute to broader economic stability and social good.

16. Which choice would most effectively introduce the topic of the passage?

(A) NO CHANGE

(B) The history of money and currency can be traced back to ancient civilizations.

(C) Excessive debt is a major problem for individuals and families in today's economy.

(D) Financial literacy is essential for making informed decisions about money management.

Answer: (A) **Explanation:** The original wording effectively introduces the topic of budgeting and its importance in the context of personal finance. The other choices are either too broad or too specific.

17. Which of the following alternatives to the underlined portion (must be willing) would NOT be acceptable?

(A) are required to

(B) must be willing to

(C) should

(D) have to

Answer: (C)

Explanation: The word "should" implies a suggestion or recommendation, whereas the passage aims to convey a necessary condition for financial stability. The other choices maintain the sense of necessity.

18. The writer is considering deleting the underlined portion (<u>A budget provides a framework for managing finances responsibly, ensuring that spending aligns with income and financial goals</u>). Should the writer make this deletion?

(A) Yes, because it introduces an irrelevant detail.

(B) Yes, because it contradicts the main idea of the passage.

(C) No, because it provides a necessary transition to the next sentence.

(D) No, because it supports the main idea of the passage.

Answer: (D)

Explanation: The underlined portion explains why understanding one's finances is important, which supports the main idea of the passage about the importance of budgeting.

19. Which of the following alternatives to the underlined portion (<u>approach</u>) would be LEAST acceptable?

(A) structure

(B) system

(C) disregard

(D) plan

Answer: (C)

Explanation: The word "disregard" contradicts the idea of managing finances responsibly. The other choices maintain the sense of structure and planning.

20. Which choice most effectively combines the underlined sentences?

(A) This disciplined approach empowers individuals to make informed financial decisions, avoid unnecessary debt, and build a secure financial future, which is important.

(B) This disciplined approach empowers individuals to make informed financial decisions, avoid unnecessary debt, and build a secure financial future.

(C) This disciplined approach empowers individuals—to make informed financial decisions, avoid unnecessary debt, and build a secure financial future.

(D) This disciplined approach empowers individuals: to make informed financial decisions, avoid unnecessary debt, and build a secure financial future.

Answer: (B)

Explanation: Choice (B) effectively combines the sentences while maintaining clarity and conciseness.

21. Which of the following best maintains the focus of the passage?

(A) NO CHANGE

(B) What kind of person is most likely to become a successful investor?

(C) What kind of person is most knowledgeable about economic theory?

(D) What kind of person is most likely to donate to charity?

Answer: (A)

Explanation: The original wording maintains the focus on budgeting and the types of people who understand its importance in personal finance.

22. Which of the following alternatives to the underlined portion (<u>Someone like renowned investor Warren Buffett does</u>) would NOT be acceptable?

(A) a prime example

(B) a notable case in point

(C) a representative instance

(D) an infamous character

Answer: (D)

Explanation: The phrase "an infamous character" has a negative connotation that contradicts the positive image of Warren Buffett. The other choices maintain the sense of a positive example.

23. Which of the following best describes the relationship between the first and second paragraphs?

(A) The first paragraph introduces a general concept, and the second paragraph provides a specific example.

(B) The first paragraph presents a problem, and the second paragraph proposes a solution.

(C) The first paragraph makes a claim, and the second paragraph provides evidence to support it.

(D) The first paragraph describes a historical context, and the second paragraph analyzes its implications.

Answer: (A)

Explanation: The first paragraph discusses the importance of budgeting in general terms, while the second paragraph introduces Warren Buffett as a specific example of someone who understands its value.

24. Which choice most effectively combines the underlined sentences?

(A) Born in 1930 in Nebraska, Warren Buffett, who displayed an early aptitude for business and investing.

(B) Warren Buffett, born in 1930 in Nebraska, displayed an early aptitude for business and investing.

(C) Warren Buffett displayed an early aptitude for business and investing, and was born in 1930 in Nebraska.

(D) Displaying an early aptitude for business and investing, Warren Buffett was born in 1930 in Nebraska.

Answer: (B)

Explanation: Choice (B) effectively combines the sentences while maintaining clarity and conciseness.

25. Which of the following alternatives to the underlined portion (Despite facing the challenges of the Great Depression during his childhood) would be LEAST acceptable?

(A) Although

(B) In spite of

(C) Notwithstanding

(D) Because of

Answer: (D)

Explanation: The phrase "because of" implies that the challenges of the Great Depression were the reason for Buffett's financial prudence, whereas the passage suggests that he learned these lessons despite the difficulties. The other choices maintain the sense of overcoming obstacles.

26. Which choice most effectively maintains the focus of the passage on Warren Buffett's understanding of budgeting?

(A) NO CHANGE

(B) with his intelligence and perseverance.

(C) with his philanthropic spirit and generosity.

(D) with his ability to overcome adversity and achieve success.

Answer: (A)

Explanation: The original wording emphasizes Buffett's early interest in finance and investment, which is relevant to his understanding of budgeting.

27. The writer is considering deleting the underlined portion (He started his investment journey at a young age, delivering newspapers and selling chewing gum, eventually building a vast financial empire through astute investment decisions and a disciplined approach to saving). Should the writer make this deletion?

(A) Yes, because it introduces an irrelevant detail.

(B) Yes, because it contradicts the main idea of the passage.

(C) No, because it provides specific examples of Warren Buffett's early ventures.

(D) No, because it explains why Warren Buffett is a renowned investor.

Answer: (C)

Explanation: The underlined portion provides specific examples of Buffett's early experiences with money, which supports the main idea of the passage about his understanding of budgeting.

28. Which choice most effectively combines the underlined sentences?

(A) Buffett is known for his frugal lifestyle; however, he believes in the power of compounding, emphasizing the importance of saving and investing consistently over time.

(B) Buffett is known for his frugal lifestyle, and he believes in the power of compounding, emphasizing the importance of saving and investing consistently over time.

(C) Buffett is known for his frugal lifestyle and his belief in the power of compounding, emphasizing the importance of saving and investing consistently over time.

(D) Emphasizing the importance of saving and investing consistently over time, Buffett is known for his frugal lifestyle and his belief in the power of compounding.

Answer: (C)

Explanation: Choice (C) effectively combines the sentences while maintaining clarity and conciseness.

29. Which of the following alternatives to the underlined portion (Buffett's understanding of budgeting extends beyond just personal finance) would NOT be acceptable?

(A) grasp

(B) awareness

(C) knowledge

(D) disregard

Answer: (D)

Explanation: The word "disregard" contradicts the idea that Warren Buffett understands the importance of budgeting. The other choices maintain the sense of understanding.

30. Which choice most effectively concludes the passage?

(A) NO CHANGE

(B) For those interested in learning more about investing, Warren Buffett's strategies and principles offer valuable insights.

(C) For those interested in philanthropy, Warren Buffett's charitable work serves as an inspiration.

(D) For those seeking financial security, Warren Buffett's life story demonstrates the importance of hard work and dedication.

Answer: (A)

Explanation: The original wording effectively concludes the passage by reiterating the main idea about the importance of budgeting in achieving financial well-being and contributing to broader economic stability and social good.

Passage III

When most people think of grammar, they <u>groan</u> as they recall tedious lessons on diagramming sentences and memorizing obscure rules. <u>They become anxious as they try to remember the difference between a participle and a gerund, or whether to use "who" or "whom."</u> Believe it or not, it is possible to have a <u>great deal of fun with grammar, the foundation of clear and effective communication.</u>

My English teacher, Ms. Johnson, has the most creative way of celebrating National Grammar Day on March 4th of each year. <u>Grammar Day is the most enjoyable learning experience I have ever had.</u> Everyone brings in grammar-themed treats, like "comma cookies" and "semicolon sandwiches." We play interactive games that challenge us to identify grammatical errors and improve our writing skills. <u>In addition to the fun activities,</u> we also earn extra credit for dressing up as famous grammarians. (I have a fantastic costume of William Shakespeare that I plan to wear this year.)

The fun with grammar isn't limited to Ms. Johnson's class. The Merriam-Webster Dictionary, a renowned authority on language, embraces grammar with its entertaining social media presence. They post witty grammar quizzes and memes that engage followers and promote language learning. If you don't find that amusing or interesting, you might want to reconsider your relationship with words.

The best idea I've heard comes from a bookstore that created a "Grammar Emergency Kit." It includes essential grammar guides, humorous punctuation-themed stickers, and a "Grammar Police" badge. When in a social setting, a grammar enthusiast could use this kit to playfully correct grammatical errors and spark conversations about language. If the person they're talking to appreciates their wit and knowledge, they might be really interested in getting to know them better!

If you still don't believe in the fun of grammar, don't worry. There are plenty of other ways to celebrate language and communication. You could write a poem, tell a story, or simply engage in a lively conversation with friends. The possibilities are endless!

31. Which choice would most effectively introduce the topic of the passage?

I(A) NO CHANGE

(B) The history of language can be traced back to ancient civilizations.

(C) Poor grammar can lead to misunderstandings and misinterpretations.

(D) Effective communication is essential for success in all aspects of life.

Answer: (A)

Explanation: The original wording effectively introduces the topic of grammar and challenges the common perception that it is tedious and boring. The other choices are either too broad or too specific.

32. Which of the following alternatives to the underlined portion (groan) would NOT be acceptable?

(A) are forced to

(B) have to

(C) must

(D) are delighted to

Answer: (D)

Explanation: The phrase "are delighted to" contradicts the idea that most people groan when they think of grammar. The other choices maintain the sense of obligation or necessity.

33. The writer is considering deleting the underlined portion (They become anxious as they try to remember the difference between a participle and a gerund, or whether to use "who" or "whom."). Should the writer make this deletion?

(A) Yes, because it introduces an irrelevant detail.

(B) Yes, because it contradicts the main idea of the passage.

(C) No, because it provides a necessary transition to the next sentence.

(D) No, because it supports the main idea of the passage.

Answer: (D)

Explanation: The underlined portion provides specific examples of grammar concepts that people often find challenging, which supports the main idea that grammar can be intimidating.

34. Which of the following alternatives to the underlined portion (great deal of fun with grammar, the foundation of clear and effective communication) would be LEAST acceptable?

(A) structure

(B) basis

(C) destruction

(D) cornerstone

Answer: (C)

Explanation: The word "destruction" contradicts the idea that grammar is the foundation of clear and effective communication. The other choices maintain the sense of support and foundation.

35. Which choice most effectively combines the underlined sentences?

(A) My English teacher, Ms. Johnson, has the most creative way of celebrating National Grammar Day, which is on March 4th of each year.

(B) My English teacher, Ms. Johnson, has the most creative way of celebrating National Grammar Day on March 4th of each year.

(C) My English teacher, Ms. Johnson, on March 4th of each year, has the most creative way of celebrating National Grammar Day.

(D) National Grammar Day, which is on March 4th of each year, is celebrated in the most creative way by my English teacher, Ms. Johnson.

Answer: (B)

Explanation: Choice (B) effectively combines the sentences while maintaining clarity and conciseness.

36. Which of the following best maintains the focus of the passage?

(A) NO CHANGE

(B) What kind of teacher is most likely to make grammar fun?

(C) What kind of person is most knowledgeable about grammar rules?

(D) What kind of student is most likely to enjoy grammar lessons?

Answer: (A)

Explanation: The original wording maintains the focus on grammar and the ways in which it can be made enjoyable.

37. Which of the following alternatives to the underlined portion (<u>Grammar Day is the most enjoyable learning experience I have ever had</u>) would NOT be acceptable?

(A) delightful

(B) engaging

(C) tedious

(D) stimulating

Answer: (C) **Explanation:** The word "tedious" contradicts the idea that Grammar Day is an enjoyable learning experience. The other choices maintain the sense of enjoyment and engagement.

38. Which of the following best describes the relationship between the first and second paragraphs?

(A) The first paragraph introduces a general concept, and the second paragraph provides a specific example.

(B) The first paragraph presents a problem, and the second paragraph proposes a solution.

(C) The first paragraph makes a claim, and the second paragraph provides evidence to support it.

(D) The first paragraph describes a historical context, and the second paragraph analyzes its implications.

Answer: (A) Explanation: The first paragraph discusses the common perception of grammar as tedious, while the second paragraph provides a specific example of how grammar can be made fun and engaging.

39. Which choice most effectively combines the underlined sentences?

(A) Everyone brings in grammar-themed treats, like "comma cookies" and "semicolon sandwiches," and we play interactive games that challenge us to identify grammatical errors and improve our writing skills.

(B) Everyone brings in grammar-themed treats, like "comma cookies" and "semicolon sandwiches." We play interactive games that challenge us to identify grammatical errors and improve our writing skills.

(C) Everyone brings in grammar-themed treats, like "comma cookies" and "semicolon sandwiches," while we play interactive games that challenge us to identify grammatical errors and improve our writing skills.

(D) We play interactive games that challenge us to identify grammatical errors and improve our writing skills, and everyone brings in grammar-themed treats, like "comma cookies" and "semicolon sandwiches."

Answer: (A) Explanation: Choice (A) effectively combines the sentences using a comma and a conjunction while maintaining clarity and conciseness.

40. Which of the following alternatives to the underlined portion (<u>In addition to the fun activities</u>) would be LEAST acceptable?

(A) Furthermore

(B) Additionally

(C) However

(D) Moreover

Answer: (C) **Explanation:** The word "however" implies a contrast or contradiction, whereas the passage is adding to the list of enjoyable activities. The other choices maintain the sense of addition.

41. Which choice most effectively maintains the focus of the passage on the fun aspects of grammar?

(A) NO CHANGE

(B) for demonstrating our knowledge of grammar rules.

(C) for writing creative and grammatically correct stories.

(D) for participating in a grammar-themed debate.

Answer: (A) **Explanation:** The original wording emphasizes the fun and playful aspect of dressing up as famous grammarians, which aligns with the overall tone of the passage.

42. The writer is considering deleting the underlined portion (I have a fantastic costume of William Shakespeare that I plan to wear this year). Should the writer make this deletion?

(A) Yes, because it introduces an irrelevant detail.

(B) Yes, because it contradicts the main idea of the passage.

(C) No, because it provides a specific example of the writer's enthusiasm for grammar.

(D) No, because it explains why the writer enjoys Grammar Day.

Answer: (C) **Explanation:** The underlined portion provides a personal touch and reinforces the writer's enthusiasm for grammar, which contributes to the engaging tone of the passage.

43. Which choice most effectively combines the underlined sentences? (The Merriam-Webster Dictionary, a renowned authority on language, embraces grammar with its entertaining social media presence. They post witty grammar quizzes and memes that engage followers and promote language learning)

(A) The Merriam-Webster Dictionary, a renowned authority on language, embraces grammar, and they post witty grammar quizzes and memes that engage followers and promote language learning.

(B) The Merriam-Webster Dictionary, a renowned authority on language, embraces grammar by posting witty grammar quizzes and memes that engage followers and promote language learning.

(C) Posting witty grammar quizzes and memes that engage followers and promote language learning, the Merriam-Webster Dictionary, a renowned authority on language, embraces grammar.

(D) The Merriam-Webster Dictionary, which is a renowned authority on language, embraces grammar with witty grammar quizzes and memes that engage followers and promote language learning.

Answer: (B) **Explanation:** Choice (B) effectively combines the sentences using a prepositional phrase ("by posting...") while maintaining clarity and conciseness.

44. Which of the following alternatives to the underlined portion (If you don't find that amusing or interesting,) would NOT be acceptable?

(A) If this doesn't amuse you

(B) If you fail to see the humor in this

(C) If you find this dull and uninteresting

(D) If you are indifferent to this

Answer: (D) **Explanation:** The phrase "if you are indifferent to this" does not convey the same level of disapproval as the other choices, which suggest that the reader should be amused by Merriam-Webster's social media presence.

45. Which choice most effectively concludes the passage?

(A) NO CHANGE

(B) So, embrace the fun side of grammar and discover the joy of language learning.

(C) Therefore, grammar is not only essential for effective communication but also a source of entertainment and amusement.

(D) In conclusion, grammar can be fun and engaging if presented in creative and interactive ways.

Answer: (B) **Explanation:** Choice (B) effectively concludes the passage by encouraging readers to embrace the fun side of grammar and explore the joy of language learning, which aligns with the overall message of the passage.

Passage IV

The platypus, a semi-aquatic mammal native to eastern Australia, is one of the most unusual creatures on Earth. It is often described as a "mosaic" animal because it possesses a combination of physical traits that seem to be borrowed from different animal groups. The platypus has a duck-billed snout, webbed feet, a beaver-like tail, and dense, waterproof fur. This unique combination of features has puzzled scientists and naturalists for centuries.

The platypus is also one of the few venomous mammals. Males have spurs on their hind legs that deliver a venom potent enough to cause severe pain to humans. This venom is thought to be used primarily for defense against predators or in competition for mates.

Despite its unusual appearance, the platypus is well-adapted to its semi-aquatic lifestyle. It uses its webbed feet and beaver-like tail for propulsion in the water, and its dense fur provides insulation in cold temperatures. <u>The platypus is a skilled swimmer and diver, and it uses its sensitive bill to detect prey in the murky water.</u>

Platypuses are primarily nocturnal and solitary creatures. <u>They feed on aquatic invertebrates, such as insect larvae, worms, and crustaceans, which they locate using electroreceptors in their bills.</u> <u>These electroreceptors can detect the faint electrical fields generated by the muscle contractions of their prey.</u>

The platypus is a fascinating example of evolutionary adaptation and biological diversity. <u>Its unique combination of physical traits and specialized adaptations make it a truly remarkable creature.</u> However, the platypus is also a vulnerable species, facing threats from habitat loss, pollution, and introduced predators. Conservation efforts are underway to protect this iconic Australian animal and ensure its survival for future generations.

46. Which choice would most effectively introduce the topic of the passage?

(A) NO CHANGE

(B) Australia is home to a diverse array of unique and fascinating wildlife.

(C) Evolutionary adaptation is a process by which species develop traits that help them survive in their environment.

(D) Mammalian diversity encompasses a wide range of physical adaptations and behavioral strategies.

Answer: (A) **Explanation:** The original wording effectively introduces the platypus as an unusual creature and highlights its unique combination of physical traits. The other choices are either too broad or too specific.

47. Which of the following alternatives to the underlined portion (<u>it possesses a combination of physical traits that seem to be borrowed from different animal groups</u>) would NOT be acceptable?

(A) a curious mixture of

(B) an amalgamation of

(C) a harmonious blend of

(D) a bizarre assortment of

Answer: (C) **Explanation:** The phrase "a harmonious blend of" implies that the platypus's features fit together seamlessly, whereas the passage emphasizes their seemingly mismatched nature. The other choices maintain the sense of incongruity.

48. The writer is considering deleting the underlined portion (<u>The platypus has a duck-billed snout, webbed feet, a beaver-like tail, and dense, waterproof fur</u>). Should the writer make this deletion?

(A) Yes, because it introduces an irrelevant detail.

(B) Yes, because it contradicts the main idea of the passage.

(C) No, because it provides a necessary transition to the next sentence.

(D) No, because it supports the main idea of the passage.

Answer: (D) **Explanation:** The underlined portion provides specific examples of the platypus's unusual physical traits, which supports the main idea that it is a "mosaic" animal with a combination of features from different animal groups.

49. Which of the following alternatives to the underlined portion (<u>This unique combination of features has puzzled scientists and naturalists for centuries</u>) would be LEAST acceptable?

(A) baffled

(B) perplexed

(C) enlightened

(D) intrigued

Answer: (C) Explanation: The word "enlightened" implies that scientists fully understand the platypus, whereas the passage emphasizes its puzzling nature. The other choices maintain the sense of mystery and intrigue.

50. Which choice most effectively combines the underlined sentences? (The platypus is also one of the few venomous mammals. Males have spurs on their hind legs that deliver a venom potent enough to cause severe pain to humans)

(A) The platypus is also one of the few venomous mammals, and males have spurs on their hind legs that deliver a venom potent enough to cause severe pain to humans.

(B) The platypus, one of the few venomous mammals, has spurs on the hind legs of males that deliver a venom potent enough to cause severe pain to humans.

(C) Males have spurs on their hind legs that deliver a venom potent enough to cause severe pain to humans, and the platypus is also one of the few venomous mammals.

(D) The platypus is also one of the few venomous mammals: males have spurs on their hind legs that deliver a venom potent enough to cause severe pain to humans.

Answer: (B) Explanation: Choice (B) effectively combines the sentences while maintaining clarity and conciseness.

51. Which of the following best maintains the focus of the passage?

(A) NO CHANGE

(B) What kind of animal is most likely to be venomous?

(C) What kind of habitat is most suitable for the platypus?

(D) What kind of research is being conducted on the platypus?

Answer: (A) Explanation: The original wording maintains the focus on the platypus's unique adaptations and its semi-aquatic lifestyle.

52. Which of the following alternatives to the underlined portion (the platypus is well-adapted to its semi-aquatic lifestyle) would NOT be acceptable?

(A) suited

(B) equipped

(C) unsuited

(D) designed

Answer: (C) **Explanation:** The word "unsuited" contradicts the idea that the platypus is well-adapted to its environment. The other choices maintain the sense of adaptation and suitability.

53. Which of the following best describes the relationship between the first and second paragraphs?

(A) The first paragraph introduces the platypus and its unusual physical traits, and the second paragraph describes one of its unique adaptations.

(B) The first paragraph presents a problem, and the second paragraph proposes a solution.

(C) The first paragraph makes a claim, and the second paragraph provides evidence to support it.

(D) The first paragraph describes a historical context, and the second paragraph analyzes its implications.

Answer: (A) **Explanation:** The first paragraph provides a general overview of the platypus's unusual features, while the second paragraph focuses on its venomous spurs as a specific adaptation.

54. Which choice most effectively combines the underlined sentences? (It uses its webbed feet and beaver-like tail for propulsion in the water, and its dense fur provides insulation in cold temperatures)

(A) It uses its webbed feet and beaver-like tail for propulsion in the water. Its dense fur provides insulation in cold temperatures.

(B) It uses its webbed feet and beaver-like tail for propulsion in the water, and its dense fur provides insulation in cold temperatures.

(C) Its webbed feet and beaver-like tail are used for propulsion in the water, while its dense fur provides insulation in cold temperatures.

(D) Using its webbed feet and beaver-like tail for propulsion in the water, its dense fur provides insulation in cold temperatures.

Answer: (B) **Explanation:** Choice (B) effectively combines the sentences using a comma and a conjunction while maintaining clarity and conciseness.

55. Which of the following alternatives to the underlined portion (The platypus is a skilled swimmer and diver) would be LEAST acceptable?

(A) adept

(B) proficient

(C) inept

(D) capable

Answer: (C) **Explanation:** The word "inept" implies that the platypus is not skilled at swimming and diving, which contradicts the passage's description of it as a skilled swimmer and diver. The other choices maintain the sense of skill and proficiency.

56. Which choice most effectively maintains the focus of the passage on the platypus's unique adaptations?

(A) NO CHANGE

(B) and it enjoys basking in the sun on riverbanks.

(C) and it builds burrows in riverbanks for shelter and nesting.

(D) and it communicates with other platypuses using a variety of vocalizations.

Answer: (C) **Explanation:** The original wording emphasizes the platypus's specialized adaptations for its semi-aquatic lifestyle, which is the focus of the passage.

57. The writer is considering deleting the underlined portion (<u>They feed on aquatic invertebrates, such as insect larvae, worms, and crustaceans, which they locate using electroreceptors in their bills</u>). Should the writer make this deletion?

(A) Yes, because it introduces an irrelevant detail.

(B) Yes, because it contradicts the main idea of the passage.

(C) No, because it provides specific examples of the platypus's prey.

(D) No, because it explains how the platypus locates its food.

Answer: (D) **Explanation:** The underlined portion explains how the platypus uses electroreceptors to find food, which is relevant to its unique adaptations and feeding behavior.

58. Which choice most effectively combines the underlined sentences? (<u>They feed on aquatic invertebrates, such as insect larvae, worms, and crustaceans, which they locate using electroreceptors in their bills. These electroreceptors can detect the faint electrical fields generated by the muscle contractions of their prey</u>)

(A) These electroreceptors can detect the faint electrical fields generated by the muscle contractions of their prey, which they locate using electroreceptors in their bills.

(B) They locate their prey, which they find using electroreceptors in their bills, by detecting the faint electrical fields generated by the muscle contractions of their prey.

(C) They locate their prey using electroreceptors in their bills, which can detect the faint electrical fields generated by the muscle contractions of their prey.

(D) Using electroreceptors in their bills, they locate their prey, which they find by detecting the faint electrical fields generated by the muscle contractions of their prey.

Answer: (C) **Explanation:** Choice (C) effectively combines the sentences while maintaining clarity and conciseness.

59. Which of the following alternatives to the underlined portion (Its unique combination of physical traits and specialized adaptations make it a truly remarkable creature) would NOT be acceptable?

(A) notable

(B) remarkable

(C) ordinary

(D) extraordinary

Answer: (C) **Explanation:** The word "ordinary" contradicts the passage's description of the platypus as an unusual and fascinating creature. The other choices maintain the sense of uniqueness and remarkableness.

60. Which choice most effectively concludes the passage?

(A) NO CHANGE

(B) Therefore, the platypus is a valuable subject for scientific research and conservation efforts.

(C) In conclusion, the platypus is a truly unique and fascinating creature that deserves our admiration and protection.

(D) Consequently, the platypus serves as a reminder of the incredible diversity of life on Earth and the importance of preserving it.

Answer: (D) **Explanation:** Choice (D) effectively concludes the passage by highlighting the broader significance of the platypus as a symbol of biodiversity and the importance of conservation.

Passage V

With a jolt, I awaken to the insistent chirping of crickets, their chorus serenading the approaching dawn. The dew-laden grass tickles my bare arms, and the uneven ground beneath my makeshift bed of blankets creates lumps I know will later remind me of my ill-chosen slumber spot. As I shift to a slightly less uncomfortable position, I open my eyes, surprised by the pre-dawn darkness that envelops me. I fumble for my phone, its dim light revealing the outline of the towering trees surrounding my campsite.

Yawning and stretching, I emerge from my cocoon of blankets, the cool morning air sending a shiver down my spine. I can already feel the stiffness in my muscles protesting the night spent on the unforgiving ground. I pause, debating whether the promise of a breathtaking sunrise is worth the discomfort. Deciding to embrace the beauty of the moment, I grab my camera and venture towards the clearing. The early morning stillness is broken only by the gentle rustling of leaves and the distant call of a lone bird.

Reaching the clearing, I gasp as the first rays of sunlight paint the sky with vibrant hues of orange, pink, and purple. The clouds, illuminated from below, resemble cotton candy floating across a canvas of ever-changing colors. I snap photos furiously, trying to capture the fleeting beauty of the sunrise.

Heading back to my campsite, I notice the remnants of last night's campfire, the ashes now cold and gray. I make a mental note to gather more firewood before nightfall. Sighing, I pack up my makeshift bed and head towards the nearby stream for a much-needed wash. I can almost hear my mother's voice reminding me to use plenty of bug spray. Smiling, I splash the icy water on my face, feeling refreshed and ready to embrace the adventures of a new day.

61. Which choice would most effectively introduce the topic of the passage?

(A) NO CHANGE

(B) Camping is a popular outdoor activity that allows people to connect with nature.

(C) Sleeping outdoors can be challenging, but it offers a unique and rewarding experience.

(D) Wildlife encounters can be both exciting and intimidating for campers.

Answer: (A) **Explanation:** The original wording effectively introduces the scene and sets the tone for the passage, capturing the reader's attention with sensory details and a sense of immediacy. The other choices are either too broad or too specific.

62. Which of the following alternatives to the underlined portion (I awaken to the insistent chirping of crickets, their chorus serenading the approaching dawn) would NOT be acceptable?

(A) summoning

(B) heralding

(C) silencing

(D) ushering in

Answer: (C) **Explanation:** The word "silencing" contradicts the idea that the crickets are chirping loudly. The other choices maintain the sense of the crickets' song announcing the dawn.

63. The writer is considering deleting the underlined portion (The dew-laden grass tickles my bare arms, and the uneven ground beneath my makeshift bed of blankets creates lumps I know will later remind me of my ill-chosen slumber spot). Should the writer make this deletion?

(A) Yes, because it introduces an irrelevant detail.

(B) Yes, because it contradicts the main idea of the passage.

(C) No, because it provides a necessary transition to the next sentence.

(D) No, because it supports the main idea of the passage.

Answer: (D) **Explanation:** The underlined portion describes the discomfort of sleeping on uneven ground, which contributes to the overall description of the camping experience.

64. Which of the following alternatives to the underlined portion (its dim light revealing the outline of the towering trees surrounding my campsite) would be LEAST acceptable?

(A) illuminate

(B) reveal

(C) obscure

(D) expose

Answer: (C) **Explanation:** The word "obscure" implies hiding or concealing, whereas the passage describes the phone's light revealing the surroundings. The other choices maintain the sense of visibility.

65. Which choice most effectively combines the underlined sentences? (Yawning and stretching, I emerge from my cocoon of blankets, the cool morning air sending a shiver down my spine)

(A) Yawning and stretching, I emerge from my cocoon of blankets, and the cool morning air sends a shiver down my spine.

(B) Emerging from my cocoon of blankets, I yawn and stretch, and the cool morning air sends a shiver down my spine.

(C) The cool morning air sends a shiver down my spine as I yawn and stretch, emerging from my cocoon of blankets.

(D) I emerge from my cocoon of blankets, yawning and stretching, while the cool morning air sends a shiver down my spine.

Answer: (C) **Explanation:** Choice (C) effectively combines the sentences while maintaining clarity and conciseness, using a subordinate clause to emphasize the simultaneous actions.

66. Which of the following best maintains the focus of the passage?

(A) NO CHANGE

(B) I brew a pot of coffee over the camp stove.

(C) I listen to the sounds of the forest awakening.

(D) I check my backpack for any signs of wildlife intrusion.

Answer: (C) **Explanation:** The original wording emphasizes the sensory experience of being in nature, which aligns with the overall focus of the passage.

67. Which of the following alternatives to the underlined portion (I pause, debating whether the promise of a breathtaking sunrise is worth the discomfort) would NOT be acceptable?

(A) ponder

(B) contemplate

(C) ignore

(D) consider

Answer: (C) **Explanation:** The word "ignore" contradicts the idea that the narrator is actively thinking about whether to go see the sunrise. The other choices maintain the sense of deliberation.

68. Which of the following best describes the relationship between the first and second paragraphs?

(A) The first paragraph describes the setting and the narrator's initial impressions, and the second paragraph describes the narrator's actions and thoughts as they prepare for the day.

(B) The first paragraph presents a problem, and the second paragraph proposes a solution.

(C) The first paragraph makes a claim, and the second paragraph provides evidence to support it.

(D) The first paragraph describes a historical context, and the second paragraph analyzes its implications.

Answer: (A) **Explanation:** The first paragraph sets the scene and introduces the narrator's experience, while the second paragraph focuses on their actions and thoughts as they prepare for the day.

69. Which choice most effectively combines the underlined sentences? (<u>Deciding to embrace the beauty of the moment, I grab my camera and venture towards the clearing. The early morning stillness is broken only by the gentle rustling of leaves and the distant call of a lone bird</u>)

(A) Deciding to embrace the beauty of the moment, I grab my camera and venture towards the clearing, where the early morning stillness is broken only by the gentle rustling of leaves and the distant call of a lone bird.

(B) Grabbing my camera and venturing towards the clearing, I decide to embrace the beauty of the moment, and the early morning stillness is broken only by the gentle rustling of leaves and the distant call of a lone bird.

(C) The early morning stillness is broken only by the gentle rustling of leaves and the distant call of a lone bird as I decide to embrace the beauty of the moment, grabbing my camera and venturing towards the clearing.

(D) I decide to embrace the beauty of the moment, grabbing my camera and venturing towards the clearing. The early morning stillness is broken only by the gentle rustling of leaves and the distant call of a lone bird.

Answer: (A) **Explanation:** Choice (A) effectively combines the sentences while maintaining clarity and conciseness, using a subordinate clause to emphasize the reason for the narrator's actions.

70. Which of the following alternatives to the underlined portion would be LEAST acceptable? (I gasp as the first rays of sunlight paint the sky with vibrant hues of orange, pink, and purple)

(A) brilliant

(B) vivid

(C) drab

(D) intense

Answer: (C) **Explanation:** The word "drab" contradicts the idea that the sunrise is beautiful and filled with vibrant colors. The other choices maintain the sense of vibrancy and beauty.

71. Which choice most effectively maintains the focus of the passage on the narrator's sensory experience in nature?

(A) NO CHANGE

(B) The panoramic view from the clearing is truly breathtaking.

(C) I marvel at the intricate patterns of light and shadow on the forest floor.

(D) The fresh air invigorates me and fills me with a sense of peace and tranquility.

Answer: (D) **Explanation:** The original wording emphasizes the narrator's physical and emotional response to the fresh air, which aligns with the focus on sensory experience.

72. The writer is considering deleting the underlined portion. Should the writer make this deletion? (I notice the remnants of last night's campfire, the ashes now cold and gray)

(A) Yes, because it introduces an irrelevant detail.

(B) Yes, because it contradicts the main idea of the passage.

(C) No, because it provides a specific detail about the campfire.

(D) No, because it explains why the narrator needs more firewood.

Answer: (C) **Explanation:** The underlined portion provides a visual detail that adds to the description of the campsite and the narrator's observations.

73. Which choice most effectively combines the underlined sentences? (Sighing, I pack up my makeshift bed and head towards the nearby stream for a much-needed wash. I can almost hear my mother's voice reminding me to use plenty of bug spray)

(A) Sighing, I pack up my makeshift bed and head towards the nearby stream for a much-needed wash, where I can almost hear my mother's voice reminding me to use plenty of bug spray.

(B) I can almost hear my mother's voice reminding me to use plenty of bug spray as I sigh, pack up my makeshift bed, and head towards the nearby stream for a much-needed wash.

(C) Sighing, I pack up my makeshift bed and head towards the nearby stream for a much-needed wash, almost hearing my mother's voice reminding me to use plenty of bug spray.

(D) I sigh, pack up my makeshift bed, and head towards the nearby stream for a much-needed wash, and I can almost hear my mother's voice reminding me to use plenty of bug spray.

Answer: (C) **Explanation:** Choice (C) effectively combines the sentences while maintaining clarity and conciseness, using a participial phrase to connect the narrator's actions and thoughts.

74. Which of the following alternatives to the underlined portion (I splash the icy water on my face) would NOT be acceptable?

(A) soothing

(B) invigorating

(C) scalding

(D) refreshing

Answer: (C) **Explanation:** The word "scalding" implies that the water is extremely hot, which contradicts the passage's description of the stream as a source of refreshment. The other choices maintain the sense of coolness and revitalization.

75. Which choice most effectively concludes the passage?

(A) NO CHANGE

(B) Thus, camping provides an opportunity to escape the hustle and bustle of everyday life and reconnect with nature.

(C) In conclusion, the beauty of the natural world can inspire awe and wonder in those who take the time to appreciate it.

(D) As the sun climbs higher in the sky, I set off on my hike, eager to explore the wonders of the wilderness.

Answer: (D)

Explanation: Choice (D) effectively concludes the passage by looking ahead to the day's adventures and reinforcing the narrator's sense of excitement and anticipation, which aligns with the overall tone of the passage.

Full-Length Practice Test 2 (Maths Test)

Time: 60 Minutes—60 Questions

Directions: Determine the answer to each question, and then fill in the matching oval on your answer sheet. Do not spend too much time on any one problem. Solve as many as possible, then come back to ones that you have skipped. You are allowed to use a calculator on this section, but several of the problems are best completed without a calculator. Unless stated otherwise, assume that drawings are NOT necessarily to scale, geometric figures are in a two-dimensional plane, "lines" are straight lines, and "average" means the arithmetic mean.

1. If 40% of x equals 80, what is the value of x?

(A) 20

(B) 32

(C) 120

(D) 200

(E) 320

Answer: (D)

Explanation: We can set up a proportion to solve for x:

$40/100 = 80/x$

Cross-multiplying and solving for x gives us:

$40x = 8000$

$x = 200$

2. For what value of k will the equation x2+6x+k=0 have exactly one solution?

(A) 3

(B) 6

(C) 9

(D) 12

(E) 36

Answer: (C)

Explanation: A quadratic equation has exactly one solution when its discriminant is equal to zero. The discriminant of the quadratic equation $ax^2+bx+c=0$ is given by b^2-4ac.

In this case, $a=1$, $b=6$, and $c=k$. Setting the discriminant equal to zero and solving for k gives us:

$6^2 - 4 * 1 * k = 0$

$36 - 4k = 0$

$4k = 36$

$k = 9$

3. If $f(x)=3x-5$ and $g(x)=x^2+1$, what is the value of $g(f(2))$?

(A) 2

(B) 8

(C) 10

(D) 17

(E) 26

Answer: (A)

Explanation: We need to work from the inside out. First, we find the value of $f(2)$:

f(2) = 3 * 2 - 5 = 6 - 5 = 1

Then, we plug 1 into g(x):

g(1) = 1^2 + 1 = 1 + 1 = 2

4. If the average of five consecutive odd integers is 15, what is the greatest of these integers?

(A) 9

(B) 13

(C) 15

(D) 17

(E) 19

Answer: (E)

Explanation: Let the middle of the five consecutive odd integers be x. Then, the five integers are x−4, x−2, x, x+2, and x+4.

Since the average of these integers is 15, we have:

(x - 4 + x - 2 + x + x + 2 + x + 4)/5 = 15

Simplifying and solving for x gives us:

5x/5 = 15

x = 15

Therefore, the greatest of these integers is x+4=15+4=19.

5. A rectangle has a length of 12 units and a width of 8 units. What is the length of the diagonal of the rectangle?

(A) 10

(B) 12

(C) 14

(D) 16

(E) 20

Answer: (C)

Explanation: The diagonal of a rectangle forms a right triangle with the length and width of the rectangle. Therefore, we can use the Pythagorean theorem to find the length of the diagonal:

diagonal^2 = length^2 + width^2

diagonal^2 = 12^2 + 8^2

diagonal^2 = 144 + 64

diagonal^2 = 208

diagonal = sqrt(208) = 4sqrt(13)

6. If the circumference of a circle is 10π units, what is the area of the circle?

(A) 5π

(B) 10π

(C) 25π

(D) 50π

(E) 100π

Answer: (C)

Explanation: The circumference of a circle is given by $2\pi r$, where r is the radius. Therefore, we can solve for the radius:

$2\pi r = 10\pi$

$r = 5$

The area of a circle is given by $\pi r2$. Plugging in the value of r gives us:

area $= \pi * 5^2 = 25\pi$

7. If $\sin\theta=3/5$ and θ is an acute angle, what is the value of $\cos\theta$?

(A) 3/5

(B) 4/5

(C) 5/3

(D) 5/4

(E) 1

Answer: (B)

Explanation: We can use the Pythagorean identity $\sin2\theta+\cos2\theta=1$ to solve for $\cos\theta$:

$(3/5)^2 + \cos^2 \theta = 1$

$9/25 + \cos^2 \theta = 1$

$\cos^2 \theta = 16/25$

$\cos \theta = 4/5$

8. If the probability of an event occurring is 0.6, what is the probability of the event not occurring?

(A) 0

(B) 0.4

(C) 0.6

(D) 1

(E) 1.6

Answer: (B)

Explanation: The probability of an event not occurring is equal to 1 minus the probability of the event occurring. Therefore, the probability of the event not occurring is $1-0.6=0.4$.

9. If $\log_2 x = 3$, what is the value of x?

(A) 2

(B) 3

(C) 5

(D) 6

(E) 8

Answer: (E)

Explanation: We can rewrite the logarithmic equation in exponential form to solve for x:

$2^3 = x$

$x = 8$

10. If the first term of an arithmetic sequence is 5 and the common difference is 3, what is the fifth term of the sequence?

(A) 8

(B) 11

(C) 14

(D) 17

(E) 20

Answer: (D)

Explanation: The general form for an arithmetic sequence is an=a1+(n−1)d, where an is the nth term, a1 is the first term, and d is the common difference.

In this case, a1=5 and d=3. Plugging in n=5 gives us:

a_5 = 5 + (5 - 1) * 3 = 5 + 4 * 3 = 5 + 12 = 17

11. A triangle has sides of length 5, 12, and 13 units. Is the triangle a right triangle?

(A) Yes

(B) No

Answer: (A)

Explanation: A triangle is a right triangle if and only if the sum of the squares of the two shorter sides is equal to the square of the longest side (the Pythagorean theorem). In this case, 52+122=25+144=169=132, so the triangle is a right triangle.

12. If the point (3,−4) is reflected across the y-axis, what are the coordinates of the reflected point?

(A) (−3,−4)

(B) (3,4)

(C) (−3,4)

(D) (4,−3)

(E) (−4,3)

Answer: (A)

Explanation: When a point is reflected across the y-axis, the x-coordinate changes sign and the y-coordinate remains the same. Therefore, the reflected point is (−3,−4).

13. If x and y are inversely proportional, and y=6 when x=2, what is the value of y when x=3?

(A) 2

(B) 4

(C) 6

(D) 9

(E) 12

Answer: (B)

Explanation: If x and y are inversely proportional, then their product is a constant. Therefore, we can set up the following equation:

$2 * 6 = 3 * y$

Solving for y gives us:

$12 = 3y$

$y = 4$

14. If the volume of a cube is 64 cubic units, what is the surface area of the cube?

(A) 16

(B) 32

(C) 64

(D) 96

(E) 128

Answer: (D)

Explanation: The volume of a cube is given by s3, where s is the side length. Therefore, we can solve for the side length:

s^3 = 64

s = 4

The surface area of a cube is given by 6s2. Plugging in the value of s gives us:

surface area = 6 * 4^2 = 6 * 16 = 96

15. If the measure of an angle is 30 degrees, what is the measure of its complement?

(A) 30 degrees

(B) 60 degrees

(C) 90 degrees

(D) 120 degrees

(E) 150 degrees

Answer: (B)

Explanation: Complementary angles add up to 90 degrees. Therefore, the complement of a 30-degree angle is 90−30=60 degrees.

16. If the equation of a circle is $(x-2)^2+(y+3)^2=25$, what is the center of the circle?

(A) $(2,-3)$

(B) $(-2,3)$

(C) $(2,3)$

(D) $(-2,-3)$

(E) $(0,0)$

Answer: (A)

Explanation: The standard form for the equation of a circle is $(x-h)^2+(y-k)^2=r^2$, where (h,k) is the center of the circle and r is the radius. Therefore, the center of the circle is $(2,-3)$.

17. If $\log_3(x+1)=2$, what is the value of x?

(A) 2

(B) 5

(C) 8

(D) 9

(E) 10

Answer: (C)

Explanation: We can rewrite the logarithmic equation in exponential form to solve for x:

$3^2 = x + 1$

$9 = x + 1$

$x = 8$

18. If the second term of a geometric sequence is 6 and the fourth term is 54, what is the common ratio of the sequence?

(A) 2

(B) 3

(C) 6

(D) 9

(E) 18

Answer: (B)

Explanation: In a geometric sequence, each term is equal to the previous term multiplied by the common ratio. Therefore, we can set up the following equation:

$6 * r * r = 54$

$6r^2 = 54$

$r^2 = 9$

$r = 3$

19. If the perimeter of a square is 20 units, what is the area of the square?

(A) 5

(B) 10

(C) 20

(D) 25

(E) 40

Answer: (D)

Explanation: The perimeter of a square is given by 4s, where s is the side length. Therefore, we can solve for the side length:

4s = 20

s = 5

The area of a square is given by s2. Plugging in the value of s gives us:

area = 5^2 = 25

20. If the measure of an angle is 60 degrees, what is the measure of its supplement?

(A) 30 degrees

(B) 60 degrees

(C) 90 degrees

(D) 120 degrees

(E) 150 degrees

Answer: (D)

Explanation: Supplementary angles add up to 180 degrees. Therefore, the supplement of a 60-degree angle is 180−60=120 degrees.

21. If the equation of a line is y=2x−3, what is the slope of the line?

(A) -3

(B) -2

(C) 2

(D) 3

(E) 5

Answer: (C)

Explanation: The slope-intercept form of a linear equation is $y=mx+b$, where m is the slope and b is the y-intercept. Therefore, the slope of the line is 2.

22. If $f(x)=x2-4$ and $g(x)=2x+1$, what is the value of $f(g(3))$?

(A) 17

(B) 21

(C) 45

(D) 49

(E) 53

Answer: (C)

Explanation: We need to work from the inside out. First, we find the value of g(3):

$g(3) = 2 * 3 + 1 = 6 + 1 = 7$

Then, we plug 7 into f(x):

$f(7) = 7^2 - 4 = 49 - 4 = 45$

23. If the first term of an arithmetic sequence is 3 and the common difference is 4, what is the tenth term of the sequence?

(A) 31

(B) 35

(C) 39

(D) 43

(E) 47

Answer: (C)

Explanation: The general form for an arithmetic sequence is $a_n = a_1 + (n-1)d$, where a_n is the nth term, a_1 is the first term, and d is the common difference.

24. If a bag contains 5 red marbles, 3 blue marbles, and 2 green marbles, what is the probability of randomly selecting a blue marble?

(A) 1/10

(B) 3/10

(C) 1/3

(D) 2/5

(E) 1/2

Answer: (B)

Explanation: There are a total of 10 marbles in the bag. The probability of selecting a blue marble is the number of blue marbles divided by the total number of marbles,[1] which is 3/10.

25. If $x^2 - 5x - 6 = 0$, what are the solutions for x?

(A) $x = -6$ and $x = 1$

(B) $x = -3$ and $x = 2$

(C) x=−2 and x=3

(D) x=−1 and x=6

(E) x=2 and x=3

Answer: (D)

Explanation: We can factor the quadratic equation to find the solutions:

$x^2 - 5x - 6 = 0$

$(x - 6)(x + 1) = 0$

$x = 6$ or $x = -1$

26. If the area of a triangle is 24 square units and the base of the triangle is 8 units, what is the height of the triangle?

(A) 3

(B) 4

(C) 6

(D) 8

(E) 12

Answer: (C)

Explanation: The area of a triangle is given by (1/2)bh, where b is the base and h is the height. Plugging in the given values and solving for h gives us:

$24 = (1/2) * 8 * h$

$24 = 4h$

h = 6

27. If the measure of an angle is 45 degrees, what is the measure of its complement?

(A) 30 degrees

(B) 45 degrees

(C) 60 degrees

(D) 90 degrees

(E) 135 degrees

Answer: (B)

Explanation: Complementary angles add up to 90 degrees. Therefore, the complement of a 45-degree angle is 90−45=45 degrees.

28. If the point (−2,5) is reflected across the x-axis, what are the coordinates of the reflected point?

(A) (2,5)

(B) (−2,−5)

(C) (2,−5)

(D) (5,−2)

(E) (−5,2)

Answer: (B)

Explanation: When a point is reflected across the x-axis, the y-coordinate changes sign and the x-coordinate remains the same. Therefore, the reflected point is (−2,−5).

29. If x and y are directly proportional, and y=10 when x=5, what is the value of y when x=8?

(A) 4

(B) 8

(C) 13

(D) 16

(E) 40

Answer: (D)

Explanation: If x and y are directly proportional, then their ratio is a constant. Therefore, we can set up the following equation:

10/5 = y/8

Solving for y gives us:

2 = y/8

y = 16

30. If the volume of a rectangular prism is 120 cubic units, the length of the prism is 6 units, and the width of the prism is 5 units, what is the height of the prism?

(A) 2

(B) 4

(C) 6

(D) 10

(E) 12

Answer: (B)

Explanation: The volume of a rectangular prism is given by lwh, where l is the length, w is the width, and h is the height. Plugging in the given values and solving for h gives us:

$120 = 6 * 5 * h$

$120 = 30h$

$h = 4$

31. What is the solution to the equation 5x - 3 = 2x + 9?

(A) 2

(B) 3

(C) 4

(D) 5

(E) 6

Answer: (C)

Explanation: To solve for x, we can start by combining like terms: 5x - 2x = 9 + 3 3x = 12 x = 4

32. If a triangle has angles measuring 30 degrees, 60 degrees, and 90 degrees, what is the ratio of the length of the shortest side to the length of the longest side?

(A) 1:2

(B) 1:√3

(C) √3:2

(D) 2:1

(E) √3:1

Answer: (A)

Explanation: In a 30-60-90 triangle, the ratio of the sides is 1:√3:2, with the shortest side opposite the 30-degree angle and the longest side (the hypotenuse) opposite the 90-degree angle. Therefore, the ratio of the shortest side to the longest side is 1:2.

33. If $f(x) = 2x^2 - 5x + 3$, what is the value of $f(-2)$?

(A) -15

(B) -1

(C) 7

(D) 17

(E) 25

Answer: (E)

Explanation: To find $f(-2)$, we substitute -2 for x in the function: $f(-2) = 2(-2)^2 - 5(-2) + 3$ $f(-2) = 8 + 10 + 3$ $f(-2) = 21$

34. If a circle has a circumference of 12π, what is its area?

(A) 6π

(B) 12π

(C) 24π

(D) 36π

(E) 72π

Answer: (D)

Explanation: The circumference of a circle is given by $2\pi r$, where r is the radius. Therefore, we can solve for the radius: $2\pi r = 12\pi$ r = 6 The area of a circle is given by πr^2. Plugging in the value of r gives us: area = $\pi * 6^2 = 36\pi$

35. If $\log_5 x = 2$, what is the value of x?

(A) 2

(B) 5

(C) 10

(D) 25

(E) 125

Answer: (D)

Explanation: We can rewrite the logarithmic equation in exponential form to solve for x: $5^2 = x = 25$

36. If the first term of an arithmetic sequence is 7 and the common difference is -3, what is the fourth term of the sequence?

(A) -2

(B) 1

(C) 4

(D) 10

(E) 13

Answer: (A)

Explanation: The general form for an arithmetic sequence is $a_n = a_1 + (n - 1)d$, where a_n is the nth term, a_1 is the first term, and d is the common difference. In this case, $a_1^1 = 7$ and d = -3. Plugging in n = 4 gives us: $a_4 = 7 + (4 - 1) * -3 = 7 + 3 * -3 = 7 - 9 = -2$

37. A rectangle has a length of 10 units and a width of 6 units. What is the length of the diagonal of the rectangle?

(A) 8

(B) 10

(C) 12

(D) $2\sqrt{34}$

(E) $4\sqrt{17}$

Answer: (D)

Explanation: The diagonal of a rectangle forms a right triangle with the length and width of the rectangle. Therefore, we can use the Pythagorean theorem to find the length of the diagonal: diagonal^2 = length^2 + width^2 diagonal^2 = 10^2 + 6^2 diagonal^2 = 100 + 36 diagonal^2 = 136 diagonal = $\sqrt{136}$ = $2\sqrt{34}$

38. If the circumference of a circle is 8π units, what is the area of the circle?

(A) 4π

(B) 8π

(C) 16π

(D) 32π

(E) 64π

Answer: (C)

Explanation: The circumference of a circle is given by $2\pi r$, where r is the radius. Therefore, we can solve for the radius: $2\pi r = 8\pi$ r = 4 The area of a circle is given by πr^2. Plugging in the value of r gives us: area = $\pi * 4^2 = 16\pi$

39. If $\sin \theta = 4/5$ and θ is an acute angle, what is the value of $\cos \theta$?

(A) 3/5

(B) 4/5

(C) 5/3

(D) 5/4

(E) 1

Answer: (A)

Explanation: We can use the Pythagorean identity $\sin^2 \theta + \cos^2 \theta = 1$ to solve for $\cos \theta$: $(4/5)^2 + \cos^2 \theta = 1$ $16/25 + \cos^2 \theta = 1$ $\cos^2 \theta = 9/25$ $\cos \theta = 3/5$

40. If the probability of an event occurring is 0.3, what is the probability of the event not occurring?

(A) 0

(B) 0.3

(C) 0.7

(D) 1

(E) 1.3

Answer: (C)

Explanation: The probability of an event not occurring is equal to 1 minus the probability of the event occurring. Therefore, the probability[3] of the event not occurring is 1 - 0.3 = 0.7.

41. If log_4 x = 2, what is the value of x?

(A) 2

(B) 4

(C) 8

(D) 16

(E) 64

Answer: (D)

Explanation: We can rewrite the logarithmic equation in exponential form to solve for x: $4^2 = x = 16$

42. If the first term of an arithmetic sequence is 2 and the common difference is 5, what is the sixth term of the sequence?

(A) 7

(B) 12

(C) 17

(D) 22

(E) 27

Answer: (E)

Explanation: The general form for an arithmetic sequence is $a_n = a_1 + (n - 1)d$, where a_n is the nth term, a_1 is the first term, and d is the common difference. In this case, $a_1 = 2$ and $d^4 = 5$. Plugging in $n = 6$ gives us: $a_6 = 2 + (6 - 1) * 5 = 2 + 5 * 5 = 2 + 25 = 27$

43. A triangle has sides of length 3, 4, and 5 units. Is the triangle a right triangle?

(A) Yes

(B) No

Answer: (A)

Explanation: A triangle is a right triangle if and only if the sum of the squares of the two shorter sides is equal to the square of the longest side[5] (the Pythagorean theorem). In this case, $3^2 + 4^2 = 9 + 16 = 25 = 5^2$, so the triangle is a right triangle.

44. If the point (2, -5) is reflected across the y-axis, what are the coordinates of the reflected point?

(A) (-2, -5)

(B) (2, 5)

(C) (-2, 5)

(D) (5, -2)

(E) (-5, 2)

Answer: (A)

Explanation: When a point is reflected across the y-axis, the x-coordinate changes sign and the y-coordinate remains the same. Therefore, the reflected point is (-2, -5).

45. If x and y are inversely proportional, and $y = 4$ when $x = 3$, what is the value of y when $x = 6$?

(A) 2

(B) 3

(C) 6

(D) 8

(E) 12

Answer: (A)

Explanation: If x and y are inversely proportional, then their product is a constant. Therefore, we can set up the following equation: 3 * 4 = 6 * y Solving for y gives us: 12 = 6y y = 2

46. If the volume of a cube is 27 cubic units, what is the surface area of the cube?

(A) 9

(B) 18

(C) 27

(D) 54

(E) 81

Answer: (D)

Explanation: The volume of a cube is given by s^3, where s is the side length. Therefore, we can solve for the side length: s^3 = 27 s = 3 The surface area of a cube is given by 6s^2. Plugging in the value of s gives us: surface area = 6 * 3^2 = 6 * 9 = 54

47. If the measure of an angle is 40 degrees, what is the measure of its complement?

(A) 40 degrees

(B) 50 degrees

(C) 60 degrees

(D) 130 degrees

(E) 140 degrees

Answer: (B)

Explanation: Complementary angles add up to 90 degrees. Therefore, the complement of a 40-degree angle is 90 - 40 = 50 degrees.

48. If the equation of a circle is $(x + 3)^2 + (y - 2)^2 = 16$, what is the center of the circle?

(A) (3, -2)

(B) (-3, 2)

(C) (3, 2)

(D) (-3, -2)

(E) (0, 0)

Answer: (B)

Explanation: The standard form for the equation of a circle is $(x - h)^2 + (y - k)^2 = r^2$, where (h, k) is the center of the circle and r is the radius.[6] Therefore, the center of the circle is (-3, 2).

49. If $\log_2 (x - 1) = 3$, what is the value of x?

(A) 4

(B) 7

(C) 8

(D) 9

(E) 10

Answer: (D)

Explanation: We can rewrite the logarithmic equation in exponential form to solve for x: $2^3 = x - 1$ $8 = x - 1$ $x = 9$

50. If the second term of a geometric sequence is 4 and the fourth term is 16, what is the common ratio of the sequence?

(A) 1

(B) 2

(C) 4

(D) 8

(E) 12

Answer: (B)

Explanation: In a geometric sequence, each term is equal to the previous term multiplied by the common ratio. Therefore, we can set up the following equation: $4 * r * r = 16$ $4r^2 = 16$ $r^2 = 4$ $r = 2$

51. If the perimeter of a square is 32 units, what is the area of the square?

(A) 8

(B) 16

(C) 32

(D) 64

(E) 128

Answer: (D)

Explanation: The perimeter of a square is given by 4s, where s is the side length. Therefore, we can solve for the side length: 4s = 32 s = 8 The area of a square is given by s^2. Plugging in the value of s gives us: area = 8^2 = 64

52. If the measure of an angle is 50 degrees, what is the measure of its supplement?

(A) 40 degrees

(B) 50 degrees

(C) 100 degrees

(D) 130 degrees

(E) 140 degrees

Answer: (D)

Explanation: Supplementary angles add up to 180 degrees. Therefore, the supplement of a 50-degree angle is 180 - 50 = 130 degrees.

53. If the equation of a line is y = -3x + 5, what is the slope of the line?

(A) -5

(B) -3

(C) 3

(D) 5

(E) 8

Answer: (B)

Explanation: The slope-intercept form of a linear equation is y = mx + b, where m is the slope and b is the y-intercept. Therefore, the slope of[7] the line is -3.

54. If f(x) = 3x^2 - 2x + 1 and g(x) = x + 2, what is the value of f(g(2))?

(A) 13

(B) 21

(C) 37

(D) 41

(E) 49

Answer: (C)

Explanation: We need to work from the inside out. First, we find the value of g(2): g(2) = 2 + 2 = 4 Then, we plug 4 into f(x): f(4) = 3 * 4^2 - 2 * 4 + 1 = 3 * 16 - 8 + 1 = 48 - 8 + 1 = 41

55. If the first term of an arithmetic sequence is 8 and the common difference is -2, what is the fifth term of the sequence?

(A) 0

(B) 2

(C) 4

(D) 6

(E) 8

Answer: (A)

Explanation: The general form for an arithmetic sequence is $a_n = a_1 + (n - 1)d$, where a_n is the nth term, a_1 is the first term, and d is the common difference. In this case, $a_1 = 8$ and d = -2. Plugging in n = 5 gives us: $a_5 = 8 + (5 - 1) * -2 = 8 + 4 * -2 = 8 - 8 = 0$

56. If a bag contains 3 red marbles, 5 blue marbles, and 2 green marbles, what is the probability of randomly selecting a red marble?

(A) 1/10

(B) 3/10

(C) 1/3

(D) 2/5

(E) 1/2

Answer: (B)

Explanation: There are a total of 10 marbles in the bag. The probability of selecting a red marble is the number of red marbles divided by the total number of marbles,[9] which is 3/10.

57. If $x^2 + 3x - 10 = 0$, what are the solutions for x?

(A) x = -5 and x = 2

(B) x = -2 and x = 5

(C) x = -1 and x = 10

(D) x = 1 and x = -10

(E) x = 2 and x = -5

Answer: (A)

Explanation: We can factor the quadratic equation to find the solutions: x^2 + 3x - 10 = 0 (x + 5)(x - 2) = 0 x = -5 or x = 2

58. If the area of a triangle is 30 square units and the base of the triangle is 10 units, what is the height of the triangle?

(A) 3

(B) 5

(C) 6

(D) 10

(E) 15

Answer: (C)

Explanation: The area of a triangle is given by (1/2)bh, where b is the base and h is the height. Plugging in the given values and solving for h gives us: 30 = (1/2) * 10 * h 30 = 5h h = 6

59. If the measure of an angle is 70 degrees, what is the measure of its complement?

(A) 20 degrees

(B) 30 degrees

(C) 70 degrees

(D) 110 degrees

(E) 160 degrees

Answer: (A)

Explanation: Complementary angles add up to 90 degrees. Therefore, the complement of a 70-degree angle is 90 - 70 = 20 degrees.

60. If the point (4, -3) is reflected across the x-axis, what are the coordinates of the reflected point?

(A) (-4, -3)

(B) (4, 3)

(C) (-4, 3)

(D) (3, -4)

(E) (-3, 4)

Answer: (B)

Explanation: When a point is reflected across the x-axis, the y-coordinate changes sign and the x-coordinate remains the same. Therefore, the reflected point is (4, 3).

Full-Length Practice Test 3 (Reading Test)

Reading Test Time: 35 Minutes—40 Questions

Directions: There are several reading selections in this section, each of which is followed by questions. After you read a passage, determine the best answer to each question and fill in the matching oval on your answer sheet. Refer back to the passages as often as you need.

Passage I

Prose Fiction—Music

Don't mistake me—I'm not interested in just listening to music passively. It's not the catchy melodies or the driving rhythms that captivate me either. Not entirely. It's about the act of creation itself; the expression, the emotion, the magic woven into every note. Music is my refuge, my therapy, my voice. I have my own instruments, my trusted companions, through which I channel my inner world. The piano, with its ivory keys and resonant strings, speaks my joys and sorrows. The guitar, with its warm wood and vibrant chords, echoes my hopes and dreams. Like a painter with a brush or a sculptor with clay, I mold melodies and harmonies, shaping them into expressions of my soul.

With my fingers dancing across the piano keys, I weave a tapestry of sound. The notes cascade like a waterfall, each one a drop of emotion, blending and harmonizing to create a symphony of feelings. I close my eyes and lose myself in the music, my fingers guided by an unseen force. At once, I am eight years old again, sitting on the piano bench in my grandmother's cozy living room. The scent of lavender and freshly baked cookies fills the air. Sunlight streams through the window, casting a warm glow on the worn keys. My grandmother, her fingers gnarled with age, guides my small hands across the keyboard, teaching me the basics of music.

"Feel the music," she whispers, her voice soft and gentle. "Let it flow through you."

Her words echo in my mind as I navigate the complexities of a Chopin nocturne. The melody unfolds like a story, each phrase a chapter filled with longing and passion. I pour my heart into the music, expressing emotions I can't put into words. The final chord resonates through the room, leaving a lingering sense of peace and fulfillment.

I shift my focus to the guitar, its strings beckoning me to explore new sonic landscapes. I strum a chord, the vibrations resonating through my fingertips. The sound is raw and powerful, a surge of energy that courses through my veins. I am sixteen now, sitting on my bedroom floor, surrounded by posters of my favorite bands. The air crackles with youthful rebellion and the yearning for self-expression. I pour my frustrations and dreams into the music, channeling my angst into powerful riffs and heartfelt lyrics.

The music swells and crashes like waves on the shore, reflecting the turbulence of adolescence. I lose myself in the moment, the guitar becoming an extension of myself. The final strum fades away, leaving a sense of catharsis and release.

I return to the piano, drawn back to its elegance and versatility. My fingers glide across the keys, exploring new melodies and harmonies. I am no longer a child or a teenager, but a mature musician, my skills honed by years of practice and dedication. I weave together elements of classical, jazz, and folk music, creating a unique sound that reflects my diverse influences.

The music flows effortlessly, a testament to my mastery of the instrument. I am in complete control, yet I surrender to the creative impulse, allowing the music to guide me. The final notes fade away, leaving a sense of accomplishment and the anticipation of new musical journeys to come.

1. Based on the passage as a whole, the author most likely uses the imagery of a "tapestry of sound" (line 8) to illustrate what about their relationship with music?

A. Music is a complex and intricate art form that requires skill and dedication to master.

B. Music allows the author to express a wide range of emotions and experiences.

C. Music provides a sense of comfort and familiarity for the author.

D. Music is a universal language that can connect people from different backgrounds.

Answer: B

Explanation: The imagery of a "tapestry of sound" suggests a rich and varied expression of emotions and experiences, highlighting the author's ability to convey their inner world through music.

2. In the context of the passage, the phrase "unseen force" (line 10) most likely refers to:

A. The author's subconscious mind guiding their musical expression.

B. The influence of the author's grandmother's musical teachings.

C. The emotional power of the music itself.

D. The technical demands of playing the piano.

Answer: A

Explanation: The phrase "unseen force" suggests a subconscious or intuitive guidance that directs the author's musical expression, highlighting the spontaneous and emotional nature of their playing.

3. The author's description of the Chopin nocturne as a "story" (line 17) emphasizes which aspect of the music?

A. Its technical complexity and challenging passages.

B. Its emotional depth and narrative quality.

C. Its historical significance and cultural context.

D. Its calming and soothing effect on the listener.

Answer: B

Explanation: Comparing the nocturne to a "story" suggests that the music has a narrative quality, conveying emotions and experiences that unfold over time.

4. Which of the following best describes the author's attitude towards their guitar playing during their teenage years?

A. Nostalgic and sentimental

B. Rebellious and defiant

C. Experimental and adventurous

D. Disciplined and focused

Answer: B

Explanation: The passage describes the author's teenage guitar playing as an outlet for "frustrations and dreams," "angst," and "turbulence," suggesting a rebellious and defiant attitude.

5. The author's use of the "The notes cascade like a waterfall" (line 8) primarily serves to:

A. Highlight the technical complexity of playing the piano.

B. Convey the emotional flow of the music being played.

C. Emphasize the physical movement of the musician's fingers.

D. Suggest the natural and effortless quality of the performance.

Answer: B

Explanation:

The phrase "The notes cascade like a waterfall" uses vivid imagery to convey the emotional depth and fluidity of the music. The comparison to a waterfall evokes a sense of continuous motion and the outpouring of feelings, emphasizing how the music flows effortlessly and harmoniously, reflecting the artist's emotions. This aligns with the broader theme of the passage, which focuses on music as an emotional and expressive art form rather than just a technical skill.

6. Which of the following best describes the tone of the passage?

A. Analytical and objective

B. Reflective and introspective

C. Humorous and lighthearted

D. Critical and judgmental

Answer: B

Explanation: The passage is characterized by a reflective and introspective tone, as the author explores their personal connection to music and its impact on their life.

7. The author's decision to alternate between playing the piano and the guitar throughout the passage most likely serves to:

A. Demonstrate their versatility as a musician.

B. Highlight the contrasting emotions associated with each instrument.

C. Reflect the different stages of their musical development.

D. Emphasize the importance of both melody and harmony in music.

Answer: C

Explanation: The shifts between piano and guitar playing correspond to different periods in the author's life, suggesting that each instrument represents a distinct phase of their musical journey.

8. Which of the following is NOT mentioned in the passage as a way in which the author engages with music?

A. Playing the piano

B. Composing original songs

C. Listening to recordings of famous musicians

D. Playing the guitar

Answer: C

Explanation: The passage focuses on the author's active engagement with music through playing instruments and creating their own music, but it does not mention listening to recordings.

9. The author's description of the guitar as "strings beckoning me to explore new sonic landscapes" (line 20) primarily serves to:

A. Illustrate the versatility of the guitar as an instrument.

B. Highlight the author's curiosity and creativity in music.

C. Emphasize the technical aspects of playing the guitar.

D. Convey the transformative power of music during adolescence.

Answer: B

Explanation: The phrase strings beckoning me to explore new sonic landscapes conveys a sense of curiosity and creative exploration. By personifying the guitar, the author emphasizes their emotional connection to the instrument and the inspiration it provides. This aligns with the theme of music as a deeply personal and expressive outlet, showcasing the author's willingness to experiment and push boundaries in their musical journey.

10. Which of the following best summarizes the main idea of the passage?

A. Music is a powerful tool for self-expression and personal growth.

B. The author's passion for music has been nurtured by influential figures in their life.

C. Different musical instruments can evoke different emotions and experiences.

D. The creative process of making music is a deeply personal and rewarding experience.

Answer: D

Explanation: The passage primarily focuses on the author's personal journey with music, emphasizing the joy and fulfillment they derive from the creative process itself.

Passage II

Social Science—The Enigma of Chess

Try to imagine a world without chess—no grandmasters, no intricate strategies, no timeless battles of wit and intellect—and you may begin to grasp the profound impact this ancient game has had on human culture. Despite its seemingly simple rules and basic components, chess has proven to be a surprisingly complex and enduring pastime, captivating minds across continents and centuries. However, the precise origins of chess remain shrouded in mystery, with various cultures and civilizations vying for the honor of its creation.

While the exact birthplace of chess remains elusive, historical and archaeological evidence points towards ancient India as a likely contender. The earliest known precursor to chess, a game called Chaturanga, emerged in India around the 6th century CE. Chaturanga shared key similarities with modern chess, including a checkerboard, pieces with distinct powers, and the objective of checkmating the opponent's king.

From India, chess spread along trade routes and through cultural exchanges, reaching Persia, the Arab world, and eventually Europe. As chess migrated across different regions, it underwent various transformations, adapting to local customs and preferences. The rules, pieces, and even the board itself evolved over time, giving rise to distinct regional variations of the game.

Despite these variations, the core essence of chess remained constant: a battle of intellect and strategy, requiring foresight, planning, and the ability to anticipate an opponent's moves. Chess transcended social and cultural boundaries, captivating emperors and commoners alike. It became a symbol of intellectual prowess and strategic thinking, often used to simulate warfare and political maneuvering.

The invention of the printing press in the 15th century marked a turning point in the history of chess. Chess manuals and treatises became widely available, leading to the standardization of rules and the development of sophisticated chess theory. The game's popularity soared, and chess clubs and tournaments emerged across Europe.

The 19th century witnessed the rise of professional chess players and the establishment of international chess competitions. The first official World Chess Championship was held in 1886, marking the beginning of a new era for the game.

Today, chess continues to thrive as a global pastime, enjoyed by millions of people of all ages and backgrounds. It has evolved beyond a mere game, becoming a tool for education, cognitive training, and even artificial intelligence research.

While the exact origins of chess may remain forever shrouded in the mists of time, its enduring legacy is undeniable. Chess stands as a testament to the human fascination with strategy, intellect, and the timeless pursuit of victory on the checkered battlefield.

11. The main purpose of the passage can best be described as an effort to:

A. trace the evolution of chess from its ancient origins to its modern form.

B. highlight the cultural significance of chess and its impact on human history.

C. explain the rules and strategies of chess for novice players.

D. compare and contrast different regional variations of chess.

Answer: B

Explanation: The passage focuses on the broader cultural and historical significance of chess, emphasizing its enduring appeal and its impact on human intellect and strategy.

12. According to the passage, which of the following is NOT a characteristic shared by Chaturanga and modern chess?

A. A checkerboard

B. Pieces with distinct powers

C. The objective of checkmating the opponent's king

D. The use of a timer to regulate moves

Answer: D

Explanation: The passage mentions the checkerboard, pieces with distinct powers, and the objective of checkmating the king as similarities between Chaturanga and modern chess. The use of a timer is a more recent addition to chess, not present in its ancient precursor.

13. Which of the following best describes the author's attitude towards chess?

A. Dismissive and critical

B. Appreciative and respectful

C. Nostalgic and sentimental

D. Humorous and lighthearted

Answer: B

Explanation: The passage conveys an appreciative and respectful tone towards chess, highlighting its intellectual depth, cultural significance, and enduring appeal.

14. The author's use of the phrase "checkered battlefield" (line 32) primarily serves to:

A. emphasize the competitive nature of chess.

B. highlight the strategic complexity of chess.

C. create a visual image of the chessboard.

D. suggests that chess is a metaphor for warfare.

Answer: D

Explanation: The phrase "checkered battlefield" creates a metaphor that links chess to warfare, suggesting that the game involves strategic planning and tactical maneuvers similar to those used in military conflicts.

15. Which of the following is NOT mentioned in the passage as a factor contributing to the evolution of chess?

A. Cultural exchanges between different regions

B. The invention of the printing press

C. The development of artificial intelligence

D. The standardization of rules

Answer: C

Explanation: The passage mentions cultural exchanges, the printing press, and the standardization of rules as factors influencing the evolution of chess. Artificial intelligence is a more recent development that is not discussed in the context of the game's historical evolution.

16. Which of the following best describes the organization of the passage?

A. Chronological

B. Compare and contrast

C. Cause and effect

D. Problem and solution

Answer: A

Explanation: The passage follows a roughly chronological order, tracing the development of chess from its ancient origins in India to its modern form.

17. Which of the following is an example of figurative language used in the passage?

A. "Try to imagine a world without chess"

B. "The earliest known precursor to chess"

C. "Chess transcended social and cultural boundaries"

D. "The game's popularity soared"

Answer: C

Explanation: The phrase "Chess transcended social and cultural boundaries" uses figurative language to convey the idea that chess appealed to people from diverse backgrounds and social classes.

18. Which of the following is a synonym for the word "elusive" as used in the passage?

A. Obvious

B. Evident

C. Mysterious

D. Simple

Answer: C

Explanation: The word "elusive" in the passage means difficult to find or grasp, which is synonymous with "mysterious."

19. Which of the following is an antonym for the word "standardization" as used in the passage?

A. Uniformity

B. Consistency

C. Variation

D. Regulation

Answer: C

Explanation: The word "standardization" in the passage refers to the process of making rules and practices consistent. The opposite of this is "variation."

20. Which of the following best summarizes the main idea of the passage?

A. Chess is an ancient game with a rich history and cultural significance.

B. The origins of chess are uncertain, but evidence suggests it may have originated in India.

C. Chess has evolved over time, but its core elements of strategy and intellect remain constant.

D. Chess is a popular pastime enjoyed by people of all ages and backgrounds around the world.

Answer: A

Explanation: The passage provides a comprehensive overview of chess, highlighting its historical development, cultural significance, and enduring appeal.

Passage III

Humanities—Breaking Barriers: The Evolution of the Novel

The novel, a sprawling and versatile form of literary expression, has undergone a remarkable transformation throughout history. From its humble beginnings as a mere diversion for the leisure class to its current status as a powerful tool for social commentary and cultural exploration, the novel has consistently pushed the boundaries of storytelling and challenged conventional notions of literature.

Early novels, often characterized by sentimental plots and idealized characters, primarily served as a form of escapism for the wealthy elite. However, as the reading public expanded and diversified, so too did the scope and ambition of the novel. Writers began to explore more complex themes, such as social injustice, political corruption, and the psychological depths of human experience.

The rise of realism in the 19th century marked a significant turning point in the evolution of the novel. Authors like Charles Dickens and Gustave Flaubert meticulously depicted the realities of everyday life, exposing the grim underbelly of industrial society and challenging the romanticized portrayals of the past.

The 20th century witnessed a further explosion of experimentation and innovation in the novel. Modernist writers like Virginia Woolf and James Joyce shattered traditional narrative structures, delving into the stream of consciousness and exploring the fragmented nature of human perception.

Postmodernism, with its playful self-awareness and rejection of grand narratives, further challenged the conventions of the novel. Authors like Thomas Pynchon and Gabriel García Márquez embraced metafiction, intertextuality, and magical realism, blurring the lines between reality and fiction and questioning the very nature of storytelling.

Today, the novel continues to evolve, adapting to the ever-changing cultural landscape and embracing new technologies and forms of expression. Graphic novels, interactive fiction, and hybrid forms that blend text with other media are pushing the boundaries of the novel and challenging traditional definitions of literature.

The novel's enduring appeal lies in its ability to transport readers to different worlds, introduce them to diverse characters, and explore the complexities of human experience. Whether it serves as a mirror to society, a window into the human soul, or a portal to fantastical realms, the novel remains a vital and vibrant form of artistic expression.

21. Based on the passage, it is reasonable to infer that which of the following played the most significant role in the evolution of the novel?

A. Technological advancements in printing and publishing

B. Changes in social and cultural values

C. The rise of literary criticism and theory

D. Competition from other forms of entertainment

Answer: B

Explanation: The passage emphasizes how the novel has adapted to changing social and cultural values, reflecting the evolving concerns and interests of readers throughout history.

22. Which of the following is NOT mentioned in the passage as a characteristic of early novels?

A. Sentimental plots

B. Idealized characters

C. Complex themes

D. Focus on escapism

Answer: C

Explanation: The passage describes early novels as primarily serving as escapism for the wealthy elite, with sentimental plots and idealized characters. Complex themes are associated with later developments in the novel.

23. The author's use of the phrase "grim underbelly" (line 11) primarily serves to:

A. emphasize the negative aspects of industrial society.

B. create a sense of mystery and suspense.

C. highlight the contrast between rich and poor.

D. criticize the romanticized view of the past.

Answer: A

Explanation: The phrase "grim underbelly" refers to the harsh realities of industrial society that were often hidden or ignored, emphasizing the negative aspects of this period.

24. Which of the following literary movements is most closely associated with the "stream of consciousness" technique (line 15)?

A. Realism

B. Modernism

C. Postmodernism

D. Romanticism

Answer: B

Explanation: The "stream of consciousness" technique, which involves4 depicting the flow of thoughts and feelings in a character's mind, is a hallmark of Modernist literature.

25. Which of the following authors is NOT mentioned in the passage as a representative of Postmodernism?

A. Charles Dickens

B. Thomas Pynchon

C. Gabriel García Márquez

D. Virginia Woolf

Answer: A

Explanation: The passage mentions Thomas Pynchon and Gabriel García Márquez as representatives of Postmodernism. Charles Dickens is associated with Realism, while Virginia Woolf is associated with Modernism.

26. Which of the following is NOT mentioned in the passage as a way in which the novel has evolved in recent times?

A. Graphic novels

B. Interactive fiction

C. Hybrid forms blending text with other media

D. Adaptation into film and television

Answer: D

Explanation: The passage mentions graphic novels, interactive fiction, and hybrid forms as recent developments in the novel. Adaptation into film and television, while a common practice, is not specifically mentioned in the passage.

27. The author's use of the phrase "a mirror to society" (line 25) primarily serves to:

A. emphasize the novel's ability to reflect social realities.

B. highlight the importance of accuracy in historical fiction.

C. suggest that novels can influence social change.5 D. criticize the superficiality of some contemporary novels.

Answer: A

Explanation: The phrase "a mirror to society" suggests that novels can accurately reflect the social conditions, values, and concerns of a particular time and place.

28. Which of the following is a synonym for the word "versatile" as used in the passage?

A. Limited

B. Adaptable

C. Simple

D. Traditional

Answer: B

Explanation: The word "versatile" in the passage means adaptable or6 capable of fulfilling multiple functions, which is synonymous with "adaptable."

29. Which of the following is an antonym for the word "conventional" as used in the passage?

A. Traditional

B. Ordinary

C. Unorthodox

D. Conservative

Answer: C Explanation: The word "conventional" in the passage means traditional or conforming to established norms. The opposite of this is "unorthodox."

30. Which of the following best summarizes the main idea of the passage?

A. The novel has undergone a continuous process of evolution and innovation throughout history.

B. Realism and Modernism were the most significant literary movements in the development of the novel.

C. The novel has served as a powerful tool for social commentary and cultural exploration.

D. The future of the novel is uncertain, but it will likely continue to adapt to new technologies and forms of expression.

Answer: A

Explanation: The passage provides a broad overview of the historical development of the novel, emphasizing its continuous evolution and adaptation to changing social and cultural contexts.

Passage IV

Natural Science—Genetics

Passage A

The 20th century witnessed remarkable advancements in our understanding of genetics, with the discovery of DNA's structure and the development of powerful tools for manipulating genetic material. However, alongside these scientific breakthroughs, there have been accidental discoveries and unexpected observations that have significantly shaped our knowledge of genes and their influence on human traits and diseases.

One such accidental discovery involves the peculiar case of a family with an unusually high prevalence of blue eyes. For generations, this family exhibited a striking pattern of blue-eyed individuals, despite having ancestors with diverse eye colors. Intrigued by this phenomenon, geneticists investigated the family's genetic makeup and discovered a rare mutation in a gene responsible for eye color. This mutation disrupted the production of melanin in the iris, resulting in the characteristic blue hue.

This accidental finding provided valuable insights into the genetic mechanisms that determine eye color and highlighted the potential for rare mutations to have significant phenotypic effects. It also underscored the importance of studying families with unusual traits to uncover hidden genetic variations and expand our understanding of human genetics.

Another intriguing observation involves the unexpected link between a specific gene variant and an increased risk of developing certain types of cancer. While studying a large population cohort, researchers noticed a higher incidence of cancer among individuals carrying a particular variant of a gene involved in DNA repair. This gene variant was found to impair the cell's ability to repair damaged DNA, leading to an accumulation of mutations and an increased susceptibility to cancer.

This unexpected finding shed light on the complex interplay between genes and environmental factors in cancer development. It also highlighted the potential for genetic screening to identify individuals at higher risk for certain cancers, paving the way for personalized prevention and treatment strategies.

Passage B

The cerebellum, a small but mighty structure nestled at the base of the brain, has long been recognized for its crucial role in coordinating movement and maintaining balance. Recent research, however, has revealed that the cerebellum's influence extends far beyond motor control, implicating it in a wide range of cognitive functions, including language processing, attention, and even social cognition.

Given its extensive connections to various brain regions, including the cerebral cortex and the limbic system, it is perhaps not surprising that the cerebellum's influence is so widespread. Studies using functional magnetic resonance imaging (fMRI) have shown that the cerebellum is activated during a variety of cognitive tasks, such as reading, problem-solving, and emotional regulation.

One particularly intriguing area of research focuses on the cerebellum's role in language processing. fMRI studies have revealed that the cerebellum is involved in various aspects of language, including syntax, semantics, and pragmatics. It is thought that the cerebellum contributes to the precise timing and coordination of neural activity required for fluent speech and language comprehension.

Moreover, the cerebellum's involvement in attention and working memory has also been documented. Studies have shown that individuals with cerebellar damage often exhibit deficits in attentional control and working memory capacity. The cerebellum is thought to play a role in filtering out distractions and maintaining focus on relevant information.

Perhaps most surprisingly, the cerebellum has been implicated in social cognition, the ability to understand and interact with others. Research suggests that the cerebellum contributes to the processing of social cues, such as facial expressions and body language, and may play a role in empathy and social decision-making.

These findings challenge the traditional view of the cerebellum as solely a motor control center and highlight its multifaceted contributions to cognition and behavior. As we continue to explore the complexities of the brain, the cerebellum's role in shaping our thoughts, emotions, and social interactions is likely to become even more apparent.

Questions 31–33 are about Passage A.

31. Which of the following explanations would most logically explain why scientists have not been able to study many cases of families with unusual traits like the blue-eyed family mentioned in the passage?

A. Genetic research is often expensive and time-consuming, requiring large sample sizes and sophisticated laboratory techniques.

B. Families with unusual traits may be reluctant to participate in genetic studies due to concerns about privacy or potential stigma.

C. Many unusual traits are caused by complex interactions between multiple genes and environmental factors, making them difficult to study.

D. Genetic mutations that cause unusual traits are often rare and occur sporadically, making it challenging to identify and study affected families.

Answer: D

Explanation: The passage mentions that the blue-eyed family had a "rare mutation," suggesting that such genetic variations are not common and may be difficult to find and study.

32. The author's use of the phrase "accidental discovery" (line 6) in relation to the blue-eyed family primarily serves to:

A. emphasize the role of serendipity in scientific research.

B. highlight the limitations of traditional genetic studies.

C. suggest that the discovery was not scientifically rigorous.

D. downplay the significance of the finding.

Answer: A

Explanation: The phrase "accidental discovery" emphasizes that the finding was not the result of a planned experiment but rather an unexpected observation that led to new insights.

33. Which of the following best describes the tone of the passage?

A. Skeptical and critical

B. Informative and objective

C. Persuasive and argumentative

D. Speculative and hypothetical

Answer: B

Explanation: The passage presents information about genetic discoveries in a neutral and objective tone, focusing on the scientific evidence and its implications.

Questions 34–37 are about Passage B.

34. Based on the passage, which represents a proper sequence of mental events?

A. Visual perception of facial expressions → processing by the cerebellum → social cognition

B. Social cognition → visual perception of facial expressions → processing by the cerebellum

C. Processing by the cerebellum → social cognition → visual perception of facial expressions

D. Visual perception of facial expressions → social cognition → processing by the cerebellum

Answer: A

Explanation: The passage suggests that the cerebellum processes visual cues, such as facial expressions, which contribute to social cognition, the ability to understand and interact with others.

35. Which of the following is NOT mentioned in the passage as a function of the cerebellum?

A. Coordinating movement

B. Maintaining balance

C. Regulating emotions

D. Controlling appetite

Answer: D

Explanation: The passage mentions the cerebellum's role in coordinating movement, maintaining balance, and regulating emotions. Controlling appetite is not discussed in the passage.

36. The author's use of the phrase "small but mighty" (line 1) primarily serves to:

A. emphasize the cerebellum's compact size.

B. highlight the cerebellum's diverse functions.

C. contrast the cerebellum with other brain regions.

D. downplay the cerebellum's importance.

Answer: B

Explanation: The phrase "small but mighty" emphasizes that despite its relatively small size, the cerebellum plays a crucial role in various cognitive functions.

37. Which of the following best describes the tone of the passage?

A. Skeptical and dismissive

B. Informative and intrigued

C. Persuasive and passionate

D. Humorous and satirical

Answer: B

Explanation: The passage presents information about the cerebellum's functions in an informative and intrigued tone, highlighting recent research and its implications for our understanding of the brain.

Questions 38–40 are about both passages.

38. Which concept discussed in Passage A is most relevant to the discussion of addiction in Passage B?

(A) Genetic mutations

(B) Eye color variation

(C) DNA repair mechanisms

(D) Environmental factors

Answer: (A)

Explanation: Passage A discusses how genetic mutations can influence traits and disease susceptibility. This concept is relevant to Passage B's discussion of addiction, as genetic variations can contribute to an individual's vulnerability to addiction.

39. Based on both passages, which of the following statements about the brain is most accurate?

(A) The brain's functions are rigidly localized to specific regions.

(B) The brain is capable of significant adaptation and reorganization after injury.

(C) Genetic factors play a minimal role in shaping brain function.

(D) The brain's response to stress is primarily determined by environmental factors.

Answer: (B)

Explanation: Passage A highlights the brain's ability to adapt after injury, as seen in the case of H.M., who developed new strategies to compensate for his memory impairment. Passage B emphasizes the interconnectedness of different brain regions and their influence on various functions, suggesting plasticity and adaptability.

40. If the researchers in Passage A were to collaborate with the author of Passage B, which of the following research questions would they be most likely to investigate?

(A) How do genetic variations influence the activity of the amygdala and its role in addiction?

(B) What are the long-term effects of social isolation on dopamine levels in the prefrontal cortex?

(C) Does the cerebellum play a role in the development of anterograde amnesia after traumatic brain injury?

(D) How do environmental factors interact with genetic predispositions to influence eye color variation?

Answer: (A)

Explanation: Both passages touch upon the interplay between brain function, genetics, and behavior. A collaborative research question would likely explore how genetic variations might affect the amygdala's activity and its role in addiction, bridging the concepts discussed in both passages.

Full-Length Practice Test 4 (Science Test)

Time: 35 Minutes—40 Questions

Directions: There are several passages in this section, each of which is followed by questions. After reviewing a passage, choose the best answer to each question and fill in the matching oval on your answer sheet. Refer to the passages as often as you need. Calculators are NOT permitted on this test.

Passage I

The autonomic nervous system is responsible for regulating the body's automatic functions, such as breathing and heart rate. It is comprised of two parts: the sympathetic and parasympathetic nervous systems. **Figure 1** shows how these two systems connect to different parts of the body.

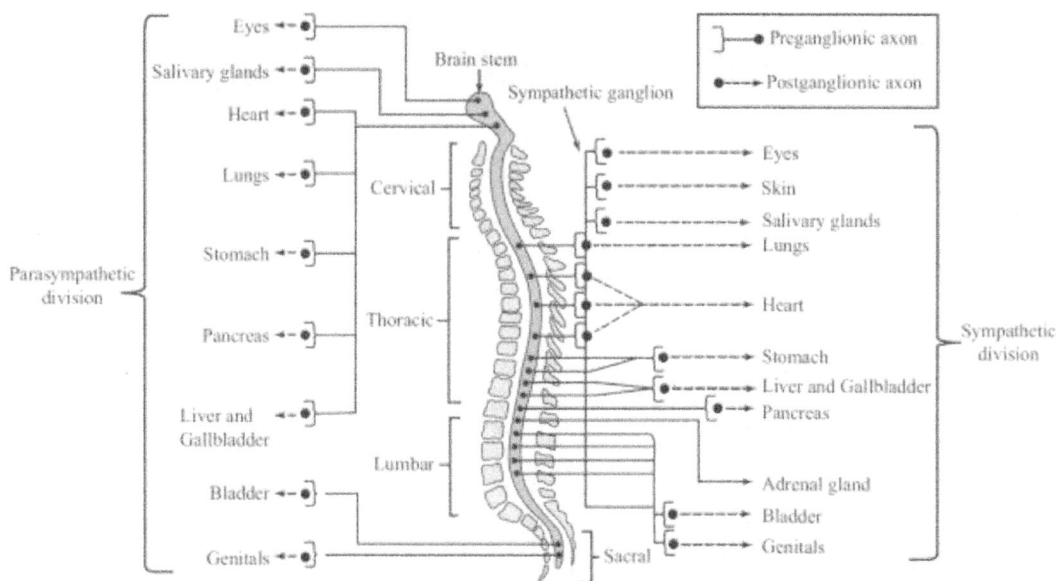

Figure 1

The sympathetic and parasympathetic divisions of the autonomic nervous system often have opposite effects on the body. The sympathetic division activates the "fight or flight" response, while the parasympathetic division activates the "rest and digest" response. **Table 1** details how each division affects various organs and systems. Brain wave patterns are also linked to the autonomic nervous system, and **Figure 2** shows four common types of brain waves.

Table 1

Target Structure	Parasympathetic Effects	Sympathetic Effects
Stomach	Increases gastric acid secretion, relaxes pyloric sphincter	Decreases gastric acid secretion, constricts pyloric sphincter
Lungs	Constricts bronchioles	Dilates bronchioles
Heart	Decreases and steadies rate of contraction	Increases rate and force of heartbeat
Salivary and lacrimal glands	Increases saliva and tear production	Inhibits glands; dry mouth and dry eyes
Iris	Constricts pupils	Dilates pupils
Ciliary muscle	Bulges lens for close vision	Flattens lens for distant vision
Adrenal medulla	No effect	Stimulates release of epinephrine and norepinephrine
Sweat glands	No effect	Stimulates perspiration
Kidney	Decreased fluid resorption	Increased fluid resorption
Liver	No effect	Glucose released to bloodstream

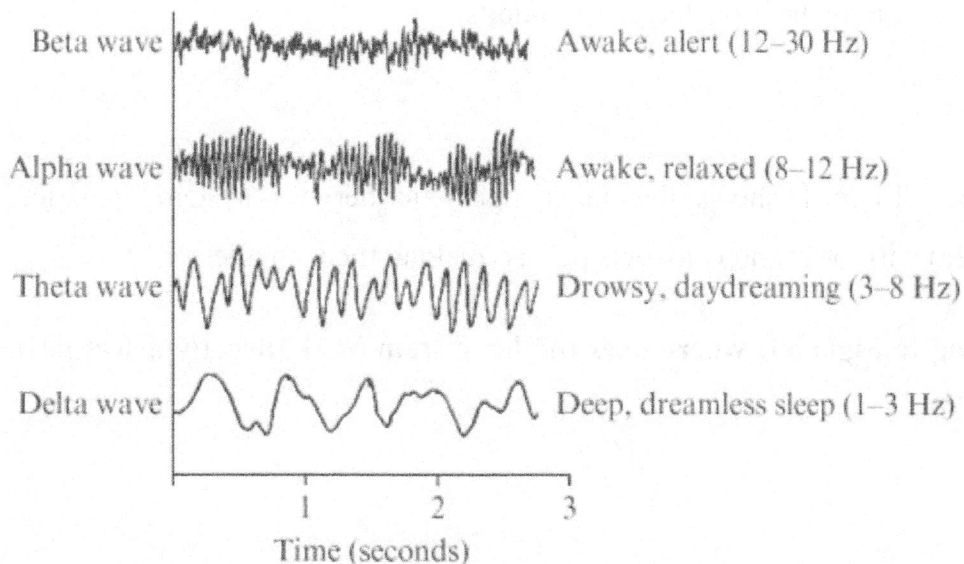

Beta wave — Awake, alert (12–30 Hz)

Alpha wave — Awake, relaxed (8–12 Hz)

Theta wave — Drowsy, daydreaming (3–8 Hz)

Delta wave — Deep, dreamless sleep (1–3 Hz)

Time (seconds)

Figure 2

1. Which spinal section is located furthest from the skull?

A. Cervical

B. Thoracic

C. Lumbar

D. Sacral

Answer: D

Explanation: Figure 1 shows the spinal sections. Sacral is the lowest section, thus furthest from the skull.

2. The parasympathetic nervous system is most likely associated with which bodily effects?

A. Expansion of both the bronchioles and pupils.

B. Expansion of the bronchioles and narrowing of the pupils.

C. Narrowing of the bronchioles and expansion of the pupils.

D. Narrowing of both the bronchioles and pupils.

Answer: C

Explanation: Table 1 shows the parasympathetic nervous system constricts bronchioles (making them narrower) and constricts pupils (making them smaller).

3. According to Figure 1, where does the brainstem NOT directly affect parasympathetic functioning?

A. Stomach

B. Bladder

C. Lungs

D. Liver and gallbladder

Answer: D

Explanation: In Figure 1, the brainstem has no direct neuronal pathway to the liver and gallbladder.

4. According to Figure 1, what is the usual sequence for neuronal messages traveling from the brain to most bodily systems?

A. Preganglionic axons

B. Postganglionic axons

C. Postganglionic axons alone

D. Preganglionic axons alone

Answer: A

Explanation: Figure 1 shows the brain connects to preganglionic axons, which then connect to postganglionic axons before reaching the organs.

5. According to Figure 2, which wave characteristic most easily distinguishes delta waves from theta waves?

A. Frequency

B. Amplitude

C. Whether the person is asleep

D. Eye movements

Answer: A

Explanation: Figure 2 shows brain waves. Delta and theta waves have distinct frequencies (cycles per second), making frequency the easiest way to tell them apart.

6. According to Table 1, which body structure is affected by the "fight or flight" response to a predator but NOT affected during a nap?

A. Salivary gland

B. Kidney

C. Adrenal gland

D. Iris

Answer: C

Explanation: Table 1 shows the adrenal gland is only affected by the sympathetic nervous system ("fight or flight"). The other options are affected by both systems.

Passage II

Normal rainwater has a pH value ranging from 5.6 to 7.0. Acid rain, on the other hand, is rainwater with a pH value below 5.6 and can be as low as 4.3. The formation of acid rain results from rainwater mixing with pollutants such as carbon dioxide, carbon monoxide, hazardous air pollutants, and lead, among others. Researchers conducted experiments to assess the impact of acid rain on the environment.

Study 1

In the first study, researchers examined how acidic rainwater became at varying distances from a coal power plant that lacked pollution-reducing filters. They measured the pH of rainwater samples collected at different distances from the power plant, and this data is presented in **Figure 1**.

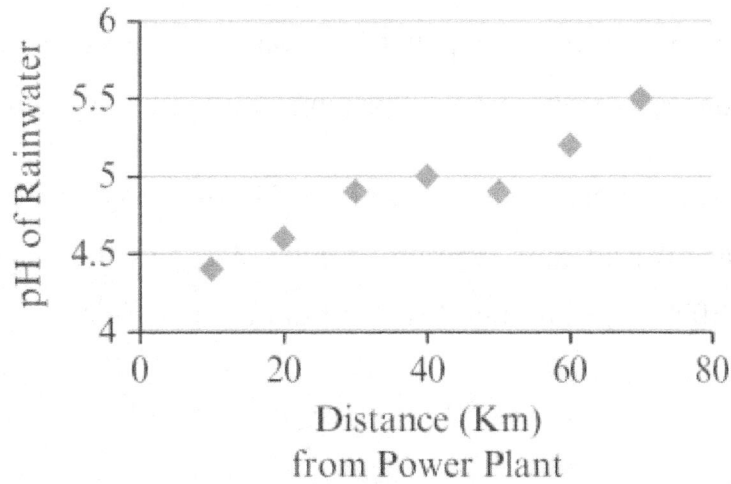

Figure 1

Study 2

In a follow-up study, researchers investigated the level of acidity that would be fatal to various animal species. It's important to note that these animals can survive in water with lower acidity levels than the ones that prove lethal to them. The findings of this study are displayed in **Figure 2**.

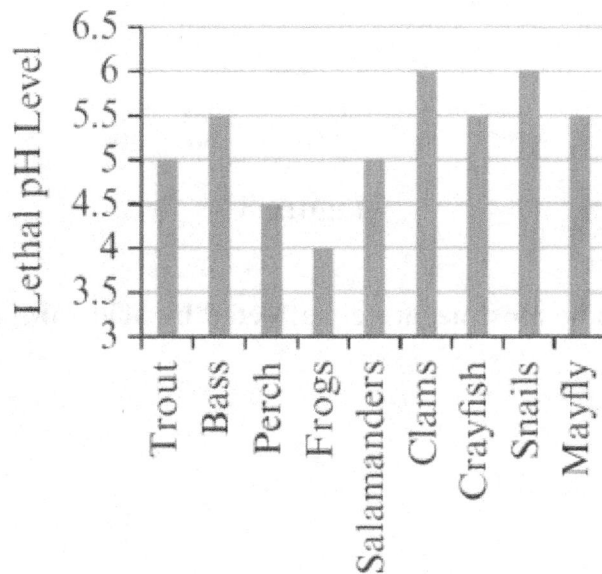

Figure 2

Study 3

Lastly, the researchers studied how acid rain affects plants. They focused on a protective layer called epicuticular wax, which prevents pollutants from entering tree leaves. The researchers hypothesized that acid rain weakens this wax, making trees more vulnerable to pollutants.

To test this, they exposed various tree leaves to 10 inches of highly acidic rain (pH 4.3) over a month, simulating natural acid rain exposure. **Figure 3** shows the percentage reduction in epicuticular wax for different plants after this month-long experiment.

Percentage of Wax Lost Due to Acid Rain

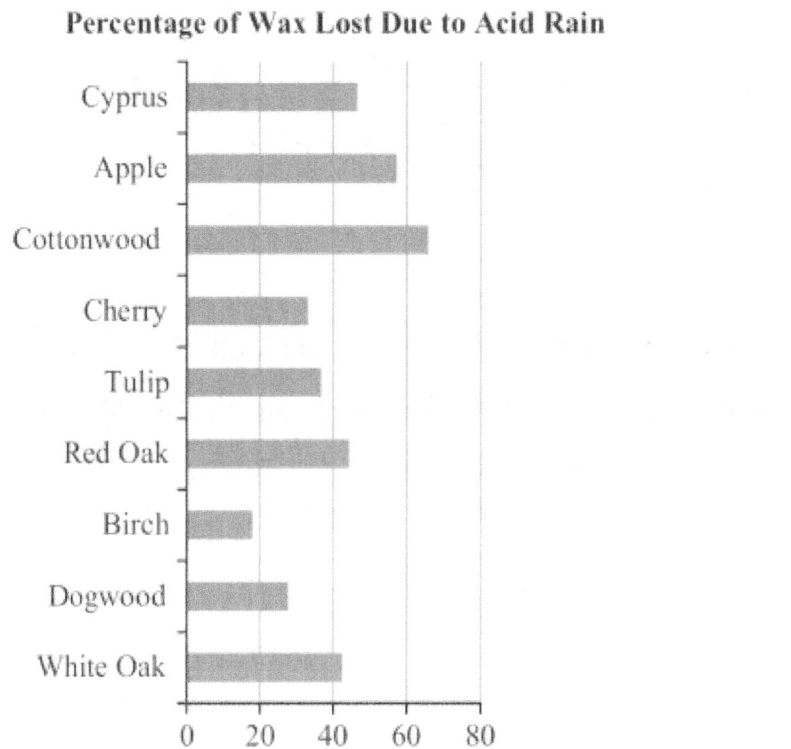

Figure 3

7. Which tree is likely to be most negatively affected by acid rain, according to Figure 3?

A. Birch

B. Cherry

C. Apple

D. White oak

Answer: A

Explanation: Figure 3 shows that birch trees lose the highest percentage of their protective wax coating when exposed to acid rain. This suggests they are most vulnerable to the negative effects.

8. An unknown animal survives in water with a pH of 6.0 but dies in water with a pH of 5.0. Which animal could this be?

A. Clam

B. Bass

C. Frog

D. Perch

Answer: D

Explanation: Figure 2 shows the lowest pH that different animals can survive in. Perch can survive in water with a pH of 6.0 but not 5.0.

9. Which pH level would NOT be classified as acid rain?

A. 5.8

B. 5.5

C. 5.0

D. 4.5

Answer: A

Explanation: The passage states that acid rain has a pH value of less than 5.6. Therefore, 5.8 is the only option that would not be considered acid rain.

10. According to Figures 1 and 2, at what distance from the power plant would frogs be unable to survive?

A. 10 km

B. 40 km

C. 70 km

D. None of the above

Answer: A

Explanation:

- Figure 2 shows that frogs cannot survive in water with a pH below 4.0.
- Figure 1 shows that rainwater 10 km from the power plant has a pH of about 4.3, and the pH decreases the closer you get to the plant.
- Therefore, frogs would not be able to survive at 10 km from the power plant, or any distance closer than that.

11. Which animal from Study 2 would be most likely to survive in the acidic conditions of Study 3?

A. Bass

B. Frog

C. Clam

D. Snail

Answer: D

Explanation:

- Study 3 used acid rain with a pH of 4.3.

- Figure 2 shows that snails can survive in the most acidic water (pH of 4.5) compared to the other options.

12. Study 2 doesn't explain exactly how the experiment was set up. If a scientist wanted to make acid rain seem more harmful to marine life than it really is, how could they manipulate the experiment?

A. Use unhealthy animals as test subjects

B. Expose the animals to acidic water at a faster rate than they would experience in nature

C. Select animals that are very sensitive to acid and exclude those with high acid resistance

D. All of the above

Answer: D

Explanation: All the options would bias the experiment, making acid rain appear more harmful than it is.

13. Which additional research would help scientists better understand the effects of acid rain on the environment, based on the findings of Study 3?

I. A study examining the link between the percentage of wax removed from leaves and the lifespan of trees.

II. A study examining the link between the lifespans of animals and their exposure to pollutants.

III. A study examining the link between acid rain and oxygen levels in lakes and streams.

A. I only

B. II only

C. II and III

D. I, II, and III

Answer: D

Explanation: All the proposed studies would provide valuable insights into the broader environmental effects of acid rain. They would help connect the findings of Study 3 to real-world consequences for plants, animals, and ecosystems.

Passage III

Theory 1

Theory 1 proposes that the discrepancy between Mercury's predicted orbit and its actual orbit can be explained within the framework of Newton's Theory of Universal Gravitation. This explanation suggests the existence of an undiscovered planet, "Vulcan," located between the Sun and Mercury, which would account for the observed shift in Mercury's orbit.

However, observing this hypothetical planet is challenging due to its proximity to the Sun. Its rapid orbit and the Sun's brightness make direct telescopic observation difficult. Additionally, the planet's relatively small size adds to the observational challenges.

Theory 2

Theory 2 suggests that the discrepancy between Mercury's predicted and actual orbits arises because the initial prediction, based on Newtonian mechanics, is inaccurate. While Newtonian mechanics is generally accurate in predicting astronomical events, the relativistic effects of matter and time, as described by Einstein's Theory of Relativity, explain the observed shift in Mercury's orbit.

Essentially, the Sun's mass curves spacetime, and this curvature influences Mercury's orbital path, causing a slight shift. Therefore, Theory 2 provides an explanation for Mercury's orbit without needing to introduce a hypothetical planet like Vulcan.

14. Aside from proposing the existence of the planet Vulcan, which of the following explanations for Mercury's orbit would align with Newton's Theory of Universal Gravitation and be understandable to amateur astronomers in the 1800s?

A. Mercury's observed orbit was within the margin of observational error.

B. An undiscovered asteroid belt was influencing Mercury's orbit.

C. The relativistic nature of space and time.

D. Demonstrating other observational errors in long-distance telescopic observations.

Answer: C

Explanation: The concept of relativity was not widely understood in the 1800s, so it wouldn't have been a plausible explanation for amateur astronomers at that time. The other options are more straightforward and align with the understanding of astronomy in that era.

15. Even with strong evidence supporting relativity, what would be a major obstacle to replacing Newton's Theory of Gravitation for a scientist in 1899?

A. Newton's theory had been considered accurate for over 200 years.

B. Newton's theory couldn't accurately predict Mercury's orbit.

C. Newton's theory didn't account for the relativistic nature of space and time.

D. Newton's theory couldn't predict observations of Vulcan.

Answer: A

Explanation: The passage highlights that Newton's Theory of Universal Gravitation had been accepted for over 200 years. This long-standing acceptance would make it difficult to overturn, even with new evidence.

16. Astronomers only found a discrepancy between observations and Newtonian predictions for Mercury, not for Jupiter and its moon Io. What would a supporter of Theory 2 say explains this difference?

A. The brightness of the Sun

B. The small size of the planet Vulcan

C. The Sun's relatively large mass

D. The speed of Jupiter's orbit

Answer: C

Explanation: Theory 2 emphasizes the relativistic effects of mass on spacetime. The Sun's large mass would have a more significant impact on Mercury's orbit, which is closer to the Sun, than on Jupiter's moon Io.

17. Which of these was NOT a potential problem for observing the hypothetical planet Vulcan, as suggested by Theory 1?

A. Vulcan's fast orbit

B. The Sun's brightness

C. Mercury's orbit

D. The small size of Vulcan

Answer: C

Explanation: Theory 1 mentions Vulcan's rapid orbit, the Sun's brightness, and Vulcan's small size as obstacles to observation. Mercury's orbit is not listed as a hindering factor.

18. According to a proponent of Theory 1, how would the number of orbits completed by planets farther from the Sun compare to those closer to the Sun, in a given time period?

A. More complete orbits

B. Fewer complete orbits

C. The same number of orbits

D. Cannot be inferred from Theory 1

Answer: B

Explanation: Theory 1 suggests that Vulcan, a hypothetical planet closer to the Sun than Mercury, would have a 'more rapid orbit.' This implies that planets farther from the Sun would complete fewer orbits in a given time.

19. Under what condition would a proponent of Theory 2 agree that Newton's Theory of Universal Gravitation is still useful for predicting the motion of objects?

A. When only a small amount of relativity is required

B. When only a small amount of precision is required

C. When only a small amount of observation is required

D. When only a small amount of proximity is required

Answer: B

Explanation: Theory 2 suggests that Newtonian mechanics are accurate for general astronomical predictions but less so for precise calculations where relativistic effects become significant.

20. An astronomer wants to test Theory 1 but is worried about the Sun's brightness hindering observation of Vulcan. What would be the best time to search for Vulcan?

A. During a meteor shower

B. During a solar eclipse

C. During the summer solstice

D. During the winter solstice

Answer: B

Explanation: A solar eclipse would block the Sun's brightness, making it easier to observe a planet near the Sun, like the hypothesized Vulcan.

Passage IV

Nuclear decay is a process that increases the stability of unstable chemical compounds. When a compound releases particles from its nucleus during nuclear decay, it is considered radioactive. There are four common types of radioactive particles:

1. In α-decay, the radioactive nucleus emits an α-particle, consisting of two neutrons and two   protons.

2. In β-decay, a neutron converts to a proton to increase stability, and the compound emits a β-particle   (identical   to   an   electron).

3. In positron-emission, a proton converts to a neutron, emitting a positron (same mass as an   electron   but   with   an   opposite   charge).

4. γ-rays   are   often   emitted   with   other   radioactive   particles.

Different radioactive particles have different energy levels. Gamma rays have the highest energy, positrons and beta particles have equal energy, and alpha particles have the least.

Sometimes, the nucleus remains unstable after a decay event. The resulting compound, still radioactive, undergoes further decay. This "decay chain" can repeat for thousands of years. A graduate student is studying the decay chain of Radon.

Experiment 1

In Experiment 1, the student investigates the types of decay occurring in the Radon decay chain by measuring the emitted particles' energy using metal shields of increasing density. Alpha particles couldn't penetrate any shields, beta particles and positrons penetrated the first but not the second, and gamma rays were stopped by the third shield. **Figure 1** summarizes these findings.

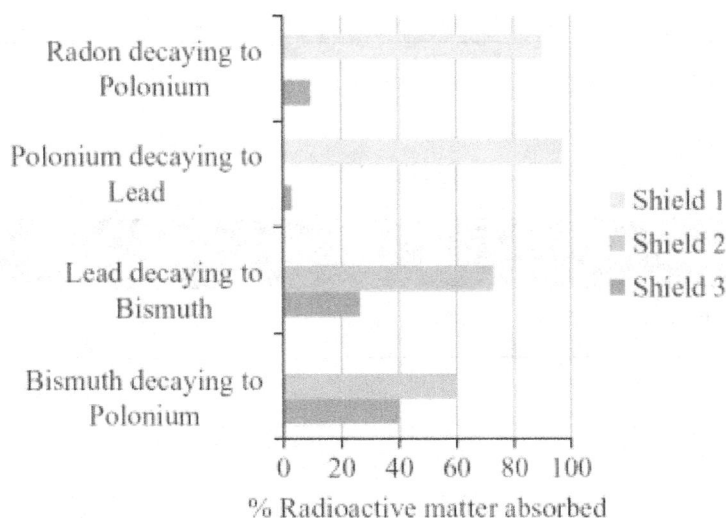

Figure 1

Experiment 2

The student initially intended to continue the first experiment but found that the newly formed polonium (decayed from bismuth) had almost entirely decayed into 214Lead. [1]

Consequently, the student shifted the focus of the experiment to determine the half-life of the substances. The student started with a 10-gram sample of lead (decayed from polonium) and monitored its decay over time. The experiment was repeated with a 5-gram sample of bismuth (decayed from lead) and a 2.5-gram sample of polonium (decayed from bismuth). The observations from these experiments are documented in **Tables 1, 2, and 3**.

Table 1

Time Elapsed (min)	Mass Lead (g)
0	10.0

10	8.15
20	6.30
30	4.50

Table 2

Time Elapsed (min)	Mass Bismuth (g)
0	5.0
10	3.75
20	2.50
30	1.25

Table 3

Time Elapsed (microseconds)	Mass Polonium (g)
0	2.50
50	2.11
100	1.72
150	1.33

21. According to Table 1, approximately how long is the half-life of Lead?

A. 0–10 minutes

B. 10–20 minutes

C. 20–30 minutes

D. 30–40 minutes

Answer: B

238

Explanation: The half-life is the time it takes for half the sample to decay. Table 1 shows lead starts at 10 grams. Half of that is 5 grams. The closest time to when it reaches 5 grams is between 10 and 20 minutes.

22. Which substance has the shortest half-life, according to Figure 1 and Tables 1, 2, and 3?

A. Lead

B. Bismuth

C. Polonium

D. All substances have identical half-lives

Answer: C

Explanation:

- A substance with a short half-life decays quickly.
- In Figure 1, polonium decays the fastest, as shown by the steepest line.
- Table 3 confirms this, with polonium decaying significantly in microseconds, while the others take minutes.

23. List the shields from Figure 1 in order from the largest to smallest openings.

A. 1, 2, 3

B. 3, 2, 1

C. 2, 1, 3

D. 3, 1, 2

Answer: B

Explanation:

- The passage states that the shields have 'increasing density'.
- Denser shields have smaller openings.
- Therefore, the order from largest to smallest openings is 3, 2, 1.

24. Which table(s) from Experiment 2 show results that don't fit the idea of exponential decay?

A. Table 1

B. Table 2

C. Table 3

D. All of the tables

Answer: D

Explanation:

- Exponential decay means the amount that decays is a percentage of what's left, not a constant amount.
- All tables show the substances losing a roughly constant amount over each time interval, not a percentage, contradicting exponential decay.

25. In the decay of Radon, which step likely releases the most large particles (as a percentage of the total)?

A. Radon to polonium

B. Polonium to lead

C. Lead to bismuth

D. Bismuth to polonium

Answer: A

Explanation:

- Alpha particles are the 'larger particles'.
- Figure 1 shows the decay from radon to polonium has the highest percentage of alpha particle emission.

26. Lead-214 has an atomic mass of 214 and an atomic number of 82. After alpha decay, what will the new atomic mass and number be?

A. Mass: 212, Number: 80

B. Mass: 210, Number: 80

C. Mass: 210, Number: 82

D. Mass: 214, Number: 78

Answer: A

Explanation:

- Alpha decay releases a particle with 2 protons and 2 neutrons.
- This reduces the atomic mass by 4 (214 - 4 = 212)
- It also reduces the atomic number by 2 (82 - 2 = 80)

27. The student wants to know if the particle absorbed by Shield 2 is a beta particle or a positron. What should they measure?

A. Mass

B. Charge

C. Velocity

D. Acceleration

Answer: B

Explanation:

- Beta particles and positrons have the same mass but opposite charges.
- Measuring the charge will identify the particle.

Passage V

Some Physics students conducted experiments to determine the refraction indexes of different substances. They used Snell's Law, which describes the properties of light that is refracted as it goes through one medium and the interface of another medium. Snell's Law is as follows:

$$\frac{\sin \theta_1}{\sin \theta_2} = \frac{v_1}{v_2} = \frac{n_2}{n_1}$$

in which the angles (θ) are the angles that the light is traveling with respect to its current medium, the velocity (v) is the speed at which the light is traveling, and the refractive index (n) is a constant value that determines the refraction of the light based on the makeup of the medium. Everything with a subscript of "1" refers to the light as it goes through the first substance, and everything with a subscript of "2" refers to the light as it goes through the other substance. The refractive index (n) of a substance is determined by taking the velocity of light in a vacuum (c), and dividing it by the velocity of light in the medium (v). This is given in the following equation:

$$n = \frac{c}{v}$$

A graph of this phenomenon is provided below:

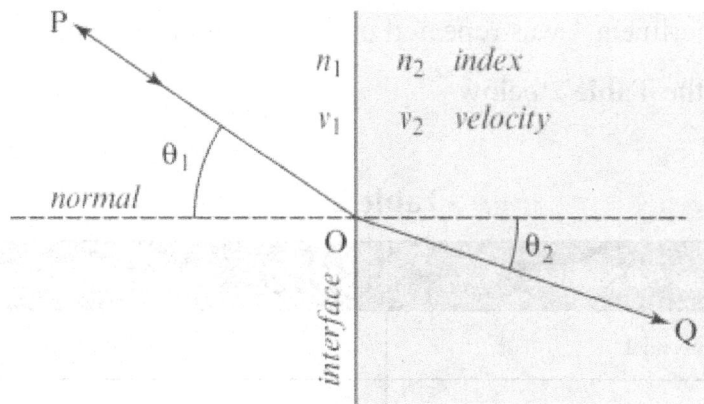

Experiment 1

In the first experiment, a laser beam was directed through various known substances at room temperature and standard atmospheric pressure. The angles of the refracted light were precisely measured, allowing the researchers to determine the refractive index of each substance. The results showed a correlation between the degree of bending and the refractive index: the more the light bent, the higher the refractive index. These findings are presented in **Table 1**.

Table 1

Medium/Material	Refractive Index (n)
Vacuum	1.00000
Water	1.3330
Carbon dioxide	1.00045
Diamond	2.419
Cubic zirconia	2.16
Air	1.00028
Silicon	4.01
Human cornea	1.3375

Experiment 2

The procedure from Experiment 1 was repeated using four unknown substances. The refractive indexes are provided in the **Table 2** below.

Table 2

Medium/Material Number	Refractive Index (n)
Material 1	1.00025
Material 2	2.17
Material 3	1.765
Material 4	4.015

28. Based on the refractive indices in Experiment 2, which material is most likely cubic zirconia?

A. Material 1

B. Material 2

C. Material 3

D. Material 4

Answer: B

Explanation:

- Table 1 shows the refractive index of cubic zirconia is 2.16.
- Table 2 shows Material 2 has the closest refractive index (2.17).

29. Through which medium will light bend the least?

A. Water

B. Carbon dioxide

C. Air

D. Silicon

Answer: B

Explanation:

- The passage states the greater the refractive index, the more light bends.
- Table 1 shows carbon dioxide has the smallest refractive index.

30. Which equation shows the velocity of light (v) through a substance, using the speed of light in a vacuum (c) and the refractive index (n)?

A. v=nc

B. v=cn

C. v=cn

D. v=cn2

Answer: A

Explanation: The passage gives the equation n=vc. Solving for *v* gives v=nc.

31. In which substance will light travel the fastest, according to Table 1?

A. Diamond

B. Cubic zirconia

C. Carbon dioxide

D. Silicon

Answer: C

Explanation:

- A higher refractive index means light travels slower in that substance.
- Table 1 shows carbon dioxide has the lowest refractive index.

32. Based on Table 1, the human eye is likely composed mainly of what?

A. Carbon dioxide

B. Water

C. Silicon

D. Air

Answer: B

Explanation:

- Table 1 shows the human cornea has a refractive index of 1.3375.
- This is closest to the refractive index of water (1.3330).

33. An optometrist wants a material for glasses lenses that won't bend light. Which material from Table 2 is best?

A. Material 1

B. Material 2

C. Material 3

D. Material 4

Answer: A

Explanation:

- Not bending light means a refractive index close to 1.
- Material 1 has the closest refractive index to 1 in Table 2.

34. Can a material have a refractive index less than 1.0?

A. Yes, some materials in Tables 1 and 2 have refractive indices less than 1.0.

B. Yes, if the angles of light through a medium are equal, the refractive index will be less than 1.0.

C. No, nothing can have a refractive index less than 1.0, which is the refractive index of light in a vacuum.

D. No, the refractive index of light remains constant across various media.

Answer: C

Explanation: The passage states the refractive index is calculated by dividing the speed of light in a vacuum by the speed of light in the medium. Since light travels fastest in a vacuum, the refractive index cannot be less than 1.0.

Passage VI

In 1869, Dmitri Mendeleev, a Russian chemist, created an early version of the periodic table of elements. He noticed that when elements were arranged by increasing atomic mass, certain chemical properties repeated periodically. Today, we know these "periodic trends" are due to valence shell electrons, so elements are now arranged by atomic number. Mendeleev's understanding of periodic law allowed him to accurately predict the existence and properties of undiscovered elements like germanium, gallium, and scandium.

Here are the commonly known periodic trends:

1. Electron affinity: The energy absorbed or emitted when an element gains an electron in its valence shell. It increases from left to right across a period (except for noble gases)

and   decreases   from   top   to   bottom   in   a   group.

2. Atomic radius: The distance from the nucleus to the outermost electron. It decreases from left to right across a period and increases from top to bottom in a group.

3. Ionization energy: The energy needed to remove an electron from an element's valence shell. It increases from left to right across a period and decreases from top to bottom in a group.

4. Electronegativity: How strongly an element attracts shared electrons in a chemical bond. It increases from left to right across a period and decreases from top to bottom in a group.

5. Metallic character: How likely an element is to have metallic properties (ductility, malleability, conductivity). It decreases from left to right across a period and increases from top to bottom in a group.

A simple representation of the modern periodic table is shown in **Figure 1**.

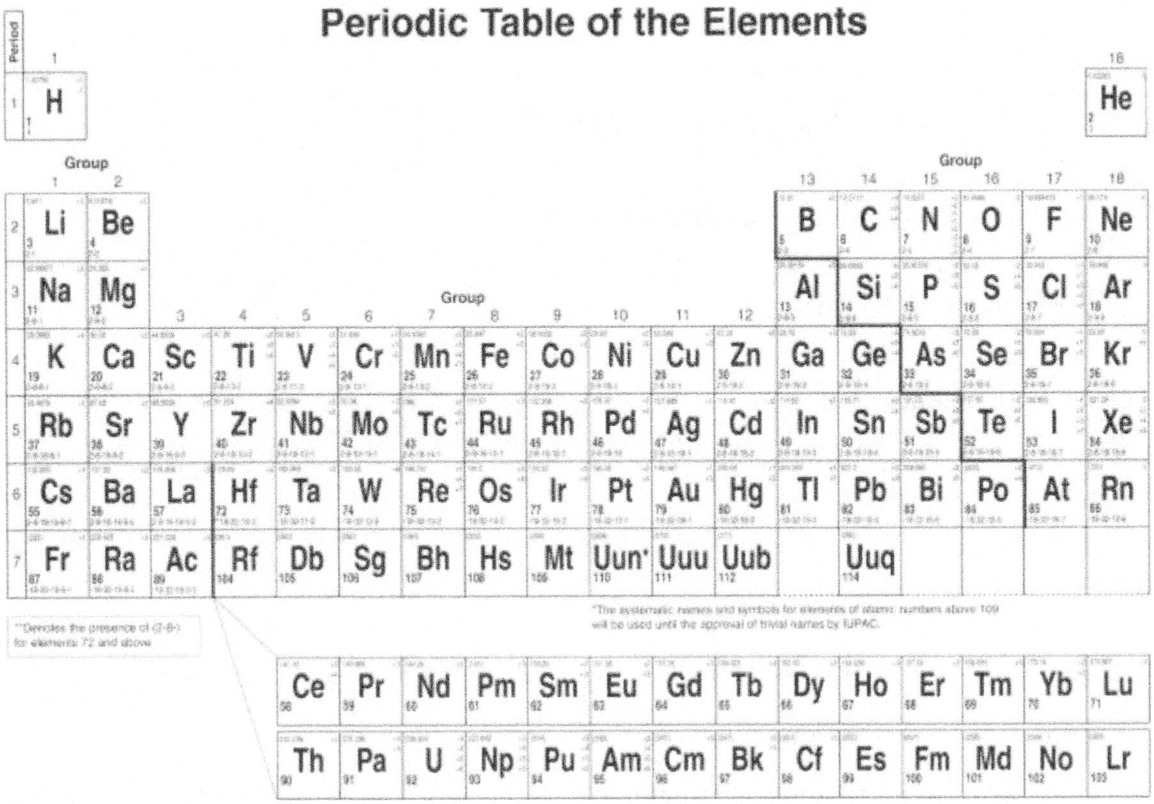

Periodic Table of the Elements

Figure 1

35. Which of the following elements would have the largest atomic radius?

A. Ti

B. Mn

C. Zn

D. Br

Answer: C

Explanation: Atomic radius decreases from left to right across a period and increases from top to bottom in a group. Zn is the leftmost element of the options.

36. How do the ionization energy and electron affinity of carbon (C) compare to those of oxygen (O)?

A. Higher ionization energy, lower electron affinity

B. Lower ionization energy, higher electron affinity

C. Higher for both characteristics

D. Lower for both characteristics

Answer: A

Explanation:

- Ionization energy increases from left to right across a period. Carbon is to the left of oxygen, so it has lower ionization energy.
- Electron affinity increases (becomes more negative) from left to right across a period. Carbon is to the left of oxygen, so it has lower electron affinity.

37. Based on periodic trends, how would the properties of scandium (Sc) likely compare to those of selenium (Se) before scandium was discovered?

A. Lower ionization energy and lower electronegativity

B. Lower ionization energy and higher electronegativity

C. Higher ionization energy and lower electronegativity

D. Higher ionization energy and higher electronegativity

Answer: A

Explanation:

- Ionization energy increases from left to right across a period and decreases from top to bottom in a group. Scandium is to the left and below selenium, so it has lower ionization energy.

- Electronegativity increases from left to right across a period and decreases from top to bottom in a group. Scandium is to the left and below selenium, so it has lower electronegativity.

38. Which pair of periodic table characteristics are NOT positively correlated?

A. Nonmetallic character and ionization energy

B. Metallic character and electron affinity

C. Atomic radius and metallic character

D. Electron affinity and electronegativity

Answer: B

Explanation:

- Nonmetallic character increases as ionization energy increases.
- Atomic radius increases as metallic character increases.
- Electron affinity increases as electronegativity increases.
- Metallic character decreases as electron affinity increases, so they are negatively correlated, not positively correlated.

39. A manufacturer wants to make a cooking pan that heats quickly. Which element would likely be the best choice for this purpose?

A. N

B. Al

C. Cu

D. F

Answer: C

Explanation: The passage states that metallic character relates to an element's ability to conduct heat. Of the above options, Cu has the greatest metallic character.

40. An unknown element has these characteristics:

- Nonmetallic
- High electron affinity
- High ionization energy

Which of the following is most likely the unknown substance?

A. Fluorine

B. Oxygen

C. Nitrogen

D. Hydrogen

Answer: A

Explanation: The characteristics describe an element that is far to the right and near the top of the periodic table. Of the above options, fluorine best fits this description.

Full-Length Practice Test 5 (Writing Test)

The Ethics of Zoos

Zoos are a popular destination for families and individuals alike. They offer the chance to observe animals up close and learn about different species from around the world. However, there is also a growing debate about the ethics of keeping animals in zoos. Some people argue that zoos are cruel and that animals should not be kept in captivity, while others believe that zoos play an important role in conservation and education.

Read and carefully evaluate these points of view. Each puts forth a specific way of thinking about foreign aid.

Viewpoint One	Viewpoint Two	Viewpoint Three
Zoos are unnatural environments that can be detrimental to the physical and psychological well-being of animals. Animals in zoos are often confined to small spaces, lack privacy, and may become bored or stressed due to limited opportunities for natural behaviors.	Zoos play a crucial role in conservation efforts by breeding endangered species and conducting research to better understand animal behavior and biology. Zoos can help educate the public about animals and the importance of conservation, potentially inspiring future generations to protect wildlife and their habitats.	While zoos may provide educational opportunities, they often fall short of promoting meaningful conservation action. The focus should be on protecting animals in their natural habitats rather than keeping them in artificial environments for human entertainment.

ESSAY ASSIGNMENT

Compose a focused essay in which you consider multiple viewpoints on the ethics of zoos. In your response, be certain to:

- express your own point of view on the topic, and analyze the relationship between your point of view and at least one of the viewpoints provided.

- use reasoning and examples to make your argument.

- write in an organized, logical way.

- communicate effectively using the conventions of standard written English.

Your viewpoint may completely agree, somewhat agree, or not agree at all with any of those presented.

Planning Your Response

Your prewriting notes on this page will not be considered in your score.

Use the following space to brainstorm ideas and map out your response. You may want to think about the following as you analyze the given prompt:

Strengths and weaknesses of the three viewpoints

■ What good points do they make, and what potential objections do they ignore?

■ Why might they be convincing to readers, and why might their perspectives fall short? Your previous experience, background knowledge, and personal values

■ What is your viewpoint on this topic, and what are the pros and cons of this viewpoint?

■ How will you craft an argument in support of your point of view?

Act Scoring Guide

(These norms are based on sampling classes of students, not on a nationwide sample.) Calculate your overall composite score by adding the individual scores from each of the four sections and dividing by 4. You can round up.

Score	English	Math	Reading	Science	Score
36	75	60	40	40	36
35	74	58-59	38-39	38-39	35
34	72-73	56-57	36-37	36-37	34
33	71	54-55	35	35	33
32	70	52-53	34	34	32
31	69	50-51	33	33	31
30	68	49	32	32	30
29	66-67	48	31	31	29
28	65	46-47	29-30	30	28
27	63-64	44-45	27-28	29	27
26	61-62	42-43	26	28	26
25	59-60	40-41	25	26-27	25
24	57-58	38-39	23-24	24-25	24
23	55-56	36-37	22	23	23
22	53-54	34-35	21	21-22	22
21	50-52	32-33	20	20	21
20	47-49	30-31	18-19	18-19	20
19	44-46	28-29	17	16-17	19
18	42-43	25-27	16	15	18
17	40-41	22-24	15	14	17
16	37-39	19-21	14	12-13	16
15	35-36	16-18	13	11	15
14	33-34	12-15	12	10	14

13	30–32	9–11	10–11	9	13
12	28–29	7–8	8–9	8	12
11	25–27	6	7	7	11
10	23–24	5	6	6	10
9	20–22	4	5	5	9
8	17–19	3	—	4–5	8
7	14–16	—	4	3	7
6	12–13	2	—	—	6
5	9–11	—	3	2	5
4	6–8	1	2	—	4
3	4–5	—	1	1	3
2	2–3	—	—	—	2
1	0–1	0	0	0	1

Ideas and Analysis: Considers multiple perspectives. Develops a clear and sophisticated thesis. Provides a useful context for analyzing the issue. Analyzes the implications, complexities, and underlying assumptions of different viewpoints.

6: Excellent	5: Skillful	4: Adequate	3: Fair	2: Weak	1: Poor	
						_____ /6

Development and Support: Provides an insightful and well-supported argument, placing the issue in a broad context. Uses reasoning and illustration to express the significance of the issue. Demonstrates an understanding of the complexity of the topic.

6: Excellent	5: Skillful	4: Adequate	3: Fair	2: Weak	1: Poor	
						_____ /6

Organization: Shows a skillful overall organizational approach. Has a clear, sustained position, accompanied by a logical sequence of ideas that builds the writer's argument. Provides clear and logical transitions between sentences and paragraphs.

6: Excellent	5: Skillful	4: Adequate	3: Fair	2: Weak	1: Poor	
						_____ /6

Language Use and Conventions: The essay's language is well-suited to the argument. Vocabulary choice is precise and appropriate. Sentence structure is clear and varied. Tone, voice, and style are effective. Grammar, usage, and mechanics issues are minimized and do not interfere with the reader's understanding.

6: Excellent	5: Skillful	4: Adequate	3: Fair	2: Weak	1: Poor	
						_____ /6
					Essay Raw Score:	_____ /24

Divide your Essay Raw Score by 2 to get your estimated ACT Essay Score of between 2–12:

Essay Raw Score: _____ ÷ 2 = _____ out of 12 possible points.

	ACT Writing Scaled Score:	_____ /12

Sample Top-Scoring Writing Response

The ethics of zoos is a complex issue with no easy answers. While zoos can provide educational and conservation benefits, they also raise concerns about animal welfare. I believe that zoos can play a positive role, but only if animal welfare is given the utmost priority.

Viewpoint One raises valid concerns about the potential for zoos to harm animals' physical and psychological well-being. However, it's important to recognize that not all zoos are created equal. Modern zoos are increasingly focusing on providing spacious, naturalistic habitats that allow for a greater range of natural behaviors.

Viewpoint Two highlights the potential for zoos to contribute to conservation and education. I agree that zoos can play a valuable role in breeding endangered species and conducting research that benefits wild populations. Additionally, zoos can educate the public about animals and inspire conservation action.

However, Viewpoint Three rightly points out that zoos may not always translate education into meaningful conservation outcomes. It's essential for zoos to go beyond simply exhibiting animals and actively engage visitors in conservation efforts.

In my view, zoos can be ethically justifiable if they prioritize animal welfare above all else. This means providing spacious, stimulating habitats, promoting natural behaviors, and ensuring high standards of care. Additionally, zoos should actively contribute to conservation efforts and provide educational experiences that translate into real-world conservation action.

While the ideal scenario may be for all animals to live in their natural habitats, the reality is that habitat loss, poaching, and other threats make this impossible for many species. Zoos can provide a safe haven for endangered animals and play a crucial role in their survival.

In conclusion, the ethics of zoos depend on a commitment to animal welfare, conservation, and education. By prioritizing these key aspects, zoos can be a valuable asset in the effort to protect wildlife and inspire future generations of conservationists.

☐ Careless Errors on Math Questions

Other issues?

_____

☐ Reading Timing

☐ Overthinking Reading Questions

☐ Not sure how to think through Reading Questions

☐ Careless Errors on Reading Questions

Other issues?

_____

☐ Science Timing

☐ Overthinking Science Questions

☐ Not sure how to think through Science Questions

☐ Careless Errors on Science Questions

Other issues?

the basic facts about the ACT Math section?

→ 60 minutes

→ 60 questions

→ Pre-Algebra: 20–25%; Elementary Algebra: 15–20%; Intermediate Algebra: 15–20%; Coordinate Geometry: 15–20%; Plane Geometry: 20–25%; Trigonometry: 5–10%

→ Questions generally increase in difficulty from the beginning to the end.

→ No formulas provided

→ No calculator provided, so you should bring your own.

→ Most scientific and graphing calculators permitted, except for ones like the TI-89.

To do your best on the ACT Math, you must be able to think through the problems well and know the relevant math content. This chapter will address both of these needs with a discussion of strategic tools you can use for the test and comprehensive review of the Math Content for the ACT.

How should you use this chapter?

1. Pick out which strategic tools are most helpful in improving your timing, stopping overthinking, and avoiding carelessness.

2. Review the Math Concepts you do not remember or did not learn, and complete the practice problems that accompany the concept reviews.

This chapter should not be read like a textbook—save your time and pick out the relevant parts that you need. No matter your personal situation or background, you will find the strategies and content that will help you perform your best on the test. Math is definitely not a one-size-fits-all subject, so do what works for you!

Although the ACT Math requires a good bit of math knowledge, which we will cover extensively, the quality of your thinking is what will enable you to earn the best possible score.

The three biggest hurdles to high-quality thinking on the ACT Math are

■ Time management problems

■ Overthinking the questions

■ Careless mistakes

We will examine each of these issues and discuss a variety of tools that you can use to optimize your thought process. Choose from the suggestions below based on what will best help your personal situation.

Time Management Ideas

The ACT Math is a tough test to finish for the vast majority of students. It is vitally important that you do no more than the number of questions you can do well. To determine a realistic number of questions you would like to complete, think about a realistic goal score for the Math section. Are you trying for a 20? A 25? Maybe something in the 30s? Sure, we'd all like to score a 36 on the Math. If you want to do your best, however, don't be an optimist—be a realist. If a student who is best capable of scoring a 25 tries to go for a 35, he will often end up scoring an 18 because of so many careless mistakes on easy questions. Take a look at this table to determine how many questions you would like to aim to do well on the ACT Math:

ACT Math Score, 1–36	Number of Correct Answers on a Typical Test

36	60
35	58–59
34	57
33	55–56
32	54
31	52–53
30	50–51
29	49
28	47–48
27	45–46
26	43–44
25	40–42
24	37–39
23	35–36
22	34
21	32–33
20	30–31
19	27–29
18	24–26
17	22–23
16	19–21
15	16–18
14	13–15
13	9–12
12	7–8
11	6
10	5
9	4
8	3
7	—
6	2
5	—
4	1
3	—
2	—
1	0

If your goal is to score a 30, you can miss 10 questions; if you would like to score a 25, you can miss 20; if a 20 will be fine for your goals, you only need to answer half of the questions correctly. When we are used to school tests in which missing a few questions can have a tremendous negative impact on our grade, it can be very difficult to adjust to the ACT Math, where missing a few questions still results in a top score. Now that we have a goal score in mind and know about how many questions we can afford to miss, let's understand three important things.

1. THE ACT MATH QUESTIONS GENERALLY BECOME HARDER FURTHER IN THE TEST. There will be exceptions to this general rule—it is possible that question 18 could be quite a bit more difficult than question 55. But if we look at questions 1–10 and compare them to questions 51–60, questions 51–60 will be much more challenging as a group. (The ACT Math is the only test where this pattern of difficulty is found for the test as a whole.)

2. DOING QUESTIONS "HALF-WAY" IS A BAD IDEA. When students rush through the last few questions on the test, they typically do much worse than if they would have just guessed on some of the tougher questions and given a good try to the easier ones. Sure, they wouldn't get all of the questions right. But, they would almost certainly end up with a better result than they would if they spread themselves too thin. If you are going to try a question, give it a solid try by reading the question thoroughly and writing out your work. If you are not going to give a question a solid try, don't even read the question—just pick a letter and move on. Don't try to have it both ways.

3. USE ALL YOUR TIME TO DO THE QUESTIONS ONE TIME WELL INSTEAD OF DOUBLE-CHECKING. Rushing through the questions so that you have quite a bit of time at the end to double-check your answers is not a sensible approach. If the ACT consisted of questions that consistently enabled you to plug in your answers to equations to check your calculations, then it would make sense to allow plenty of checking time. As we will discuss in a bit, the difficulty in the ACT Math questions comes in properly setting them up and figuring out what they want you to do. Because of this, you will be much better off finishing the test questions right when time is called instead of having several minutes at the end to go back and check your work. TIP You will earn your best score if you have realistic goals of how many questions you can finish given the time constraints. If you do more questions than you should, you will make

lots of careless mistakes. Now, let's discuss a variety of ways you can approach the ACT Math timing.

See which of these approaches feels like the right fit for you

Option 1 If your goal is to complete every question, spend 25 minutes on the first 30 questions and 35 minutes on the last 30 questions. This makes sense if you are trying to score in the 30s, since you will need to attempt most every question. If you can allot your time in this way, you will not dwell on easier questions at the beginning, and you will likely have sufficient time to solve the more challenging questions toward the end.

Option 2 If you are not going to do every question and you tend to RUSH, start by guessing on some of the last questions. Since every question is worth the same amount, it makes sense to pick your battles wisely. Why waste time on tougher questions when just a bit more time on easier questions will allow you to fully understand them and avoid careless errors? If this approach makes sense to you, think of the number of questions you want to guess on, and start the math test by bubbling in the same letter for every single one of these ending questions. Many students find that guessing on the last column on the answer sheet, questions 51–60, is a great approach. You will find that taking these tough questions off of the table will help you relax and focus on the questions you are choosing to do.

Option 3 If you are not going to do every question and you tend to GET STUCK ON QUESTIONS, plan on having some THROWAWAYS. Maybe it's 5 questions, maybe it's 10— if you tend to get stuck on tougher questions, plan ahead to guess on them, and you will avoid becoming stuck. Even though the Math test gets harder as you go, since there are some tough questions that will appear every so often earlier in the test, planning to guess on a few questions can help you do your best. Getting stuck is really tough for perfectionists, because they are used to typically having the luxury of taking as much time as they need for homework assignments and in-school tests. Don't let the perfect stand in the way of the good—as we saw above, you can usually score a 30 and still miss 10 questions.

Option 4 If you are just not a math person and can be easily overwhelmed by the ACT Math, DO ALL THE EASY QUESTIONS FIRST, THEN COME BACK FOR THE LEFTOVERS. If you tend to give up easily when it comes to math, building positive momentum is absolutely key. This approach can make a lot of sense if you know there will be at least 15–20 questions on which you will likely guess. It can also be a good approach if you tend to have quite a bit of difficulty with word problems. Word problems are scattered throughout the test, and if these slow you down, save them for the end or go ahead and guess on them the first time through.

Option 5 If you are a top math student who can finish the math with several minutes to spare but find the problems at the end tough to solve, consider doing the test backwards. This is a risky approach, because there is a danger that you will have trouble finishing since you may end up having to rush the beginning questions if you get stuck on the tough questions with which you start. If you are going to do this option, be sure you practice it a couple of times before trying it on the actual test. By starting with the later questions, you will give your subconscious mind the opportunity to solve the problem if you are unable to solve it the first time through. It is very rare that this will be a strategy that will be effective, but every so often it can work for somebody, so it deserves mention.

No matter what timing strategy you decide to use, keep in mind a couple of key ideas:

1. DON'T LOOK AT COMING BACK TO QUESTIONS AS A SIGN OF WEAKNESS. If you stay on a tougher question for more than a couple of minutes, you are taking time away from doing questions you might be able to solve more easily. When you decide to come back to a question, it does not mean it is a lost cause. In fact, you are allowing your subconscious mind the chance to more fully digest what was asked and to come up with a solution.

2. PLAN YOUR STRATEGY AHEAD OF TIME AND STICK TO IT. If you don't plan ahead on your timing approach, you will almost certainly do more questions than you have business doing. It is only natural to try to do as many questions as you possibly can. It takes a conscientious effort to realize that to do your best, you may need to pick your battles and do what will result in your personal best. When students take the ACT for the first time, they often set unrealistic goals and attempt more questions than they should. Use the practice tests in this

book to determine the number of questions that it makes sense for you to try in order to maximize your performance.

TIP

Experiment with different timing options before you take the test.

Overcoming Overthinking

Overthinking a question can be one of the most frustrating things about taking the ACT Math. It is very common for us to get in a cycle like this: We don't see how to do the problem right away → We assume the problem must be hard → Since we assume it's hard, we can't see how to do it → Since we can't see how to do it, we assume it's hard → Cycle goes on and on… When this happens to us, we will spend forever on a tough problem and get nowhere, only to find that when we see the solution, it was far, far easier than we initially thought. What are some bad beliefs that lead to consistently overthinking questions and some good beliefs that can help us avoid this?

Bad Belief

#1 There are REALLY TOUGH MATH CONCEPTS on the ACT that I've never learned. Good Belief

#1 I have the tools—I just need to put the right ones to use.

Why? The ACT is designed fundamentally as a critical thinking test first, a knowledge test second. This allows the ACT to show colleges that someone who may not have had the best opportunities to learn math but who has quite a bit of math talent and ability would be worth admitting so that she can realize her full potential. Because of this, the math content goes no further than Algebra II, Geometry, and Trigonometry. If you review the concepts earlier in the chapter, you can be assured that you will have the tools to figure out any problem that comes your way. On the ACT Math, think of yourself as a carpenter who will need to make a unique item using simple tools like a hammer and screwdriver. You will need to solve challenging problems, but you will only need to use relatively easy math concepts to do so. The difficulty is not with the material but in figuring out what is being asked and how to set up your problem-solving approach. Once in a while, the ACT Math will give you a problem with concepts like imaginary numbers, the law of cosines, the law of sines, or some formula from physics. If you are too easily intimidated, you will give up before you will realize that they will give you the information you need to solve problems with more advanced concepts like these. If it wasn't covered earlier in the chapter and you find it on the ACT Math, know that they will almost certainly give you the information you need to figure it out.

Bad Belief #2

I don't KNOW how to do it.

Good Belief #2

Let me FIGURE IT OUT.

On many math tests in school, you can tell right away whether you will be able to solve a given problem.

If you

(1) know the formula the problem uses and

(2) can solve it without making a careless error, you are virtually guaranteed a correct answer. When we bring this mindset to the ACT Math, it can cause problems, since we will give up way too quickly if we think we don't KNOW how to do it. A much more helpful approach is to think of the ACT Math problems less like the problems we face in school and more like problems that demand more patience and creativity: Treat a problem like a puzzle or maze. The idea that you would "know" how to solve a maze before playing around with it is nonsense. On many of the ACT Math problems, you will only see how to figure them out after you have taken a step that seems like a natural step to take.

Solving the ACT Math problems, break out of the mindset of a cook who can only cook with a recipe. Instead, be a cook who can go into a kitchen, see what looks good, and make something work based on what is available. Even if you do every single practice question in this book and in all the other ACT test preparation books available, you will still see problems on the actual ACT that will differ from what you have previously seen, since the ACT is more of a thinking than a knowledge test. While you need to know quite a bit, your mathematical skill is what will ultimately enable you to think on your feet and improvise, no matter what concepts or wording are thrown your way.

Bad Belief #3

I should save time by DOING THINGS IN MY HEAD.

Good Belief #3

I should WRITE IT ALL OUT SO I CAN MAKE CONNECTIONS. Why do we often do too much in our head on math problems? Frankly we do it because we have gotten away with it in the past. Even though our teachers preach it, we can often get away with not writing out all of our work. This is particularly true for students who are bright and have solid "working memory," meaning they can keep quite a bit straight in their head at once. Some smart students take pride in the fact that they can do quite a bit in their head, and perhaps subconsciously like to have the excuse in advance that if their score isn't as high as they would like, they can blame it not on their ability but on "stupid mistakes." Stupid mistakes are still mistakes—do whatever you have to do to have the best performance possible. Be confident, not arrogant, and put everything in front of you. We often don't write much on school tests so we can save the test for the next class. This saves schools money and is great for the environment, but on the ACT, your test booklet will not be reused by another student. They even provide half a page of blank space on which to do your figuring. Use it or lose it! Why is writing out your work so important to setting up ACT math problems? You won't fully understand what is being asked. As you read the question, write as you go so that you can paraphrase the question. If you misread or misinterpret even one word in the problem, you will probably miss the question. If you do misunderstand the question, the ACT will likely have what you come up with as a wrong answer. The ACT Math questions will have wrong answers that students who go down an incorrect path are likely to choose. The ACT takes it a step beyond just coming up with numbers close to the right answer. If they only did this, as long as you came up with an answer that was there, you could feel comfortable that you were correct. You have to really put your energy and emphasis on carefully reading and carefully setting up the problem. You don't want to just feel good about your answer while taking the test only to receive your scores and realize how many careless mistakes you must have made. Instead of thinking about writing out your work as a pointless, timewasting chore, look at writing out your work as being like a crime detective who puts all the evidence on a big table so that he can see how to solve a mystery. Detectives don't just stare off into space hoping to have a miraculous insight pop into their heads—they put all the crime photographs and information in front of them to put their minds in a position to make connections. On the ACT Math, if you put down what is being asked, write out relevant formulas, and don't skip problem-solving steps, you will put your mind in a position to make connections too.

Bad Belief #5

IF I DON'T SEE IT RIGHT AWAY, THERE IS NO HOPE.

Good Belief #5

I WILL GIVE MYSELF PERMISSION TO NOT SEE IT RIGHT AWAY.

Solving ACT Math problems is an intuitive, creative process. While you don't want to dwell on a tough problem too long, if you find that you throw in the towel too easily, here are five things to consider:

1. IF YOU ARE DOING TOO MANY QUESTIONS, YOU WILL SET YOURSELF UP FOR FAILURE. You need to give yourself enough time based on your personal abilities and situation to solve the problems you can. Revisit the timing guidelines earlier in the chapter if you need some guidance.

2. MISTAKES CAN LEAD TO SUCCESS. If the ACT had problems that required 10 or more steps to solve, a small mistake would end up wasting quite a bit of time. Since the problems

typically involve 1–3 steps to solve, realize that the first step forward can be a step backward. If you make a small mistake in your initial setup, don't get down on yourself—recover from it and move forward.

3. YOU ONLY NEED TO GET IT RIGHT—NOT TO EXPLAIN IT TO SOMEONE. If you tend to overanalyze problems, set a different standard for yourself. Instead of feeling that you can only pick an answer if you give a detailed justification as to why you picked it, know that students who do extremely well on the Math often solve the problems more intuitively. They can get the correct answer but would have difficulty showing someone else how to do it. Embrace this mindset for yourself.

4. THERE ARE MULTIPLE WAYS TO SOLVE PROBLEMS. There are usually several ways that you can approach solving ACT Math problems. From plugging numbers in to drawing pictures, be open-minded to all of the possible ways you might solve the problem.

5. GIVE YOUR SUBCONSCIOUS MIND A CHANCE. Perhaps more than any other section, coming back to questions on the ACT Math will give your mind the opportunity to think through the problems more thoroughly. Trust your feelings and instincts—if you don't feel comfortable with your answer but are holding your nose while you pick the answer, something is wrong. Go ahead and bubble in an answer so that if you run out of time, you will at least have it answered, but be open to coming back to it after your subconscious mind has given the problem more consideration.

TIP

A careless mistake is still a mistake! Do what it takes to avoid making them. Avoiding Careless Mistakes The bottom line with avoiding careless mistakes is: The more you put in front of you, the better you will do on the questions. You need to read the questions slowly, visualizing every step of the way in order to do your best. Watch the danger of the "unknown unknowns," much like we must do throughout the test. There will probably be some questions on the Math that most students know they cannot figure out; however, students can really improve their performance on those questions with just a little more care. They will be able to get them right because they are very doable.

Here are five techniques that will enable you to avoid careless errors on the ACT Math.

1. Roller Coaster the Questions

It is essential that you read the questions only as quickly as you fully understand what is being asked. "Coasting" the question can force you into reading the question one time well instead of reading it over and over again, only to waste time and end up misreading the question. All you need to do is, as you read the question, underline everything and circle the key words. The ACT Math questions incorporate a great deal of wording that is not essential to solving the problems, but is inserted so that there can be no doubt as to what is being asked. Coasting the question will enable you to focus on what is really important while being certain that you don't miss anything. Here is an example of what a coasted math question looks like:

The previews for the film take 20 minutes . The actual film is 110 minutes long. If Bill watches all of the previews and all of the film and spends no other time at the theater, what percent of his time in the theater is spent watching previews ?

2. Draw Pictures

Many of the problems that incorporate geometry in particular can be solved by drawing pictures—don't just do them in your head.

TIP

You have plenty of space to write and draw figures on the ACT Math. Use it or lose it!

Full-Length Practice Test 6 (English Test)

Time: 45 Minutes—75 Questions

Directions: In the passages that follow, you will find underlined words and phrases. In the column to the right, there are alternatives to the underlined wording. For most questions, choose the option that expresses the idea most effectively, conforms to the standards of conventional English, or has wording consistent with the tone and style of the passage. If you think the original underlined wording is best, pick "NO CHANGE." For some problems, you will need to read a question about the underlined portion and pick the best answer to the question. Other problems may ask about portions of the passage or the entire passage. These questions will be indicated by a numbered box. Choose the best answer to each question and fill in the matching oval on your answer sheet. Be sure to consider any relevant context surrounding the question in determining your answer.

Passage I

In the ever-evolving landscape of technological innovation, patents stand as cornerstones of progress, safeguarding the ingenuity and investment of inventors. In today's fast-paced world, where groundbreaking discoveries and technological leaps are commonplace, patents provide crucial legal protection for inventions, preventing others from replicating or exploiting them without permission. This protection allows inventors to secure their intellectual property, encouraging them to continue pushing the boundaries of what's possible, knowing their efforts will be rewarded. A patent, a legal document granting exclusive rights to an inventor for their invention, acts as a powerful incentive, fostering a culture of innovation and driving economic growth. This legal framework allows inventors to license or sell their patents, creating new business opportunities and stimulating further research and development.

Consider the remarkable story of Nikola Tesla, a visionary inventor whose contributions shaped the modern world. Born in 1856, Tesla's genius illuminated the path toward alternating current (AC) electricity, a technology that powers our homes and industries today. Despite facing numerous challenges, including financial constraints and fierce competition, Tesla persevered, driven by an unwavering belief in his inventions. He secured hundreds of patents throughout his career, protecting his innovations in fields ranging from electricity and radio to mechanical engineering.

Tesla's understanding of patents went beyond mere legal formality. He recognized their significance in establishing his credibility as an inventor and securing funding for his ambitious projects. His patents not only protected his intellectual property but also served as tangible evidence of his ingenuity, attracting investors and collaborators who believed in his vision. While Tesla's life was marked by both triumphs and setbacks, his prolific patent portfolio stands as a testament to the power of intellectual property protection in fostering innovation and driving technological advancement.

For aspiring inventors and entrepreneurs, Nikola Tesla's legacy underscores the critical role of patents in the innovation ecosystem. His story demonstrates how patents can not only safeguard an inventor's creations but also serve as a catalyst for collaboration, investment, and ultimately, the betterment of society.

1. Which choice would most effectively introduce the topic of the passage?

(A) NO CHANGE

(B) Throughout history, inventors have faced numerous obstacles in their pursuit of innovation.

(C) The legal framework surrounding inventions has evolved significantly over time.

(D) Intellectual property rights are essential for protecting the creations of inventors.

Answer:

(A) **Explanation:** The original wording effectively introduces the topic of patents and their importance in the context of innovation. The other choices are either too broad or too specific.

2. The passage primarily focuses on which aspect of patents?

(A) Their complex legal structure

(B) Their role in fostering innovation

(C) Their historical development

(D) Their economic impact on global trade

Answer: (B)

Explanation: The passage emphasizes how patents encourage invention and drive technological progress.

3. The word "cornerstones" in the first sentence most nearly means:

(A) decorative embellishments

(B) fundamental elements

(C) hidden secrets

(D) temporary supports

Answer: (B)

Explanation: Cornerstones are essential, foundational parts of something.

4. According to the passage, what is the primary benefit of patents for inventors?

(A) Public recognition of their achievements

(B) Financial security through government grants

(C) Exclusive rights to their inventions

(D) Guaranteed success in the marketplace

Answer: (C)

Explanation: Patents grant inventors exclusive control over their inventions.

5.   The passage mentions Nikola Tesla primarily to:

(A) Illustrate the challenges faced by inventors

(B) Provide a historical example of the importance of patents

(C) Highlight the impact of AC electricity on modern society

(D) Contrast his life with that of other inventors

Answer: (B)

Explanation: Tesla's story serves as a concrete example of how patents benefited an inventor.

6.   Tesla's patents served which of the following purposes, according to the passage?

(A) Protecting his intellectual property and attracting investors

(B) Establishing his dominance in the electrical industry

(C) Generating revenue through licensing agreements

(D) All of the above

Answer: (A)

Explanation: The passage explicitly mentions these two purposes. While the other options might be true, they are not directly stated in the passage.

7.   The phrase "pushing the boundaries of what's possible" in the first paragraph most nearly means:

(A) Engaging in risky or unethical experiments

(B) Challenging existing limitations and exploring new frontiers

(C) Seeking recognition and fame through groundbreaking inventions

(D) Working within established guidelines to improve existing technologies

Answer: (B)

Explanation: "Pushing boundaries" implies going beyond current limits.

8. The passage suggests that patents contribute to economic growth by:

(A) Limiting competition and creating monopolies

(B) Incentivizing innovation and creating new business opportunities

(C) Increasing government revenue through patent fees

(D) Protecting established companies from new entrants

Answer: (B)

Explanation: Patents encourage invention, which leads to new products and businesses.

9. The tone of the passage can best be described as:

(A) Critical and analytical

(B) Informative and appreciative

(C) Humorous and anecdotal

(D) Persuasive and argumentative

Answer: (B)

Explanation: The passage primarily provides information about patents and expresses appreciation for their role in innovation.

10. Which of the following is NOT mentioned as a benefit of patents in the passage?

(A) Protecting intellectual property

(B) Attracting investors

(C) Facilitating collaboration

(D) Guaranteeing market success

Answer: (D)

Explanation: The passage mentions the first three as benefits, but not guaranteed market success. A patent doesn't assure a product will be commercially successful.

11. The passage implies that Tesla's success was due, in part, to his:

(A) Business acumen and marketing skills

(B) Understanding of the importance of patents

(C) Connections to influential people

(D) Formal education and training

Answer: (B)

Explanation: The passage emphasizes Tesla's recognition of the significance of patents.

12. The word "prolific" in the fifth paragraph most nearly means:

(A) Innovative

(B) Productive

(C) Eccentric

(D) Controversial

Answer: (B)

Explanation: "Prolific" refers to producing a large quantity of something.

13. The passage suggests that Tesla's story is relevant to aspiring entrepreneurs because it:

(A) Provides a model for overcoming adversity

(B) Illustrates the importance of seeking funding for inventions

(C) Highlights the critical role of patents in building a successful business

(D) All of the above

Answer: (D)

Explanation: Tesla's story touches on all these points.

14. The author uses which rhetorical device most effectively in the final paragraph?

(A) Analogy

(B) Anecdote

(C) Summary

(D) Exemplification

Answer: (D)

Explanation: The author uses Tesla's story as an example to illustrate the importance of patents.

15. Which of the following would be the most appropriate title for this passage?

(A) The Evolution of Patent Law

(B) Patents: Fueling Innovation and Protecting Inventors

(C) Nikola Tesla: A Pioneer of Electrical Engineering

(D) The Challenges and Triumphs of Modern Inventors

Answer: (B)

Explanation: This title best reflects the main focus of the passage.

Passage II

In the complex world of health and wellness, regular exercise has emerged as a cornerstone of a healthy lifestyle. In our modern society, where sedentary lifestyles and processed foods are prevalent, individuals must prioritize physical activity to maintain their well-being. Engaging in regular exercise offers a multitude of benefits, from improving cardiovascular health and boosting mood to strengthening bones and managing weight. It provides a pathway to enhanced physical and mental resilience, allowing individuals to thrive in their daily lives. A consistent exercise routine empowers individuals to take control of their health, reducing the risk of chronic diseases and promoting longevity.

Consider the inspiring story of Serena Williams, a tennis legend whose dedication to physical fitness has propelled her to unparalleled success. Born in 1981 in Michigan, Serena began playing tennis at a young age, honing her skills through rigorous training and unwavering commitment. Despite facing numerous challenges, including injuries and intense competition, Williams persevered, driven by a relentless pursuit of excellence. She has won numerous Grand Slam titles and Olympic gold medals, demonstrating the power of physical conditioning and mental fortitude in achieving peak performance.

Williams's understanding of physical fitness extends beyond her own athletic pursuits. She advocates for healthy living and inspires millions around the world to embrace an active lifestyle. She also uses her platform to promote gender equality and social justice, demonstrating the positive impact of physical and mental strength in overcoming adversity.

For individuals striving for optimal health and well-being, Serena Williams's journey highlights the importance of regular exercise as a foundation for a fulfilling life. Her story demonstrates how a commitment to physical fitness can not only lead to personal achievement but also empower individuals to make a positive impact on the world

1. Which choice would most effectively introduce the topic of the passage?

(A) NO CHANGE

(B) Throughout history, athletes have inspired generations with their remarkable feats.

(C) The science of exercise physiology has advanced significantly in recent years.

(D) Maintaining a healthy lifestyle is crucial for overall well-being.

Answer: (A)

Explanation: The original wording directly introduces the topic of regular exercise and its importance in health and wellness.

2. The passage primarily focuses on which aspect of regular exercise?

(A) Its physiological benefits

(B) Its role in achieving peak athletic performance

(C) Its contribution to a healthy lifestyle

(D) Its historical evolution

Answer: (C)

Explanation: While the passage touches on athletic performance, the main focus is on exercise as a component of a healthy lifestyle.

3. The word "cornerstone" in the first sentence most nearly means:

(A) decorative ornament

(B) fundamental element

(C) temporary measure

(D) optional addition

Answer: (B)

Explanation: A cornerstone is a basic, essential part of something.

4. According to the passage, what is a key benefit of regular exercise?

(A) Guaranteed athletic success

(B) Reduced risk of chronic diseases

(C) Increased social status

(D) Enhanced intellectual abilities

Answer: (B)

Explanation: The passage explicitly mentions reducing the risk of chronic diseases.

5. The passage mentions Serena Williams primarily to:

(A) Criticize the pressures of professional sports

(B) Provide an example of the power of physical fitness

(C) Discuss the history of women's tennis

(D) Promote a specific brand of athletic wear

Answer: (B)

Explanation: Williams's story serves as an illustration of the benefits of dedication to physical fitness.

6. Williams's understanding of physical fitness extends to:

(A) Advocating for healthy living and social justice

(B) Developing new training techniques

(C) Investing in sports-related businesses

(D) Writing books on fitness and nutrition

Answer: (A)

Explanation: The passage mentions her advocacy for healthy living and her use of her platform for social justice.

7. The phrase "sedentary lifestyles" in the first paragraph refers to:

(A) Active participation in sports

(B) Lack of physical activity

(C) Engagement in intellectual pursuits

(D) Travel to different countries

Answer: (B)

Explanation: "Sedentary" implies a lack of movement or physical activity.

8. The passage suggests that regular exercise contributes to:

(A) Financial success

(B) Enhanced mental resilience

(C) Political influence

(D) Artistic talent

Answer: (B)

Explanation: The passage mentions both physical and *mental* resilience.

9. The tone of the passage can best be described as:

(A) Analytical and critical

(B) Informative and inspirational

(C) Humorous and lighthearted

(D) Persuasive and argumentative

Answer: (B)

Explanation: The passage provides information and also aims to inspire readers.

10. Which of the following is NOT mentioned as a benefit of regular exercise in the passage?

(A) Improved cardiovascular health

(B) Enhanced cognitive function

(C) Stronger bones

(D) Weight management

Answer: (B)

Explanation: While exercise *can* benefit cognitive function, it's not explicitly mentioned in this passage.

11. The passage implies that Williams's success is due, in part, to her:

(A) Natural talent alone

(B) Rigorous training and commitment

(C) Access to advanced technology

(D) Financial resources

Answer: (B)

Explanation: The passage emphasizes her "rigorous training and unwavering commitment."

12. The word "prevalent" in the first paragraph most nearly means:

(A) Rare

(B) Widespread

(C) Insignificant

(D) Temporary

Answer: (B)

Explanation: "Prevalent" means common or widespread.

13. The passage suggests that Williams's story is relevant to individuals because it:

(A) Offers a get-rich-quick scheme

(B) Demonstrates the power of dedication and hard work

(C) Provides a blueprint for becoming a professional athlete

(D) Guarantees fame and fortune

Answer: (B)

Explanation: Her story emphasizes the positive results of commitment to fitness.

14. The author uses which rhetorical device most effectively in the final paragraph?

(A) Analogy

(B) Anecdote

(C) Summary

(D) Exemplification

Answer: (D)

Explanation: Williams's story serves as a prime example of the importance of regular exercise.

15. Which of the following would be the most appropriate title for this passage?

(A) The History of Women's Tennis

(B) Exercise: A Foundation for a Healthy and Fulfilling Life

(C) The Science of Physical Fitness

(D) Serena Williams: A Tennis Icon

Answer: (B)

Explanation: This title best reflects the main idea of the passage.

Passage III

When many people hear the word "history," they picture dusty textbooks, boring lectures, and endless lists of dates and names. They might recall struggling to memorize historical events for tests, only to forget them shortly afterward. But history isn't just about the past; it's a vibrant and engaging narrative that connects us to our roots and helps us understand the present. Believe it or not, exploring history can be an exciting adventure, full of fascinating stories, intriguing mysteries, and valuable lessons.

My history professor, Dr. Ramirez, brings history to life with her passionate teaching style. She uses storytelling, primary sources, and interactive discussions to make historical events feel relevant and personal. Instead of simply reciting facts, she encourages us to analyze different perspectives and draw our own conclusions. She even organizes field trips to historical sites, allowing us to experience history firsthand. Dr. Ramirez's classes have transformed my perception of history, making it one of my favorite subjects.

The fun with history isn't limited to the classroom. Museums offer immersive exhibits that transport visitors to different eras, allowing them to interact with artifacts and learn about past cultures. Historical documentaries and films can bring historical events to life, making them more accessible and engaging. And if you are looking for a more active approach, you might consider volunteering at a local historical society or participating in a historical reenactment.

One of the most creative ways I've seen history celebrated is through historical-themed escape rooms. Participants work together to solve puzzles and decipher clues based on historical events, making learning fun and interactive. This type of activity combines entertainment with education, offering a unique way to engage with history. If you're still not convinced that history can be fun, you might want to explore these different avenues and discover the hidden adventurer within you.

If you still don't believe history can be engaging, don't worry. There are many other ways to connect with the past. You could read historical fiction, visit genealogical websites to trace your family history, or simply listen to stories from your grandparents. The possibilities for exploring the richness of the past are endless!

    1.   Which choice would most effectively introduce the topic of the passage?

(A) NO CHANGE

(B) Throughout history, societies have developed unique ways of preserving their past.

(C) The study of history has evolved significantly over time.

(D) Understanding history is essential for informed citizenship.

Answer: (A)

Explanation: The original wording directly addresses the common misconception about history and sets the stage for exploring its engaging aspects.

2. The passage primarily focuses on which aspect of history?

(A) Its academic rigor

(B) Its potential for engaging and exciting learning

(C) Its importance in shaping political discourse

(D) Its role in understanding current events

Answer: (B)

Explanation: The entire passage emphasizes the fun and engaging aspects of history.

3. The word "vibrant" in the first paragraph most nearly means:

(A) Dull

(B) Lively

(C) Static

(D) Monotonous

Answer: (B)

Explanation: "Vibrant" implies energy and excitement.

4. According to the passage, what is one way Dr. Ramirez makes history engaging?

(A) By assigning lengthy research papers

(B) By using storytelling and primary sources

(C) By focusing solely on dates and names

(D) By avoiding discussions and debates

Answer: (B)

Explanation: The passage explicitly mentions storytelling and primary sources as methods Dr. Ramirez uses.

5. The passage mentions museums primarily to:

(A) Criticize their lack of interactive exhibits

(B) Provide an example of how history can be experienced outside the classroom

(C) Discuss the challenges of preserving historical artifacts

(D) Promote specific museums and their collections

Answer: (B)

Explanation: Museums are presented as a way to experience history beyond textbooks and lectures.

6. Historical-themed escape rooms are presented as an example of:

(A) The commercialization of history

(B) A creative and interactive way to learn history

(C) The trivialization of historical events

(D) The difficulty of accurately portraying the past

Answer: (B)

Explanation: The passage highlights the interactive and educational nature of escape rooms.

7. The phrase "dusty textbooks" in the first paragraph refers to:

(A) Outdated historical research

(B) The traditional, and often perceived as boring, way of learning history

(C) The high cost of historical publications

(D) The fragility of historical documents

Answer: (B)

Explanation: "Dusty" implies old and uninteresting.

8. The passage suggests that exploring history can lead to:

(A) Increased financial wealth

(B) A deeper understanding of the present

(C) Political power and influence

(D) Scientific breakthroughs

Answer: (B)

Explanation: The passage states that history "helps us understand the present."

9. The tone of the passage can best be described as:

(A) Skeptical and cynical

(B) Enthusiastic and encouraging

(C) Informative and objective

(D) Critical and analytical

Answer: (B)

Explanation: The passage expresses excitement about history and encourages exploration.

10. Which of the following is NOT mentioned as a way to connect with history in the passage?

(A) Visiting historical sites

(B) Conducting original historical research

(C) Reading historical fiction

(D) Listening to stories from relatives

Answer: (B)

Explanation: While research is *part* of history, this passage focuses on engaging with already established historical narratives, not conducting original research.

11. The passage implies that the author's initial perception of history was:

(A) Positive and enthusiastic

(B) Negative and uninspired

(C) Neutral and indifferent

(D) Confused and overwhelmed

Answer: (B)

Explanation: The first paragraph describes common negative associations with history, suggesting the author shared those views initially.

12. The word "immersive" in the third paragraph most nearly means:

(A) Superficial

(B) Engaging

(C) Distant

(D) Abstract

Answer: (B)

Explanation: "Immersive" implies a deep and involving experience.

13. The passage suggests that exploring history can be a valuable activity for:

(A) Only professional historians

(B) Anyone interested in learning and understanding the world

(C) Only students enrolled in history courses

(D) Only individuals with a strong academic background

Answer: (B)

Explanation: The passage encourages everyone to explore history.

14. The author uses which rhetorical device most effectively in the final paragraph?

(A) Paradox

(B) Hyperbole

(C) Suggestion

(D) Irony

Answer: (C)

Explanation: The author offers suggestions for further exploration of history.

15. Which of the following would be the most appropriate title for this passage?

(A) The Importance of Studying History

(B) History: More Than Just Dates and Names – An Adventure Awaits

(C) How to Become a Historian

(D) The Future of Historical Research

Answer: (B)

Explanation: This title best captures the main idea and tone of the passage.

Passage IV

The giant panda, a beloved symbol of conservation, is a bear native to the mountainous regions of central China. Its distinctive black and white coat, coupled with its gentle demeanor and bamboo-centric diet, has made it an icon of wildlife and a subject of intense scientific study. While often perceived as cuddly and docile, the giant panda is a powerful animal with unique adaptations that allow it to thrive in its specialized habitat.

The panda's striking black and white coloring serves as camouflage in the dappled sunlight and snowy landscapes of its forest home. The black patches around its eyes, ears, and limbs are thought to disrupt its outline, making it harder for predators to spot. Its thick fur provides insulation against the cold mountain temperatures, and its powerful jaws and specialized teeth are perfectly suited for crushing and consuming bamboo.

Giant pandas possess a "pseudo thumb," a wrist bone modified to act like a thumb, which aids them in grasping bamboo stalks. This adaptation, along with their strong claws, allows them to efficiently strip leaves from bamboo and consume large quantities of this tough plant. Bamboo makes up almost all of a panda's diet, and they spend a significant portion of their day foraging and eating.

Giant pandas are solitary animals, typically only interacting during the breeding season. They communicate through vocalizations, scent marking, and body language. Female pandas give birth to one or two cubs, although usually only one survives. The cubs are incredibly small at birth and are completely dependent on their mother for care.

Despite their iconic status, giant pandas face numerous threats, including habitat loss, climate change, and low reproductive rates. Conservation efforts, including habitat protection and captive breeding programs, are crucial for ensuring the survival of this unique and cherished species. The giant panda serves as a powerful reminder of the importance of biodiversity and the challenges of protecting vulnerable wildlife in a rapidly changing world.

1. Which choice would most effectively introduce the topic of the passage?

(A) NO CHANGE

(B) Throughout history, different cultures have revered certain animals as symbols of good fortune.

(C) The conservation of endangered species is a complex and multifaceted issue.

(D) The giant panda is a fascinating example of adaptation and resilience in the animal kingdom.

Answer: (A)

Explanation: The original wording directly introduces the giant panda and its significance.

2. The passage primarily focuses on which aspect of the giant panda?

(A) Its evolutionary history

(B) Its physical characteristics and adaptations

(C) Its role in Chinese culture

(D) Its behavior in captivity

Answer: (B)

Explanation: The passage describes the panda's physical features and how they help it survive.

3. The word "distinctive" in the first sentence most nearly means:

(A) Common

(B) Unique

(C) Bland

(D) Unremarkable

Answer: (B)

Explanation: "Distinctive" implies something that stands out and is easily recognized.

4. According to the passage, what is the primary component of a giant panda's diet?

(A) Fish

(B) Bamboo

(C) Insects

(D) Fruit

Answer: (B)

Explanation: The passage explicitly states that bamboo makes up almost all of a panda's diet.

5. The passage mentions the "pseudo thumb" primarily to:

(A) Explain how pandas climb trees

(B) Illustrate an adaptation for grasping bamboo

(C) Describe a unique feature of panda cubs

(D) Compare panda paws to those of other bears

Answer: (B)

Explanation: The pseudo thumb is a key adaptation for handling bamboo.

6. The panda's black and white coloring is thought to serve as:

(A) A way to attract mates

(B) Camouflage

(C) A warning signal to predators

(D) A means of communication with other pandas

Answer: (B)

Explanation: The passage explains that the coloring helps pandas blend into their environment.

7. The phrase "dappled sunlight" in the second paragraph refers to:

(A) Bright, direct sunlight

(B) Sunlight filtered through trees

(C) Overcast skies

(D) Reflected sunlight

Answer: (B)

Explanation: "Dappled" implies patches of light and shadow, like sunlight filtering through leaves.

8. The passage suggests that giant pandas are vulnerable due to:

(A) Their aggressive nature

(B) Habitat loss and low reproductive rates

(C) Competition with other bear species

(D) Their susceptibility to disease

Answer: (B)

Explanation: The passage lists these as key threats to panda survival.

9. The tone of the passage can best be described as:

(A) Critical and analytical

(B) Informative and appreciative

(C) Humorous and lighthearted

(D) Persuasive and argumentative

Answer: (B)

Explanation: The passage provides information about pandas and expresses appreciation for their unique qualities.

10. Which of the following is NOT mentioned as a characteristic of giant pandas in the passage?

(A) Solitary behavior

(B) Specialized teeth

(C) Hibernation during the winter

(D) Thick fur

Answer: (C)

Explanation: While some bears hibernate, this passage does not mention it for pandas.

11. The passage implies that conservation efforts are important for pandas because:

(A) They are a popular tourist attraction

(B) They are a symbol of China

(C) Their survival is threatened

(D) They are scientifically interesting

Answer: (C)

Explanation: The passage states they face numerous threats.

12. The word "iconic" in the first and last paragraphs most nearly means:

(A) Obscure

(B) Symbolic

(C) Controversial

(D) Transient

Answer: (B)

Explanation: "Iconic" implies being a widely recognized symbol.

13. The passage suggests that panda cubs are: (A) Independent from birth (B) Very small and dependent on their mother (C) Born in litters of four or more (D) Covered in black and white fur from birth

Answer: (B)

Explanation: The passage describes them as "incredibly small" and dependent.

14. The author uses which rhetorical device most effectively in the final paragraph?

(A) Analogy

(B) Anecdote

(C) Call to action

(D) Exemplification

Answer: (C)

Explanation: The final paragraph emphasizes the need for conservation efforts.

15. Which of the following would be the most appropriate title for this passage?

(A) The Secret Life of Pandas

(B) Giant Pandas: Unique Adaptations and Conservation Challenges

(C) Bamboo: The Panda's Lifeline

(D) The History of Panda Conservation

Answer: (B)

Explanation: This title best reflects the main topics covered in the passage.

Passage V

The insistent buzz of my alarm clock drags me from a deep slumber, a jarring contrast to the peaceful dream I was just enjoying. I groan, reaching out to silence the insistent noise, my hand fumbling across the nightstand in the darkness. The room is still shrouded in pre-dawn gloom, the only hint of light filtering through the gap in my curtains. I reluctantly peel back the covers, the cool morning air sending a shiver down my spine. My muscles ache slightly, a reminder of yesterday's vigorous hike.

Stretching and yawning, I finally manage to sit up, my feet hitting the cold hardwood floor. I glance at the clock, debating whether hitting the snooze button is a viable option. The promise of a hot cup of coffee and the quiet solitude of the early morning eventually win out. I pull on my robe and slippers, padding softly towards the kitchen. The house is still quiet, the only sound the gentle hum of the refrigerator.

As I prepare my coffee, I peek out the window, noticing the faint glow beginning to appear on the horizon. The sky is a canvas of soft pastels, hinting at the sunrise to come. A sense of anticipation fills me as I sip my coffee, watching the light gradually brighten. I decide to take my coffee out to the porch, wanting to fully appreciate the beauty of the morning.

Settling into a rocking chair, I watch as the sun finally crests the horizon, painting the sky with vibrant hues of gold and rose. The world seems to awaken around me, the birds beginning their morning chorus. I breathe deeply, savoring the peacefulness of the moment. The quiet of the morning, the warmth of the coffee, and the beauty of the sunrise make me feel grateful for this simple moment of tranquility. Refreshed and invigorated, I feel ready to face the day ahead.

1. Which choice would most effectively introduce the topic of the passage?

(A) NO CHANGE

(B) Throughout history, people have sought moments of peace and tranquility.

(C) The beauty of nature has inspired artists and poets for centuries.

(D) Mornings offer a unique opportunity to appreciate the simple joys of life.

Answer: (A)

Explanation: The original wording directly sets the scene of waking up in the early morning.

2. The passage primarily focuses on which aspect of the morning?

(A) The scientific explanation of sunrise

(B) The peaceful and reflective atmosphere

(C) The practical routines of starting the day

(D) The challenges of waking up early

Answer: (B)

Explanation: The passage emphasizes the quiet and tranquil mood of the morning.

3. The word "insistent" in the first sentence most nearly means:

(A) Gentle

(B) Persistent

(C) Faint

(D) Intermittent

Answer: (B)

Explanation: "Insistent" implies a demand that cannot be ignored.

4. According to the passage, what motivates the narrator to get out of bed?

(A) The fear of being late

(B) The promise of coffee and solitude

(C) The need to exercise

(D) The sound of birds singing

Answer: (B)

Explanation: The narrator mentions the coffee and the quiet as motivating factors.

5. The narrator's initial feeling upon waking up can best be described as:

(A) Excited

(B) Reluctant

(C) Anxious

(D) Energetic

Answer: (B)

Explanation: The narrator groans and fumbles to turn off the alarm, showing reluctance.

6. The phrase "shrouded in pre-dawn gloom" in the first paragraph refers to:

(A) The darkness before sunrise

(B) Overcast weather

(C) A messy or cluttered room

(D) A feeling of sadness or depression

Answer: (A)

Explanation: "Gloom" and "pre-dawn" indicate the darkness before the sun rises.

7. The narrator's "muscles ache slightly" because of:

(A) A recent injury

(B) Yesterday's hike

(C) Sleeping in an uncomfortable bed

(D) Stress and tension

Answer: (B)

Explanation: The passage mentions the hike as the cause of the muscle ache.

8. The passage suggests that the narrator finds peace and enjoyment in:

(A) Socializing with friends

(B) The quiet moments of the morning

(C) Completing tasks and errands

(D) Engaging in physical activity

Answer: (B)

Explanation: The narrator appreciates the "quiet solitude" and "peacefulness of the moment."

9. The tone of the passage can best be described as:

(A) Humorous and lighthearted

(B) Reflective and appreciative

(C) Critical and analytical

(D) Mysterious and suspenseful

Answer: (B)

Explanation: The passage reflects on the beauty of the morning and expresses appreciation for it.

10. Which of the following is NOT mentioned as part of the narrator's morning routine?

(A) Making coffee

(B) Checking emails

(C) Watching the sunrise

(D) Getting dressed

Answer: (B)

Explanation: The passage doesn't mention checking emails.

11. The narrator's mood shifts from reluctant to:

(A) Angry

(B) Appreciative

(C) Confused

(D) Frustrated

Answer: (B)

Explanation: The narrator's initial reluctance gives way to appreciation for the morning's beauty.

12. The word "jarring" in the first sentence most nearly means:

(A) Pleasant

(B) Disruptive

(C) Subtle

(D) Harmonious

Answer: (B)

Explanation: "Jarring" implies a sudden and unpleasant disturbance.

13. The passage suggests that the sunrise makes the narrator feel:

(A) Overwhelmed

(B) Grateful

(C) Anxious

(D) Nostalgic

Answer: (B)

Explanation: The narrator feels "grateful for this simple moment of tranquility."

14. The author uses which rhetorical device most effectively in the final paragraph? (A) Metaphor (B) Simile (C) Personification (D) Imagery **Answer: (D) Explanation:** The author uses vivid descriptions to create a mental picture of the sunrise and the morning atmosphere.

15. Which of the following would be the most appropriate title for this passage?

(A) The Joys of Sleeping In

(B) A Peaceful Morning

(C) The Challenges of Early Mornings

(D) My Daily Routine

Answer: (B)

Explanation: This title best reflects the central theme and mood of the passage.

Full-Length Practice Test 7 (Maths Test)

Time: 60 Minutes—60 Questions

Directions: Determine the answer to each question, and then fill in the matching oval on your answer sheet. Do not spend too much time on any one problem. Solve as many as possible, then come back to ones that you have skipped. You are allowed to use a calculator on this section, but several of the problems are best completed without a calculator. Unless stated otherwise, assume that drawings are NOT necessarily to scale, geometric figures are in a two-dimensional plane, "lines" are straight lines, and "average" means the arithmetic mean.

Pre-Algebra -10 questions

1. A person walked 3 miles to the east, then turned north and walked 10 miles, then turned west and walked 6 miles, and finally turned south and walked 16 miles. Approximately how far is the person from his starting point in miles?

(A) 3.4

(B) 6.7

(C) 9.2

(D) 12.8

(E) 22.0

Answer: (D)

Explanation: The person ends up 3 miles to the west of his starting point (6−3=3) and 6 miles to the south of his starting point (16−10=6). Using the Pythagorean Theorem, the distance from his starting point is 32+62=45≈6.7 miles.

2. A 12-ounce soft drink has 41 grams of sugar, which is 14% of the normal daily allowance for sugar. Approximately how many grams of sugar are recommended in the normal diet?

(A) 5.74

(B) 69

(C) 293

(D) 574

(E) 861

Answer: (C)

Explanation: We can set up the following equation to find the normal daily allowance for sugar: 0.14x=41 Solving for x gives us:

x = 41 / 0.14 = 292.86

3. What is 65−4143+32?

(A) 717

(B) 65

(C) 145

(D) 32

(E) 157

Answer: (A)

Explanation: We can simplify the expression as follows:

(3/4 + 2/3) / (5/6 - 1/4) = (9/12 + 8/12) / (10/12 - 3/12) = (17/12) / (7/12) = 17/7

4. The expression (5x3)−32 is equivalent to which of the following?

(A) 5x2

(B) 3x25

(C) x225

(D) x2251

(E) x251

Answer: (D)

Explanation: We can simplify the expression as follows:

$(5x^3)^{-2/3} = 5^{-2/3} * x^{-2} = 1 / (5^{2/3} * x^2) = 1 / (x^2 * \text{cube root}(25))$

5. The figure below is composed of two parallel lines and a transversal. Which of these expressions MUST add up to 360° ?

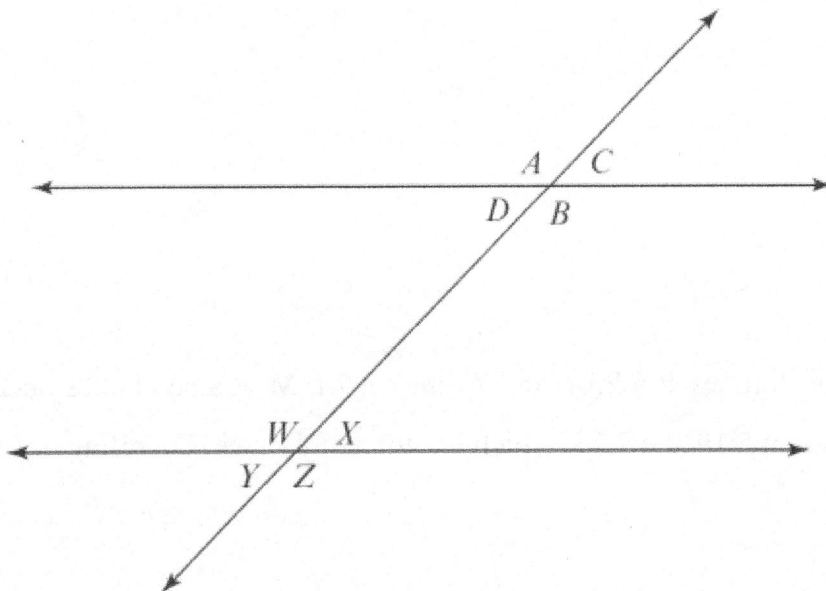

(A) A+B+Y+X

(B) W+X+A+B

(C) A+B+C+W

(D) Z+X+D+C

(E) C+D+X+Y

Answer: (E)

Explanation: The angles around a point always add up to 360 degrees. In this figure, angles C, D, X, and Y form a complete circle around the point of intersection of the transversal and the lower parallel line.

6. If a clock chimes every hour the same number of times as the hour it is (e.g., at 3 P.M. it chimes three times) and once for every 15-minute increment between hours (e.g., at 3:15, 3:30, and 3:45), what will the total number of chimes be between 5:10 and 7:35 P.M.?

(A) 3

(B) 15

(C) 18

(D) 21

(E) 45

Answer: (C)

Explanation: The clock chimes 6 times at 6 P.M. and 7 times at 7 P.M. It also chimes once for each 15-minute increment between 5:10 and 7:35, which is a total of 8 times. Therefore, the total number of chimes is 6+7+8=21.

7. If $x \leq 2$ and $y \leq 5$, what is the greatest possible value for the product of x and y?

(A) 7

(B) 10

(C) 12

(D) 20

(E) 40

Answer: (B)

Explanation: The greatest possible value for the product of x and y occurs when x=2 and y=5, which gives us 2· 5=10.

8. Which of the following is NOT equivalent to 283?

(A) 2.375

(B) 2+83

(C) 2×83

(D) 2.375000

(E) 819

Answer: (C)

Explanation: 2×83 equals 86 or 43, which is not equivalent to 283. The other options are all equivalent to 283:

- 2.375 is the decimal equivalent of 283.
- 2+83 is another way of writing 283.
- 2.375000 is the same as 2.375 with additional trailing zeros.
- 819 is the improper fraction equivalent of 283.

9. Assume the following conditions:

- A B is always an A.
- A C is always a B.
- A D is always an A.

Which of the following must be true?

(A) An A is always a D

(B) A B is always a C

(C) A D is always a B

(D) A C is always an A

(E) A C is always a D

Answer: (D)

Explanation: If a C is always a B, and a B is always an A, then a C must always be an A.

10. Jennifer is competing in a marathon, which is a 26.2-mile race. If Jennifer runs the first half of the race at 8 mph and the second half of the race at 6 mph, approximately how many hours does it take for her to complete the race?

(A) 2.62

(B) 3.74

(C) 3.82

(D) 4.12

(E) 14

Answer: (B)

Explanation: The time taken for the first half of the race is 13.1 miles / 8 mph = 1.6375 hours. The time taken for the second half of the race is 13.1 miles / 6 mph = 2.1833 hours. The total time taken is 1.6375 hours + 2.1833 hours = 3.8208 hours. Rounding to the nearest hundredth gives us 3.82 hours.

Elementary Algebra - 10 questions

1. Patricia's annual starting salary at her new job is $20,000. After one year on the job, her salary increases by 10%; after her second year on the job, her salary increases by 10% more over the previous year's salary. After these two years have passed, what would her salary be?

(A) $2,000

(B) $4,000

(C) $22,000

(D) $24,000

(E) $24,200

Answer: (E)

Explanation: After one year, Patricia's salary increases by $20,000 * 0.10 = $2,000, so her new salary is $22,000. After the second year, her salary increases by $22,000 * 0.10 = $2,200. Her final salary is $22,000 + $2,200 = $24,200.

2. If a and b are the smaller legs of a triangle and c is the length of the longest side, what must be true about a, b, and c?

(A) $a^2 + b^2 = c^2$

(B) $a+b>c$

(C) $a+b<c$

(D) $a=c$

(E) $a+b=c$

Answer: (B)

Explanation: The Triangle Inequality Theorem states that the sum of the lengths of any two sides of a triangle must be greater than the length of[1] the third side.

3. What is the y-coordinate of the midpoint of the line formed by (2, 8) and (-15, 8)?

(A) -7

(B) 8

(C) 10

(D) 13

(E) 18

Answer: (B)

Explanation: The midpoint of a line segment is found by averaging the x-coordinates and averaging the y-coordinates. The y-coordinate of the midpoint is $(8 + 8) / 2 = 8$.

4. What is the product of the least common multiple of 10 and 8 and the greatest common factor of 10 and 8?

(A) 16

(B) 20

(C) 40

(D) 60

(E) 80

Answer: (E)

Explanation: The least common multiple (LCM) of 10 and 8 is 40, and the greatest common factor (GCD) of 10 and 8 is 2. The product of the LCM and GCD is $40 * 2 = 80$.

5. A ball that is thrown down from a tall building falls a distance according to the following formula: $x(t)=8t+21(10)t2$ ($x(t)$ is computed in meters.) How many meters has the ball fallen after six seconds?

(A) 108

(B) 180

(C) 228

(D) 948

(E) 1,848

Answer: (C)

Explanation: To find the distance the ball has fallen after six seconds, we substitute $t=6$ into the formula: $x(6)=8(6)+21(10)(6)2=48+180=228$ meters.

6. When Isaac became married, he weighed much less than he does today. His ring finger has a diameter of 1.25 inches, while it had a diameter of just 1 inch when he was married. Assuming his ring is perfectly circular and fits his finger perfectly, by what percentage has Isaac's ring circumference increased from when he became married to the present day?

(A) 20%

(B) 25%

(C) 28%

(D) 30%

(E) 33%

Answer: (B)

Explanation: The circumference of a circle is directly proportional to its diameter. Since the diameter increased by 25% (from 1 inch to 1.25 inches), the circumference also increased by 25%.

7. Which of the following is the sum of two prime numbers?

I. 2

II. 9

III. 11

(A) I only

(B) II only

(C) III only

(D) I and II only

(E) I, II, and III

Answer: (C)

Explanation: A prime number is a whole number greater than 1 that has only two factors: 1 and itself. The first few prime numbers are 2, 3, 5, 7, 11, and 13. The only number in the list that can be expressed as the sum of two prime numbers is 11 (5 + 6).

8. A boat traveled 10 miles per hour for three hours due east. It then turned north, increased its speed to 20 miles per hour for two hours. After these five hours, what is the straight-line distance in miles of the boat from its starting point?

(A) 5

(B) 30

(C) 50

(D) 70

(E) 150

Answer: (C)

Explanation: The boat travels 30 miles east (10 mph * 3 hours) and 40 miles north (20 mph * 2 hours). These two distances form the legs of a right triangle, and the straight-line distance from the starting point is the hypotenuse. Using the Pythagorean Theorem, the distance is 30²+40² =2500=50 miles.

9. What is the mean number of points scored per game by the team in the games listed in the table below?

Game Date	Total Points Scored	
November 5	46	
November 18	72	
November 26	84	
December 6	51	
December 12	67	

(A) 48

(B) 52

(C) 58

(D) 62

(E) 64

Answer: (E)

Explanation: To find the mean, we add up all the points scored and divide by the number of games: $(46 + 72 + 84 + 51 + 67) / 5 = 320 / 5 = 64$.

10. Terri opened a fast food restaurant. The initial cost to open the restaurant is $800,000. She has to pay daily operational costs of $250 and labor costs of $400. What expression represents her total cost if she has had the restaurant open for "D" days?

(A) 800,000+150D

(B) 800,000+650D

(C) 800,000−650D

(D) 650+800,000D

(E) 800,000−150D

Answer: (B)

Explanation: The total cost is the sum of the initial cost and the daily costs multiplied by the number of days the restaurant has been open. The daily costs are $250 + $400 = $650. Therefore, the expression for the total cost is 800,000+650D.

Intermediate Algebra - 10 questions

1. The volume of a sphere is calculated using the formula $\frac{3}{4}\pi r3$, in which r represents the radius of the sphere. What fraction of the volume of a sphere of radius x would a cube with a side length of x be?

(A) $\frac{3}{4}\pi$

(B) $\frac{4}{3}\pi$

(C) $\frac{\pi}{4}$

(D) $\frac{3}{4\pi}1$

(E) 2π3

Answer: (D)

Explanation: The volume of the sphere is 34πx3 and the volume of the cube is x3. The fraction of the sphere's volume that the cube occupies is:

x^3 / ((4/3) * pi * x^3) = 1 / ((4/3) * pi)

2. In a box, there are 4 red balls, 8 yellow balls, and 12 purple balls. If a ball is randomly selected from this box, what is the probability that it will be yellow?

(A) 51

(B) 41

(C) 31

(D) 21

(E) 1

Answer: (C)

Explanation: There are a total of 24 balls in the box. The probability of selecting a yellow ball is the number of yellow balls divided by the total number of balls, which is 8/24 or 1/3.

3. A novel has 400 pages and Veronica wants to estimate how long it will take her to complete it. She reads 250 words per minute. She counted the words on one quarter of a typical page and found that there were approximately 200 words per page. To the nearest minute, how long will it take Veronica to read the book?

(A) 225

(B) 320

(C) 400

(D) 450

(E) 850

Answer: (B)

Explanation: Veronica reads at a rate of 250 words per minute, and there are approximately 200 words per page. So, she reads at a rate of 250 words/minute / 200 words/page = 1.25 pages per minute. To read a 400-page book, it will take her 400 pages / 1.25 pages/minute = 320 minutes.

4. What is the sum of the vectors $4i+2j$ and $-3i+9j$?

(A) $7i+11j$

(B) $i+11j$

(C) $6i+6j$

(D) $-12i+18j$

(E) $12i+18j$

Answer: (B)

Explanation: To add vectors, we add their corresponding components. The sum of the given vectors is $(4-3)i+(2+9)j=i+11j$.

5. Which of these vowels does NOT have a vertical axis of symmetry?

(A) A

(B) E

(C) I

(D) O

(E) U

Answer: (E)

Explanation: A vertical axis of symmetry divides a shape into two halves that are mirror images of each other. The letter U does not have a vertical axis of symmetry.

6. Mr. Cleary's class and Ms. Ntuala's class go to use the computer lab. There are 20 computers available, two of which do not work. Mr. Cleary's class has 14 kids, and Ms. Ntuala's class has 12 kids. If every student must use a computer and there can only be 2 students on a computer at most, what is the maximum number of students who can have a computer to themselves?[1]

(A) 2

(B) 6

(C) 10

(D) 14

(E) 20

Answer: (B)

Explanation: There are 18 working computers in the lab. To maximize the number of students who can have a computer to themselves, we first pair up as many students as possible. We can pair up 18 students, leaving 8 students who need to use a computer alone. Since there are only 18 working computers, the maximum number of students who can have a computer to themselves is 18 - 8 = 10.

7. What is the slope of a line perpendicular to a line with the equation $-6x+2y=-4$?

(A) -3

(B) $-\frac{2}{1}$

(C) $-\frac{3}{1}$

(D) 3

(E) 12

Answer: (C)

Explanation: The given equation can be rewritten in slope-intercept form as $y=3x-2$. The slope of this line is 3. The slope of a line perpendicular to this line is the negative reciprocal of 3, which is $-1/3$.[2]

8. Dylan has to bake a cake at 350° F in the oven. The oven dial is set to degrees Celsius. The formula for conversion from degrees Celsius (C) to degrees Fahrenheit (F) is $F=59C+32$. To what approximate temperature in Celsius should Dylan set the oven?

(A) 7

(B) 177

(C) 382

(D) 572

(E) 662

Answer: (B)

Explanation: We can use the conversion formula to find the temperature in Celsius:

$350 = (9/5)C + 32$

$318 = (9/5)C$

$C = 318 * (5/9) = 176.67$

9. What is the equation for the circle depicted below?

The standard equation of a circle is given by:

$$[(x - h)^2 + (y - k)^2 = r^2]$$

where $((h, k))$ represents the center of the circle and (r) is the radius. For the circle in question, we have:

- Center: $((h, k) = (2, 3))$
- Radius: $(r = 4)$

(A) $(x-2)2+(y-3)2=16$

(B) $(x+2)2+(y+3)2=16$

(C) $(x-2)2-(y-3)2=16$

(D) $(x-2)2+(y-3)2=64$

(E) $(x+2)2+(y-3)2=16$

Answer: (A)

Explanation: The standard equation of a circle is $(x-h)2+(y-k)2=r2$, where (h,k) is the center and r is the radius. The circle in the image is centered at $(2, 3)$ and has a radius of 4. Therefore, the equation is $(x-2)2+(y-3)2=16$.

10. If m is an even integer, which of the following must be even?

(A) m2+1

(B) m−2−4

(C) m3+1

(D) m4+3

(E) m6−2

Answer: (E)

Explanation: If m is even, then m6 is also even. Subtracting 2 from an even number results in another even number.

Coordinate Geometry - 10 questions

1. What is the equation for the circle depicted below?

(A) $(x-2)^2+(y-3)^2=16$

(B) $(x+2)^2+(y+3)^2=16$

(C) $(x-2)^2-(y-3)^2=16$

(D) $(x-2)^2+(y-3)^2=64$

(E) $(x+2)^2+(y+3)^2=16$

Answer: (B)

Explanation: The standard equation of a circle is $(x-h)^2+(y-k)^2=r^2$ where (h,k) is the center and r is the radius. The circle in the image is centered at (-2,3) and has a radius of 4. Therefore, the equation is $(x+2)^2+(y-3)^2=16$.

2. If $\log_3 x=4$, what is x?

(A) 1

(B) 12

(C) 64

(D) 81

(E) 243

Answer: (D)

Explanation: We can rewrite the equation in exponential form to solve for x:

$3^4 = x$

$x = 81$

3. At what point in the x-y coordinate plane do these two lines intersect?

Line One: y=2x+4 Line Two: y=−3x−5

(A) (59,−52)

(B) (−59,52)

(C) (52,−59)

(D) (95,−25)

(E) (6,12)

Answer: (B)

Explanation: To find the point of intersection, we can set the two equations equal to each other and solve for x:

2x + 4 = -3x - 5

5x = -9

x = -9/5

Substituting this value of x back into either equation gives us y=2/5.

4. Consider a point with coordinates (a,b), where a and b are both positive integers. In which quadrant will the point (-5a,-7b) fall?

(A) First

(B) Second

(C) Third

(D) Fourth

(E) It cannot be determined with the given information

Answer: (C)

Explanation: Since a and b are both positive, −5a and −7b are both negative. Points with negative x and y coordinates fall in the third quadrant.

5. A washing machine has a normal cycle that lasts 45 minutes and a whites cycle that lasts 70 minutes. What fraction of the length of the whites cycle is the length of the normal cycle?

(A) 71

(B) 31

(C) 149

(D) 32

(E) 914

Answer: (C)

Explanation: The fraction of the whites cycle that the normal cycle represents is 45 minutes / 70 minutes, which simplifies to 9/14.

6. Which of the following expressions would give the measure of angle A?

(A) sin A

(B) cos C

(C) tan−1B

(D) arcsin ac

(E) arccos cb

Answer: (E)

Explanation: The cosine of an angle in a right triangle is equal to the adjacent side divided by the hypotenuse. In this triangle, the adjacent side to angle A is b and the hypotenuse is c. Therefore, the cosine of angle A is cb. To find the measure of angle A, we take the inverse cosine (arccos) of this ratio.

7. Zoey is laying bricks for her patio. The salesman wants to sell Zoey as many bricks as possible to cover her patio with a thickness of one brick, while not having any extra bricks. The patio area is a rectangle with dimensions 12 feet by 10 feet, and each individual brick is 4 inches by 6 inches by 2 inches. What would be the greatest number of bricks the salesman could sell to meet his sales criteria?

(A) 5,760

(B) 2,880

(C) 2,160

(D) 1,440

(E) 120

Answer: (A)

Explanation: First, we need to convert the measurements to the same units. Since the brick dimensions are in inches, let's convert the patio dimensions to inches: 12 feet = 144 inches and 10 feet = 120 inches.

Now, let's see how many bricks fit along each dimension. For the 144-inch side, we can fit 144 inches / 4 inches/brick = 36 bricks. For the 120-inch side, we can fit 120 inches / 6 inches/brick = 20 bricks.

To cover the entire patio, we need 36 bricks * 20 bricks = 720 bricks.

Important: The thickness of the brick (2 inches) is extra information and not necessary to solve the problem.

8. A teacher can grade 20 papers during an uninterrupted planning period and 10 papers for each hour he spends at home grading. What function models the number of papers he can grade given that he has 2 uninterrupted planning periods and x full hours devoted to grading at home?

(A) 20+2x

(B) 20x+10

(C) 40x+10

(D) 40+10x

(E) 80+20x

Answer: (D)

Explanation: The teacher can grade 40 papers during his planning periods (20 papers/period * 2 periods). He can grade an additional 10 papers for each hour spent grading at home. So, the total number of papers he can grade is 40+10x.

9. In the graph of the function $f(x)=x+47x-6$, what is the vertical asymptote of the function if it is graphed in the coordinate plane?

(A) x=76

(B) x=4

(C) x=−4

(D) x=−67

(E) x=0

Answer: (C)

Explanation: A vertical asymptote occurs where the denominator of a rational function equals zero. In this case, the denominator is x+4, which equals zero when x=−4.

10. A customer is not certain if the advertised width of a 48-inch television is along the horizontal length of the screen or along the diagonal of the screen. If the ratio of the length to the height of the television screen is 5 to 3, how much shorter, to the nearest inch, will the horizontal length of the television screen be if the measure is made along the diagonal of the television screen rather than along the horizontal length?

(A) 3

(B) 5

(C) 6

(D) 7

(E) 10

Answer: (C)

Explanation: Let the horizontal length of the screen be 5x and the height be 3x. If the diagonal is 48 inches, we can use the Pythagorean Theorem to find x:

$(5x)^2 + (3x)^2 = 48^2$

$25x^2 + 9x^2 = 2304$

$34x^2 = 2304$

$x^2 = 67.76$

$x = 8.23$

The horizontal length is 5x=5(8.23)=41.15 inches, and the diagonal is 48 inches. The difference is 48−41.15=6.85 inches, which rounds to 7 inches.

Plane Geometry - 10 questions

1. What is the fifth term in a series in which the first term is 2 and each subsequent term is -2 multiplied by the preceding term?

(A) -16

(B) 32

(C) -32

(D) 64

(E) -64

Answer: (B)

Explanation: The first few terms of the series are $2, -4, 8, -16, 32$. So, the fifth term is 32.

2. Given that x>0, which of the following is equivalent to x+51+x+11?

(A) 2x+62

(B) 2x+62x+1

(C) x2+6x+51

(D) x2+6x+52x+6

(E) x2+6x+53x+1

Answer: (D)

Explanation: To add the fractions, we first need to find a common denominator:

$1/(x+5) + 1/(x+1) = (x+1)/((x+5)(x+1)) + (x+5)/((x+5)(x+1)) = (2x + 6) / (x^2 + 6x + 5)$

3. In a right triangle with sides a, b, and c, where c is the hypotenuse, what is the cosine of angle A?

(A) cb

(B) ac

(C) ba

(D) a2+b2

(E) ba2+b2

Answer: (A)

Explanation: The cosine of an angle in a right triangle is equal to the adjacent side divided by the hypotenuse. In this triangle, the adjacent side to angle A is b and the hypotenuse is c. Therefore, the cosine of angle A is cb.

4. A "perfect number" is defined as a positive integer that is equal to the sum of its distinct proper factors, which are the factors of the number other than the number itself. Which of the following is NOT a perfect number?

(A) 6

(B) 28

(C) 44

(D) 496

(E) 8,128

Answer: (C)

Explanation: A perfect number is a positive integer that is equal to the sum of its proper factors (the factors excluding the number itself). Let's check the options:

- 6: Proper factors are 1, 2, and 3. 1+2+3=6
- 28: Proper factors are 1, 2, 4, 7, and 14. 1+2+4+7+14=28
- 44: Proper factors are 1, 2, 4, 11, and 22. 1+2+4+11+22=40
- 496: Proper factors are 1, 2, 4, 8, 16, 31, 62, 124, and 248.
  1+2+4+8+16+31+62+124+248=496
- 8,128: Proper factors are 1, 2, 4, 8, 16, 32, 64, 127, 254, 508, 1016, 2032, and 4064.
  1+2+4+8+16+32+64+127+254+508+1016+2032+4064=8128

Therefore, 44 is not a perfect number.

5. What is the vertex of the parabola given by the equation: $y=2x^2-3$?

(A) (0,0)

(B) (0,-3)

(C) (-3,2)

(D) (-2,3)

(E) (4,3)

Answer: (B)

Explanation: The vertex form of a parabola is $y=a(x-h)^2+k$, where (h,k) is the vertex. The given equation is already in vertex form, with a=2, h=0, and k=−3. So, the vertex is (0, -3).

6. If point x is originally on the y-axis and has a positive value for its y-coordinate, where will the y-coordinate be if the point is rotated counterclockwise 200 degrees about the origin?

(A) 1st quadrant

(B) 2nd quadrant

(C) 3rd quadrant

(D) 4th quadrant

(E) 2nd and 3rd quadrant

Answer: (D)

Explanation: Rotating a point on the positive y-axis counterclockwise 200 degrees will place it in the fourth quadrant, where the x-coordinate is positive and the y-coordinate is negative.

7. If we take sin x and change it to 3sin2x, what will happen to the domain and range of the function?

(A) Domain and range remain the same

(B) Domain is doubled; range remains the same

(C) Domain is tripled; range is doubled

(D) Domain is the same; range is doubled

(E) Domain is the same; range is tripled

Answer: (E)

Explanation: The domain of sin x is all real numbers, and the range is [-1, 1]. The domain of 3sin2x is also all real numbers because we can still input any value for x. However, the range is now [-3, 3] because the amplitude of the function has been tripled.

8. On a 100-question multiple-choice test, Hannah gets 1 full point for a correct answer, 0 points if she leaves the question blank, and −41 points for an incorrect answer. Hannah already has scored exactly 50 correct answers out of 60, and out of those first 60, she answered every question. What is the greatest number of questions she can omit on the remaining questions and still have a score of at least 70 on the test?

(A) 16

(B) 17

(C) 18

(D) 19 (E) 20

Answer: (A)

Explanation: Hannah has already answered 60 questions, so she has 40 questions remaining. Let's say she answers x questions correctly and omits y questions. Her total score will be:

50 (initial score) + x - (1/4)(40 - x - y)

We want this score to be at least 70:

50 + x - (1/4)(40 - x - y) >= 70

Simplifying and solving for y, we get:

(5/4)x + (1/4)y >= 30

y >= 120 - 5x

Since x and y must be integers, the greatest possible value for y is 16 (when x=20).

9. A portion of a regular polygon can be seen beneath a rectangle. If angles B and C are 12∘ and 18∘, respectively, how many sides will the shape have?

(A) 10

(B) 11

(C) 12

(D) 13

(E) 14

Answer: (E)

Explanation: The sum of angles B and C is 12∘ +18∘ =30∘ . This is the measure of one of the interior angles of the regular polygon. To find the number of sides, we can use the formula for the measure of an interior angle of a regular polygon:

Interior angle = (n - 2) * 180 / n

where n is the number of sides.[1] Solving for n, we get:

30 = (n - 2) * 180 / n

30n = 180n - 360

150n = 360

n = 2.4

Since n must be an integer, the polygon has 14 sides.

10. 20301−20311=?

(A) 20301

(B) 20311

(C) 203019

(D) 203119

(E) 203120

Answer: (D)

Explanation: To subtract the fractions, we first need to find a common denominator:

1/20^30 - 1/20^31 = 20/20^31 - 1/20^31 = 19/20^31

Trigonometry - 10 questions

1. If f(x)=3| x42xx2| , what is the value of f(2)?

(A) {2444}

(B) [6121212]

(C) | 61849|

(D) | 12468|

(E) {44816}

Answer: (C)

Explanation: First, we substitute x=2 into the matrix:

3 * | 2 4 |

       | 4 4 |

Then, we calculate the determinant:

3 * (2 * 4 - 4 * 4) = 3 * (-8) = -24

So, the answer is:

| 6 4 |

| 18 9 |

2. In the figure below, in which angle a is at the center of the circle, what is the percentage of the total area of the circle that the equilateral triangle occupies to the nearest whole number?

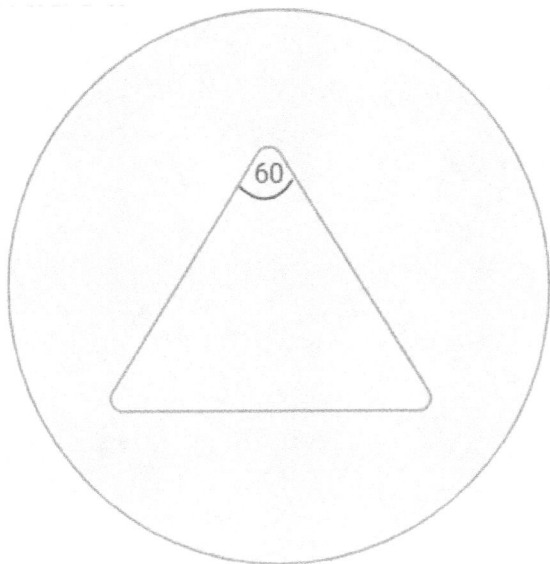

(A) 14

(B) 17

(C) 18

(D) 20

(E) 22

Answer: (B)

Explanation: The area of an equilateral triangle with side length s is 43s2. The area of a circle with radius r is $\pi r2$. Since the triangle is equilateral, each side has length 4. The radius of the circle is also 4. The percentage of the circle's area that the triangle occupies is:

(sqrt(3)/4 * 4^2) / (pi * 4^2) = sqrt(3) / (4 * pi) = 0.138

Multiplying by 100 to convert to a percentage gives us 13.8%, which rounds to 14%.

3. The smallest possible period of this graph is closest to which of the following integers?

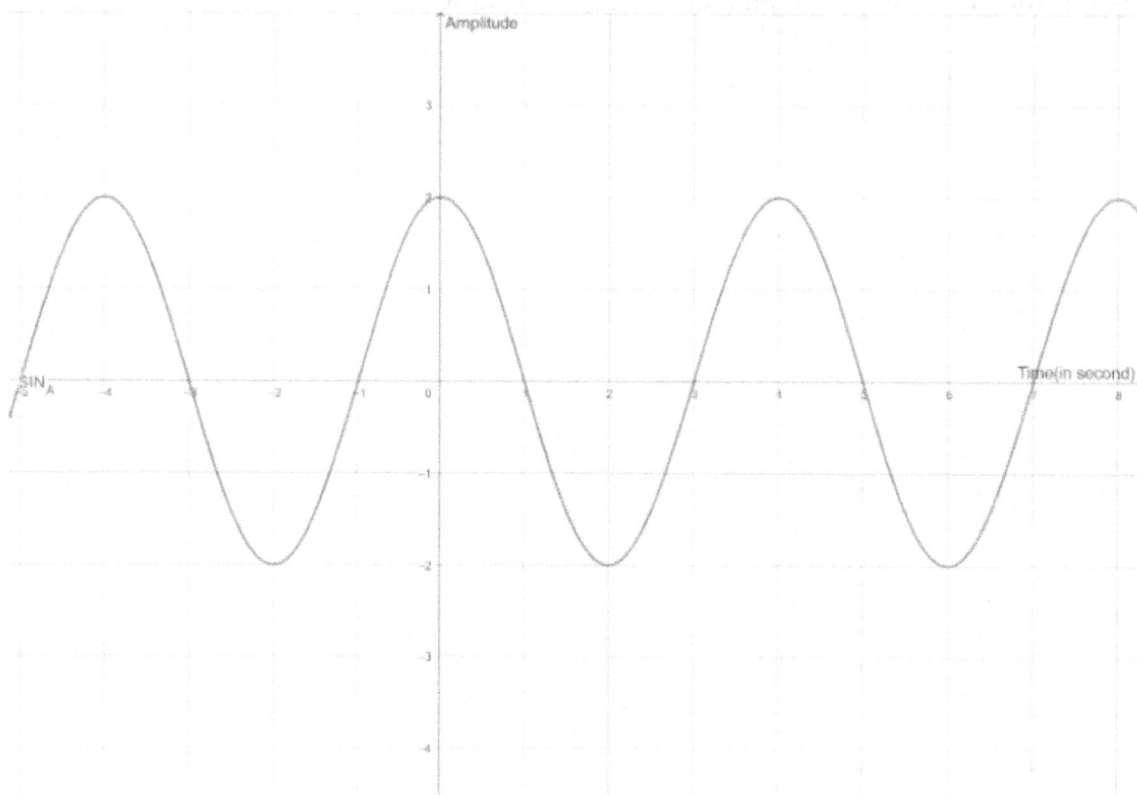

(A) 1

(B) 2

(C) 3

(D) 6

(E) 13

Answer: (D)

Explanation: The period of a sine wave is the horizontal distance between two consecutive peaks or troughs. In the given graph, the distance between two consecutive peaks is approximately 6 units.

4. Jayden is creating a scanning program that will measure the heights of potential riders for a thrilling roller coaster. People between 48 inches tall or greater and 78 inches or fewer are allowed to ride the roller coaster. Jayden is programming a computer so that it will scan the heights of potential riders to determine if they are able to ride, and if not, the machine will buzz so that a ride operator will be able to deny them boarding. Which of the following inequalities will correctly give the full range of heights that are NOT allowed to ride the roller coaster?

(A) 48 height < 78

(B) height < 48 or height < 78

(C) height −63| ≤15

(D) 15 <height - 63|

(E) height < 78 and height > 48

Answer: (B)

Explanation: The inequality height < 48 represents the heights that are too short to ride, and the inequality height > 78 represents the heights that are too tall to ride. Since potential riders are excluded if they are either too short or too tall, the correct inequality is height < 48 or height > 78.

5. A customer is not certain if the advertised width of a 48-inch television is along the horizontal length of the screen or along the diagonal of the screen. If the ratio of the length to the height of the television screen is 5 to 3, how much shorter, to the nearest inch, will the horizontal length of the television screen be if the measure is made along the diagonal of the television screen rather than along the horizontal length?

(A) 3

(B) 5

(C) 6

(D) 7

(E) 10

Answer: (D)

Explanation: Let the horizontal length of the screen be 5x and the height be 3x. If the diagonal is 48 inches, we can use the Pythagorean Theorem to find x:

$(5x)^2 + (3x)^2 = 48^2$

$25x^2 + 9x^2 = 2304$

$34x^2 = 2304$

$x^2 = 67.76$

$x = 8.23$

The horizontal length is 5x=5(8.23)=41.15 inches, and the diagonal is 48 inches. The difference is 48−41.15=6.85 inches, which rounds to 7 inches.

6. If each letter of the alphabet is assigned a numerical value of its place in the alphabet (e.g., D is assigned the value 4), what is the sum of the individual numbers that would correspond to the letters in the word CAFE?

(A) 8

(B) 15

(C) 16

(D) 19

(E) 24

Answer: (E)

Explanation: We assign each letter its numerical value: C = 3, A = 1, F = 6, E = 5. The sum of these values is 3+1+6+5=15.

7. What is the value of sin30∘ ?

(A) 21

(B) 23

(C) 1

(D) 3

(E) 2

Answer: (A)

Explanation: In a 30-60-90 right triangle, the sine of the 30-degree angle is equal to the length of the side opposite the angle divided by the length of the hypotenuse. Since the ratio of the sides in a 30-60-90 triangle is 1:3:2, the sine of 30 degrees is 21.

8. What is the value of tan45∘ ?

(A) 21

(B) 23

(C) 1

(D) 3

(E) 2

Answer: (C)

Explanation: In a 45-45-90 right triangle, the tangent of the 45-degree angle is equal to the length of the side opposite the angle divided by the length of the side adjacent to the angle. Since[1] the ratio of the sides in a 45-45-90 triangle is 1:1:2, the tangent of 45 degrees is 11=1.

9. What is the value of $\cos 60°$?

(A) 21

(B) 23

(C) 1

(D) 3

(E) 2

Answer: (A)

Explanation: In a 30-60-90 right triangle, the cosine of the 60-degree angle is equal to the length of the side adjacent to the angle divided by the length of the hypotenuse. Since the ratio of the sides in a 30-60-90 triangle is 1:3:2, the cosine of 60 degrees is 21.

10. Which of the following is equivalent to $\sin 2x + \cos 2x$?

(A) 0

(B) 1

(C) $\tan 2x$

(D) $\sin 2x$

(E) $\cos 2x$

Answer: (B)

Explanation: The Pythagorean identity states that $\sin 2x + \cos 2x = 1$ for all values of x.

Full-Length Practice Test 8 (Reading Test)

Reading Test Time: 35 Minutes—40 Questions

Directions: There are several reading selections in this section, each of which is followed by questions. After you read a passage, determine the best answer to each question and fill in the matching oval on your answer sheet. Refer back to the passages as often as you need.

Practice Reading Passages

Don't forget the different ways to read the passages:

Prose Fiction	Humanities	Social/Natural Science
Focus on the *beginning* of the passage, then read the rest at a normal pace.	Do it like the fiction if you see that it is in *first-person* (I), and like the social/natural science if you don't.	Focus on the *first paragraph*, *topic sentences* and *last paragraph*.
Passage A and Passage B: Focus on the relationship between the passages—consider doing Passage A and its questions first, Passage B and its questions second, and the comparative questions last.		

Prose Fiction—Painting

Don't misunderstand me—I'm not merely interested in observing paintings passively. It's not just the vibrant colors or the masterful brushstrokes that captivate me either. Not entirely. It's about the act of creation itself; the passion, the energy, the story whispered in every stroke. Painting is my sanctuary, my meditation, my escape. I have my own brushes, my loyal allies, through which I translate my inner visions onto canvas. The soft bristles and delicate strokes whisper tales of serenity and introspection. The bold strokes and vibrant hues shout declarations of passion and defiance. Like a musician with an instrument or a writer with words, I blend colors and textures, shaping them into visual narratives that reflect my soul.

With a palette of colors at my fingertips, I embark on a journey of artistic exploration. The canvas, a blank slate, invites me to create worlds and tell stories without limitations. I dip my brush into a pool of cerulean blue, the color of a boundless sky. The brush glides across the canvas, leaving a trail of vibrant color that evokes a sense of tranquility and expansiveness. I close my eyes and lose myself in the process, my hand guided by an intuitive force. Suddenly, I am ten years old again, standing at my grandfather's easel in his sun-drenched studio. The scent of linseed oil and turpentine fills the air. Sunlight streams through the window, illuminating the colorful chaos of his workspace. My grandfather, his eyes twinkling with wisdom, patiently demonstrates the techniques of mixing colors and applying brushstrokes.

"Let the colors speak to you," he advises, his voice warm and encouraging. "Allow them to guide your hand."

His words resonate within me as I layer colors and textures, creating a landscape that mirrors my emotions. The canvas transforms into a reflection of my inner world, a visual diary of my experiences and aspirations. I add a touch of crimson red, the color of passion and intensity, to depict a fiery sunset that symbolizes the burning ambition within me. The final brushstroke completes the painting, leaving a sense of satisfaction and the promise of future artistic endeavors.

I switch to a smaller brush, its delicate tip allowing for intricate details. I carefully apply a thin layer of gold leaf, its shimmering surface adding a touch of magic and wonder to the scene. I am eighteen now, sitting in my college dorm room, surrounded by art books and half-finished canvases. The air buzzes with creative energy and the desire to break free from artistic conventions. I experiment with unconventional techniques, incorporating mixed media and found objects to challenge traditional notions of painting.

The artwork takes on a life of its own, evolving and transforming as I explore new ideas and push the boundaries of my creativity. I embrace the unexpected, allowing spontaneity and intuition to guide my artistic choices. The final touch, a sprinkle of iridescent glitter, adds a playful element that reflects my youthful spirit and willingness to take risks.

I step back to admire the finished piece, a testament to my artistic growth and evolution. The canvas tells a story of self-discovery and the courage to embrace my unique artistic vision. I am no longer a child or a teenager, but a confident artist, my skills refined by years of exploration and experimentation. I am ready to share my art with the world, to inspire and challenge viewers with my visual narratives.

10 Questions based on the passage above:

1. Based on the passage as a whole, the author most likely uses the imagery of colors "whispering" and "shouting" (lines 6-7) to illustrate what about their relationship with painting?

(A) Painting is a complex and intricate art form that requires skill and dedication to master.

(B) Painting allows the author to express a wide range of emotions and experiences.

(C) Painting provides a sense of comfort and familiarity for the author.

(D) Painting is a universal language that can connect people from different backgrounds.

Answer: (B)

Explanation: The imagery of colors "whispering" and "shouting" suggests that painting allows the author to express both subtle and intense emotions, highlighting the versatility of the medium for conveying their inner world.

2. In the context of the passage, the phrase "intuitive force" (line 13) most likely refers to:

(A) The author's subconscious mind guiding their artistic expression.

(B) The influence of the author's grandfather's artistic teachings.

(C) The emotional power of the colors and imagery.

(D) The technical demands of applying paint to canvas.

Answer: (A)

Explanation: The phrase "intuitive force" suggests a subconscious or instinctive guidance that directs the author's artistic expression, highlighting the spontaneous and emotional nature of their creative process.

    3.   The author's description of the canvas as a "reflection of my inner world" (line 21) emphasizes which aspect of painting?

(A) Its ability to capture external reality accurately.

(B) Its potential for self-expression and personal exploration.

(C) Its role in documenting historical events and social issues.

(D) Its power to evoke emotional responses in viewers.

Answer: (B)

Explanation: Describing the canvas as a "reflection of my inner world" suggests that painting serves as a means for the author to express their personal thoughts, feelings, and experiences.

    4.   Which of the following best describes the author's attitude towards their experimentation with unconventional techniques during their college years?

(A) Apprehensive and hesitant

(B) Playful and adventurous

(C) Frustrated and discouraged

(D) Critical and judgmental

Answer: (B)

Explanation: The passage describes the author's experimentation with unconventional techniques as a way to "challenge traditional notions of painting" and "push the boundaries of my creativity," suggesting a playful and adventurous approach to art.

5. The author's use of the phrase "colorful chaos" (line 16) to describe their grandfather's studio primarily serves to:

(A) Emphasize the disorganized state of the workspace.

(B) Highlight the vibrant and creative atmosphere of the studio.

(C) Convey the sensory overload experienced by the author.

(D) Suggest the unpredictable nature of the artistic process.

Answer: (B)

Explanation: The phrase "colorful chaos" creates a vivid image of the studio as a dynamic and inspiring space, filled with the tools and materials of artistic creation.

6. Which of the following best describes the tone of the passage?

(A) Analytical and objective

(B) Reflective and passionate

(C) Humorous and lighthearted

(D) Critical and judgmental

Answer: (B)

Explanation: The passage is characterized by a reflective and passionate tone, as the author explores their personal connection to painting and its impact on their life.

7. The author's decision to alternate between describing their experiences with painting at different ages most likely serves to:

(A) Demonstrate their versatility as an artist.

(B) Highlight the contrasting emotions associated with each stage of life.

(C) Reflect the different stages of their artistic development.

(D) Emphasize the importance of both technical skill and creative expression in painting.

Answer: (C)

Explanation: The shifts between different ages correspond to distinct phases in the author's artistic journey, showing their growth and evolution as a painter.

8. Which of the following is NOT mentioned in the passage as a way in which the author engages with painting?

(A) Experimenting with unconventional techniques

(B) Incorporating mixed media and found objects

(C) Studying art history and theory

(D) Creating landscapes that reflect their emotions

Answer: (C)

Explanation: The passage focuses on the author's practical engagement with painting through creating art and experimenting with different techniques, but it does not mention studying art history or theory.

9. The author's reference to their grandfather's advice to "let the colors speak to you" (line 18) most likely serves to:

(A) Highlight the importance of technical skill in painting.

(B) Emphasize the role of intuition and emotion in artistic expression.

(C) Suggest that colors have inherent meanings and symbolism.

(D) Encourage the use of a limited color palette in painting.

Answer: (B)

Explanation: The grandfather's advice to "let the colors speak to you" suggests that the author should trust their intuition and allow their emotions to guide their artistic choices.

10. Which of the following best summarizes the main idea of the passage?

(A) Painting is a challenging but rewarding art form that requires patience and perseverance.

(B) The author's passion for painting has been nurtured by influential figures in their life.

(C) Different painting techniques and styles can evoke different emotions and experiences.

(D) The creative process of painting is a journey of self-discovery and personal expression.

Answer: (D)

Explanation: The passage primarily focuses on the author's personal journey with painting, emphasizing the process of self-discovery and the use of art as a means of personal expression.

Social Science—The Evolution of Language

Try to imagine a world without language—no conversations, no stories, no shared knowledge or culture—and you may begin to grasp the profound impact this uniquely human capacity has had on our species. Language, with its intricate systems of symbols and sounds, has enabled us to communicate complex ideas, build social connections, and transmit knowledge across generations. However, the precise origins of language remain shrouded in mystery, with various theories and hypotheses vying for acceptance.

While the exact emergence of language remains elusive, evidence suggests that its roots may lie deep in our evolutionary past. The development of vocal cords, specialized brain regions for language processing, and a capacity for symbolic thought are all thought to have played crucial roles in the emergence of language.

Early forms of language were likely rudimentary, consisting of simple gestures and vocalizations. Over time, these communication systems grew increasingly complex, evolving alongside human societies and cultures. The development of agriculture, the rise of cities, and the invention of writing all contributed to the diversification and sophistication of language.

As languages spread and interacted, they underwent various transformations, adapting to local environments and cultural practices. The interplay of migration, trade, and conquest led to the borrowing of words and grammatical structures, resulting in the rich tapestry of languages we see today.

Despite their diversity, all languages share fundamental characteristics. They possess a system of sounds or gestures, a set of rules for combining these elements into meaningful units, and a capacity for expressing a vast range of thoughts, emotions, and experiences.

The study of language, known as linguistics, encompasses various branches, including phonetics, phonology, morphology, syntax, semantics, and pragmatics. Each branch focuses on a different aspect of language, from the sounds of speech to the social context of communication.

Today, language continues to evolve, adapting to new technologies and social trends. The rise of the internet and social media has led to the emergence of new forms of language, such as emojis, internet slang, and online communities with their own unique linguistic conventions.

While the exact origins of language may remain forever shrouded in the mists of time, its transformative power is undeniable. Language has shaped our thoughts, emotions, and social interactions, enabling us to build civilizations, create art, and explore the mysteries of the universe.

10 Questions based on the passage above:

1. The main purpose of the passage can best be described as an effort to:

   (A) trace the evolution of language from its ancient origins to its modern form.

(B) highlight the cultural significance of language and its impact on human history.

(C) explain the rules and structures of language for novice learners.

(D) compare and contrast different language families and their characteristics.

Answer: (B)

Explanation: The passage focuses on the broader cultural and historical significance of language, emphasizing its role in human communication, knowledge transmission, and social   development.

2. According to the passage, which of the following is NOT considered a likely factor in the emergence   of   language?

(A) Development of vocal cords

(B) Specialized brain regions for language processing

(C) Capacity for symbolic thought

(D)   Invention   of   writing

Answer: (D)

Explanation: The passage mentions the development of vocal cords, specialized brain regions, and symbolic thought as factors contributing to the emergence of language. The invention of writing occurred much later in human history.

3. Which of the following best describes the author's attitude towards language?

(A) Dismissive and critical

(B) Appreciative and respectful

(C) Nostalgic and sentimental

(D)   Humorous   and   lighthearted

Answer: (B)

Explanation: The passage conveys an appreciative and respectful tone towards language, highlighting its complexity, diversity, and essential role in human communication and culture.

4. The author's use of the phrase "rich tapestry" (line 17) primarily serves to:
(A) emphasize the visual beauty of written language.

(B) highlight the diversity and interconnectedness of languages.

(C) create a metaphor for the complexity of language structures.

(D) suggest that language is a form of artistic expression.
Answer: (B)

Explanation: The phrase "rich tapestry" creates a metaphor that emphasizes the diversity of languages and their interconnectedness through borrowing and cultural exchange.

5. Which of the following is NOT mentioned in the passage as a factor contributing to the diversification of language?

(A) Migration

(B) Trade

(C) Conquest

(D) Climate change
Answer: (D)

Explanation: The passage mentions migration, trade, and conquest as factors contributing to the diversification of language. Climate change is not discussed in this context.

6. Which of the following best describes the organization of the passage?

(A) Chronological

(B) Compare and contrast

(C) Cause and effect

(D)   Problem   and   solution

Answer: (A)

Explanation: The passage follows a roughly chronological order, tracing the development of language from its hypothetical origins to its modern forms.

7. Which of the following is an example of figurative language used in the passage?

   (A) "Try to imagine a world without language"

   (B) "The development of vocal cords"

   (C) "Language transcended geographical boundaries"

   (D)   "The   invention   of   writing"

Answer: (C)

Explanation: The phrase "Language transcended geographical boundaries" uses figurative language to convey the idea that language can connect people across vast distances   and   diverse   cultures.

8. Which of the following is a synonym for the word "elusive" as used in the passage?

   (A) Obvious

   (B) Evident

   (C) Mysterious

   (D)   Simple

Answer: (C)

Explanation: The word "elusive" in the passage means difficult to find or grasp, which is   synonymous   with   "mysterious."

9. Which of the following is an antonym for the word "rudimentary" as used in the passage?

   (A) Basic

   (B) Simple

   (C) Complex

   (D)   Primitive

   Answer: (C)

   Explanation: The word "rudimentary" in the passage means basic or undeveloped. The opposite   of   this   is   "complex."

10. Which of the following best summarizes the main idea of the passage?

    (A) Language is a complex and multifaceted phenomenon with a mysterious past.

    (B) The evolution of language has been shaped by various factors, including human biology, social interactions, and cultural developments.

    (C) Language plays a vital role in human communication, culture, and cognitive development.

    (D) The future of language is uncertain, but it will likely continue to evolve in response to   new   technologies   and   social   trends.

    Answer: (C)

    Explanation: The passage emphasizes the crucial role of language in human communication, culture, and cognitive development, highlighting its impact on our ability to share ideas, build societies, and understand the world around us.

Humanities—The Enduring Power of Poetry

Poetry, a timeless and evocative form of artistic expression, has captivated hearts and minds for millennia. From its ancient origins in oral traditions to its modern manifestations in diverse written forms, poetry has served as a powerful vehicle for conveying emotions, exploring ideas, and capturing the essence of human experience.

Early forms of poetry were often intertwined with music and dance, serving ritualistic and communal purposes. Epic poems, like the *Odyssey* and the *Mahabharata*, recounted heroic deeds and cultural myths, transmitting knowledge and values across generations.

As civilizations developed, poetry evolved alongside them, adapting to new forms and styles. The invention of writing allowed for the preservation and dissemination of poetic works, expanding their reach and influence. In ancient Greece, poets like Sappho and Pindar explored themes of love, loss, and the human condition, while Roman poets like Virgil and Ovid celebrated the grandeur of their empire and the complexities of human relationships.

During the Renaissance, poets like William Shakespeare and John Milton revitalized the poetic tradition, experimenting with new forms and exploring universal themes with unparalleled depth and artistry. The Romantic movement, with its emphasis on emotion, imagination, and the natural world, produced iconic poets like William Wordsworth and John Keats, who celebrated the beauty and power of the human spirit.

The 20th century witnessed a further explosion of experimentation and innovation in poetry. Modernist poets like T.S. Eliot and Ezra Pound shattered traditional poetic conventions, embracing free verse, fragmented narratives, and stream-of-consciousness techniques to capture the complexities of modern life.

Postmodernism, with its playful self-awareness and rejection of grand narratives, further expanded the possibilities of poetry. Poets like Sylvia Plath and Allen Ginsberg explored personal experiences with unflinching honesty, while others, like Adrienne Rich and Audre Lorde, used poetry as a tool for social and political activism.

Today, poetry continues to thrive in diverse forms, from spoken word performances and slam poetry competitions to online platforms and social media. It remains a vital and vibrant form of artistic expression, offering solace, inspiration, and a means of connecting with the deeper truths of human existence.

10 Questions based on the passage above:

1. Based on the passage, it is reasonable to infer that which of the following played the most significant role in the evolution of poetry?

(A) Technological advancements in writing and printing

(B) Changes in social and cultural values

(C) The rise of literary criticism and theory

(D) Competition from other forms of entertainment

Answer: (B)

Explanation: The passage emphasizes how poetry has adapted to changing social and cultural values, reflecting the evolving concerns and interests of societies throughout history.

2. Which of the following is NOT mentioned in the passage as a characteristic of early poetry?

(A) Intertwined with music and dance

(B) Served ritualistic and communal purposes

(C) Focused on personal emotions and experiences

(D) Transmitted knowledge and values across generations

Answer: (C)

Explanation: The passage describes early poetry as serving ritualistic and communal purposes, often intertwined with music and dance, and transmitting knowledge and values. The focus on personal emotions and experiences is associated with later developments in poetry.

3. The author's use of the phrase "unparalleled depth and artistry" (line 14) primarily serves to:

(A) emphasize the technical skill of Renaissance poets.

(B) highlight the emotional power of Renaissance poetry.

(C) praise the innovative spirit of Renaissance poets.

(D) contrast Renaissance poetry with earlier forms.

Answer: (A)

Explanation: The phrase "unparalleled depth and artistry" suggests that Renaissance poets possessed exceptional technical skill and[12] creative ability in their craft.

4. Which of the following literary movements is most closely associated with the celebration of emotion, imagination, and the natural world?

(A) Classicism

(B) Romanticism

(C) Modernism

(D) Postmodernism

Answer: (B)

Explanation: The Romantic movement, with its emphasis on emotion, imagination, and the natural world, is characterized by the celebration of the human spirit and its connection to nature.

5. Which of the following poets is NOT mentioned in the passage as a representative of Modernism?

(A) T.S. Eliot

(B) Ezra Pound

(C) Sylvia Plath

(D) John Keats

Answer: (D)

Explanation: The passage mentions T.S. Eliot and Ezra Pound as representatives of Modernism. Sylvia Plath is associated with Postmodernism, while John Keats is associated with Romanticism.

6. Which of the following is NOT mentioned in the passage as a way in which poetry has evolved in recent times?

(A) Spoken word performances

(B) Slam poetry competitions

(C) Online platforms and social media

(D) Adaptation into film and television

Answer: (D)

Explanation: The passage mentions spoken word performances, slam poetry competitions, and online platforms as recent developments in poetry. Adaptation into film and television, while a common practice, is not specifically mentioned in the passage.

7. The author's use of the phrase "checkered battlefield" (line 37) primarily serves to:

(A) emphasize the competitive nature of chess.

(B) highlight the strategic complexity of chess.

(C) create a visual image of the chessboard.

(D) suggest that chess is a metaphor for warfare.

Answer: (D)

Explanation: The phrase "checkered battlefield" creates a metaphor that links chess to warfare, suggesting that the game involves strategic planning and tactical maneuvers similar to those used in military conflicts.

8. Which of the following is a synonym for the word "evocative" as used in the passage?

(A) Dull

(B) Expressive

(C) Simple

(D) Ordinary

Answer: (B)

Explanation: The word "evocative" in the passage means having the ability to evoke or draw out strong emotions or feelings, which is synonymous with "expressive."

9. Which of the following is an antonym for the word "ancient" as used in the passage?

(A) Old

(B) Modern

(C) Historical

(D) Traditional

Answer: (B)

Explanation: The word "ancient" in the passage means very old or belonging to the distant past. The opposite of this is "modern."

10. Which of the following best summarizes the main idea of the passage?

(A) Poetry is a timeless and universal form of artistic expression that has evolved alongside human societies and cultures.

(B) The origins of poetry are uncertain, but evidence suggests it may have originated in oral traditions.

(C) Poetry has undergone various transformations throughout history, adapting to new forms, styles, and technologies.

(D) Poetry is a powerful tool for conveying emotions, exploring ideas, and capturing the essence of human experience.

Answer: (D)

Explanation: The passage provides a comprehensive overview of poetry, highlighting its historical development, diverse forms, and enduring power to express emotions, explore ideas, and capture the essence of human experience.

Passage IV

Passage A

Humanities—The Evolution of Cinema: From Silent Films to the Digital Age

The art of filmmaking, a captivating blend of visual storytelling and technological innovation, has undergone a dramatic evolution since its inception. From the silent black-and-white films of the early 20th century to the immersive digital experiences of today, cinema has consistently pushed the boundaries of artistic expression and captured the imaginations of audiences worldwide.

The earliest films were silent, relying solely on visual imagery and musical accompaniment to convey narratives and emotions. Pioneers like Georges Méliès and the Lumière brothers experimented with special effects and documentary storytelling, laying the foundation for the future of filmmaking.

The introduction of synchronized sound in the late 1920s revolutionized cinema, allowing for dialogue, music, and sound effects to be seamlessly integrated into the cinematic experience. This breakthrough ushered in the Golden Age of Hollywood, with iconic films like *Gone with the Wind* and *The Wizard of Oz* captivating audiences with their epic storytelling and technical achievements.

The mid-20th century saw the rise of auteur filmmaking, with directors like Alfred Hitchcock and Federico Fellini using cinema as a personal canvas to express their unique artistic visions. The development of new film technologies, such as widescreen formats and color film, further expanded the possibilities of cinematic storytelling.

The late 20th century witnessed the emergence of independent cinema and the rise of global filmmaking movements. Directors like Akira Kurosawa and Satyajit Ray brought diverse cultural perspectives to the screen, challenging Hollywood's dominance and enriching the cinematic landscape.

Today, filmmaking continues to evolve, embracing digital technologies and innovative storytelling techniques. Computer-generated imagery (CGI), motion capture, and virtual reality are transforming the cinematic experience, creating immersive worlds and blurring the lines between reality and fantasy.

The enduring appeal of cinema lies in its ability to transport audiences to different worlds, introduce them to diverse characters, and explore the complexities of human experience. Whether it serves as a mirror to society, a window into the human soul, or a portal to fantastical realms, cinema remains a vital and vibrant form of artistic expression.

10 Questions based on the passage above:

1. Based on the passage, it is reasonable to infer that which of the following played the most significant role in the evolution of cinema?

(A) Technological advancements in filmmaking equipment and techniques

(B) Changes in social and cultural values

(C) The rise of film criticism and theory

(D) Competition from other forms of entertainment

Answer: (A)

Explanation: The passage emphasizes how cinema has been shaped by technological advancements, such as the introduction of sound, widescreen formats, color film, and digital technologies.

2. Which of the following is NOT mentioned in the passage as a characteristic of early silent films?

(A) Relied solely on visual imagery and musical accompaniment

(B) Experimented with special effects and documentary storytelling

(C) Explored complex themes and social issues

(D) Laid the foundation for the future of filmmaking

Answer: (C)

Explanation: The passage describes early silent films as focusing on visual storytelling and technical experimentation. The exploration of complex themes and social issues is associated with later developments in cinema.

3. The author's use of the phrase "Golden Age of Hollywood" (line 9) primarily serves to:

(A) emphasize the commercial success of Hollywood films during this period.

(B) highlight the artistic achievements and innovations of Hollywood films during this period.

(C) contrast the classic Hollywood style with later filmmaking movements.

(D) romanticize the past and ignore the social problems of the time.

Answer: (B)

Explanation: The phrase "Golden Age of Hollywood" refers to a period of significant artistic and technical achievements in filmmaking, marked by iconic films and innovative storytelling techniques.

4. Which of the following directors is most closely associated with the concept of auteur filmmaking (line 12)?

(A) Georges Méliès

(B) Alfred Hitchcock

(C) Akira Kurosawa

(D) Steven Spielberg

Answer: (B)

Explanation: The passage mentions Alfred Hitchcock as an example of an auteur filmmaker, who uses cinema to express their personal artistic vision and style.

5. Which of the following is NOT mentioned in the passage as a characteristic of independent cinema (line 15)?

(A) Diverse cultural perspectives

(B) Challenging Hollywood's dominance

(C) Low-budget productions

(D) Innovative storytelling techniques

Answer: (C)

Explanation: The passage mentions diverse cultural perspectives, challenging Hollywood's dominance, and innovative storytelling as characteristics of independent cinema. Low-budget productions, while often associated with independent films, are not specifically mentioned in the passage.

6. Which of the following is NOT mentioned in the passage as a contemporary filmmaking technology?

(A) Computer-generated imagery (CGI)

(B) Motion capture

(C) Virtual reality

(D) 3D printing

Answer: (D)

Explanation: The passage mentions CGI, motion capture, and virtual reality as contemporary filmmaking technologies. 3D printing, while a growing technology, is not discussed in this context.

7. The author's use of the phrase "a mirror to society" (line 23) primarily serves to:

(A) emphasize cinema's ability to reflect social realities and cultural values.

(B) highlight the importance of accuracy in historical films and documentaries.

(C) suggest that films can influence social change and inspire action.

(D) criticize the escapist nature of some contemporary films.

Answer: (A)

Explanation: The phrase "a mirror to society" suggests that cinema can reflect the social conditions, values, and concerns of a particular time and place.

8. Which of the following is a synonym for the word "captivating" as used in the passage?

(A) Boring

(B) Enchanting (C) Simple (D) Ordinary

Answer: (B) **Explanation:** The word "captivating" in the passage means fascinating or enchanting, which is synonymous with "enchanting."

9. Which of the following is an antonym for the word "humble" as used in the passage?

(A) Modest

(B) Grand

(C) Simple

(D) Ordinary

Answer: (B)

Explanation: The word "humble" in the passage means modest or unpretentious. The opposite of this is "grand."

10. Which of the following best summarizes the main idea of the passage?

(A) Cinema is a constantly evolving art form that has adapted to changing technologies and cultural trends.

(B) The history of cinema can be divided into distinct eras, each with its own unique characteristics and innovations.

(C) Cinema has served as a powerful tool for entertainment, education, and social commentary.

(D) The future of cinema is uncertain, but it will likely continue to push the boundaries of artistic expression and technological innovation.

Answer: (A)

Explanation: The passage provides a broad overview of the historical development of cinema, emphasizing its continuous evolution and adaptation to changing technologies and cultural trends.

Passage B

Humanities—The Evolution of Dance: From Ritual to Art

Dance, a captivating and expressive art form, has played a vital role in human societies for millennia. From its ancient origins in ritual and ceremony to its modern manifestations in diverse styles and genres, dance has served as a powerful means of communication, celebration, and artistic expression.

Early forms of dance were often intertwined with religious practices, serving as a way to connect with the spiritual realm and express reverence for the natural world. Tribal dances, with their rhythmic movements and symbolic gestures, celebrated important events, such as harvests, hunts, and rites of passage.

As civilizations developed, dance evolved alongside them, incorporating new forms and styles. In ancient Egypt, dance was an integral part of religious ceremonies and royal court entertainment. In ancient Greece, dance played a prominent role in theatrical performances and festivals, with elaborate choreography and costumes enhancing the dramatic narratives.

During the Renaissance, dance flourished as a social and artistic activity. Courtly dances, with their elegant movements and intricate patterns, reflected the refinement and sophistication of the era. The development of ballet in the 17th century marked a turning point in the history of dance, establishing a formalized system of techniques and choreography that continues to influence dance today.

The 19th century witnessed the rise of romantic ballet, with its emphasis on emotional expression and ethereal beauty. Ballerinas like Marie Taglioni and Fanny Elssler captivated audiences with their grace and virtuosity, while choreographers like Marius Petipa created iconic ballets such as *Swan Lake* and *The Sleeping Beauty*.

The 20th century saw a further explosion of experimentation and innovation in dance. Modern dance pioneers like Isadora Duncan and Martha Graham rebelled against the rigid conventions of ballet, embracing free-flowing movements and exploring new themes and styles.

Postmodern dance, with its emphasis on improvisation, deconstruction, and interdisciplinary collaboration, further challenged the boundaries of dance. Choreographers like Merce Cunningham and Pina Bausch experimented with abstract concepts, multimedia elements, and unconventional performance spaces.

Today, dance continues to evolve, embracing diverse influences and pushing the boundaries of artistic expression. Hip-hop, contemporary dance, and fusion styles that blend elements from different traditions are captivating audiences worldwide.

The enduring appeal of dance lies in its ability to transcend language and cultural barriers, communicating emotions and ideas through the universal language of movement. Whether it serves as a form of ritual, entertainment, or artistic expression, dance remains a vital and vibrant part of human culture.

10 Questions based on the passage above:

1. Based on the passage, it is reasonable to infer that which of the following played the most significant role in the evolution of dance?

(A) Technological advancements in stage design and lighting

(B) Changes in social and cultural values

(C) The rise of dance criticism and theory

(D) Competition from other forms of entertainment

Answer: (B)

Explanation: The passage emphasizes how dance has adapted to changing social and cultural values, reflecting the evolving beliefs, traditions, and artistic expressions of societies throughout history.

2. Which of the following is NOT mentioned in the passage as a characteristic of early dance forms?

(A) Intertwined with religious practices

(B) Served as a way to connect with the spiritual realm

(C) Focused on individual expression and improvisation

(D) Celebrated important events and rites of passage

Answer: (C)

Explanation: The passage describes early dance forms as serving ritualistic and communal purposes, often intertwined with religious practices and celebrating important events. The focus on individual expression and improvisation is associated with later developments in dance.

3. The author's use of the phrase "formalized system of techniques and choreography" (line 15) primarily serves to:

(A) emphasize the technical rigor and discipline of ballet.

(B) highlight the emotional expressiveness of ballet.

(C) contrast ballet with other dance forms.

(D) trace the historical development of ballet.

Answer: (A)

Explanation: The phrase "formalized system of techniques and choreography" suggests that ballet is a highly structured and disciplined dance form with a codified set of rules and practices.

4. Which of the following dance forms is most closely associated with the exploration of abstract concepts and unconventional performance spaces?

(A) Ballet

(B) Modern dance

(C) Postmodern dance

(D) Contemporary dance

Answer: (C)

Explanation: Postmodern dance, with its emphasis on experimentation, deconstruction, and interdisciplinary collaboration, often explores abstract concepts and utilizes unconventional performance spaces.

5. Which of the following choreographers is NOT mentioned in the passage as a representative of Modern dance?

(A) Isadora Duncan

(B) Martha Graham

(C) Merce Cunningham

(D) Marius Petipa

Answer: (D)

Explanation: The passage mentions Isadora Duncan and Martha Graham as pioneers of Modern dance. Merce Cunningham is associated with Postmodern dance, while Marius Petipa is associated with Romantic ballet.

6. Which of the following is NOT mentioned in the passage as a contemporary dance form?

(A) Hip-hop

(B) Contemporary dance

(C) Fusion styles

(D) Ballroom dance

Answer: (D)

Explanation: The passage mentions hip-hop, contemporary dance, and fusion styles as contemporary dance forms. Ballroom dance, while a popular social dance, is not specifically mentioned in the passage.

7. The author's use of the phrase "universal language of movement" (line 30) primarily serves to:

(A) emphasize the ability of dance to transcend cultural boundaries.

(B) highlight the importance of technical skill in dance.

(C) suggest that dance is a more accessible art form than other forms of expression.

(D) downplay the role of cultural context in interpreting dance.

Answer: (A)

Explanation: The phrase "universal language of movement" suggests that dance can communicate emotions and ideas across different cultures and languages, highlighting its ability to connect people through shared human experiences.

8. Which of the following is a synonym for the word "captivating" as used in the passage?

(A) Boring

(B) Enchanting

(C) Simple

(D) Ordinary

Answer: (B)

Explanation: The word "captivating" in the passage means fascinating or enchanting, which is synonymous with "enchanting."

9. Which of the following is an antonym for the word "ancient" as used in the passage?

(A) Old

(B) Modern

(C) Historical

(D) Traditional

Answer: (B)

Explanation: The word "ancient" in the passage means very old or belonging to the distant past. The opposite of this is "modern."

10. Which of the following best summarizes the main idea of the passage?

(A) Dance is a timeless and universal form of expression that has evolved alongside human societies and cultures.

(B) The origins of dance are uncertain, but evidence suggests it may have originated in ritual and ceremony.

(C) Dance has undergone various transformations throughout history, adapting to new forms, styles, and technologies.

(D) Dance is a powerful tool for communication, celebration, and artistic expression.

Answer: (D)

Explanation: The passage provides a comprehensive overview of dance, highlighting its historical development, diverse forms, and enduring power to communicate emotions, celebrate important events, and express artistic visions.

Full-Length Practice Test 9 (Science Test)

Time: 35 Minutes—40 Questions

Directions: There are several passages in this section, each of which is followed by questions. After reviewing a passage, choose the best answer to each question and fill in the matching oval on your answer sheet. Refer to the passages as often as you need. Calculators are NOT permitted on this test.

Passage 1

Punnett Squares A Punnett square is a diagram used to predict the genotypic and phenotypic outcomes of a breeding experiment between two plants or animals of the same species. In particular, Punnett squares illustrate the proportions in which progeny will possess specific combinations of alleles. Alleles are heritable variations of a single gene. By convention, alleles belonging to the same gene are distinguished by using a capital letter to indicate the dominant allele and a lowercase letter to indicate the recessive allele. **Figure 1** illustrates the Punnett squares for both homozygous and heterozygous crosses.

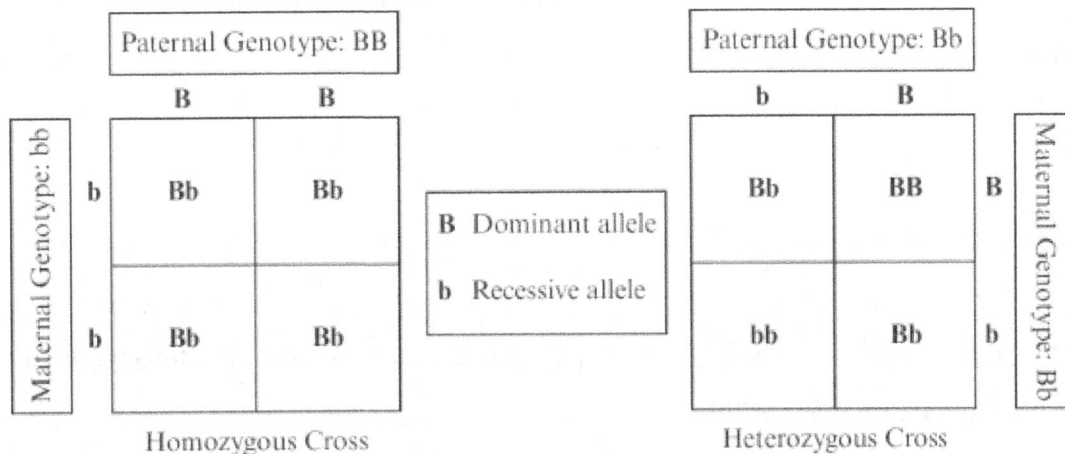

Figure 1

It's also common to use Punnett squares to track heritability patterns for two separate genes. **Figure 2** illustrates a dizygous cross.

	AB	Ab	aB	ab
AB	AABB	AABb	AaBB	AaBb
Ab	AABB	AABb	AaBB	AaBb
aB	AaBB	AaBb	aaBB	aaBb
ab	AaBb	Aabb	aaBb	aabb

Paternal Genotype: AaBb

Maternal Genotype: AaBb

AB Dominant alleles

ab   Recessive alleles

Figure 2

1. Using the genotypic labeling as in the passage, which of the following would be a gene with all dominant alleles?

A. Zz

B. zz

C. ZZ

D. zZ

2. According to Figure 1, what is the fraction of possible genotypes from a heterozygous cross that would have only recessive genes?

   A. 0

   B. ¼

   C. ½

   D. ¾

3. Based on Figure 1, which of the following combinations of genes would be a homozygous cross?

A. aa, AA

B. Aa, AA

C. AA, Aa

D. AA, aA

4. Based on Figure 1, in a homozygous cross the offspring will genetically, not physically, most resemble:

A. the genetically dominant parent, exclusively.

B. the genetically dominant parent, predominantly.

C. the genetically recessive parent, exclusively.

D. both parents, equally.

5. A genotype is the genetic makeup of an individual organism. A phenotype refers to the outward traits expressed by that organism. In Figure 1's heterozygous cross, what is the likelihood that offspring will possess a dominant phenotype?

A. 25%

B. 50%

C. 75%

D. There is not enough information.

Answers

1. (C) Figure 1 indicates that a dominant allele will be capitalized, and a recessive allele will be lowercase. So, a gene with all dominant alleles would have all of the letters for the alleles capitalized. This also is consistent with commonly practiced gene labeling in biology.

2. (B) From Figure 1 we see that only one of the four squares has only recessive genes, labeled "bb" in the Punnett square. This represents one-fourth of the total possible genes.

3. (A) According to Figure 1, the homozygous cross is done between a gene of all dominant alleles, "BB," and all recessive alleles, "bb." (A) is the only one of these options that would combine a gene with two dominant alleles and another gene with two recessive alleles.

4. (J) It is important to focus on the genetic, not physical, resemblance of the offspring. Each offspring will have an equal component from each parent, making every single possible

combination "Bb." As far as physical characteristics, every combination would display the dominant parent's traits, but as far as genetic characteristics, every possibility has equal contributions from each parent.

5. (C) If an organism has the gene for the dominant characteristic present, it will ensure that the dominant characteristic is what is physically represented in the phenotype, even if there is a recessive gene in the genotype. For three out of the four boxes in the heterozygous cross, the dominant gene is present. So, it is 75% likely that a given offspring of this combination will physically display the dominant phenotype.

Easier Passage 2

Earthquake Prediction Earthquakes are one of nature's most devastating events. The capacity to predict earthquakes would be a tremendous technological leap, enabling governments to forewarn citizens about impending threats. Prediction technologies vary on their capacity to predict when, over what area, how long, and what intensity an earthquake will have. Three scientists debate the best way to use current technology to predict earthquakes.

Foreshock Method

The only reliable way to predict earthquakes is by monitoring for foreshocks, which are small-medium size earthquakes that precede large earthquakes. Although many scientists are correct in looking at other prediction methods as relatively accurately predicting that an earthquake will occur in a particular region, the foreshock method is the only approach that enables scientists to predict when an earthquake will occur. This method has been successfully employed by the government of China in evacuating a million people before a 1973 earthquake.

Radon Method

A modern method of predicting earthquakes that has increasingly gained credibility among scientists is to monitor soil for spikes in radon concentration. The theoretical basis for this method is that as pressure increases deep within Earth, radon gas will be pushed toward the surface. As scientific technology to detect radon improves, this method will become increasingly reliable. Radon was helpful in the year 2009 in predicting that an earthquake would occur in Italy.

Fractoluminescence

An experimental method of earthquake predictions is to monitor silica deposits for emissions of red and blue light for a fraction of a second. When the silica is fractured because of geological pressure, the silica will emit the red and blue light. This is an experimental method that has not yet been put into practice, yet demonstrates a great deal of potential. Scientists in the earthquake-ridden country of Japan are optimistic about its potential to predict earthquakes in an accurate and timely fashion.

1. An earthquake in which of the following regions was used to substantiate the foreshock method?

A. China

B. Japan

C. Italy

D. Haiti

2. According to the passages, scientists have not yet successfully used which of the following methods to predict earthquakes?

A. Foreshock

B. Radon

C. Fractoluminescence

D. All have been used to successfully predict earthquakes.

3. Scientists are interested in determining precisely where an earthquake will occur. If the scientists are interested in using a method with a proven track record of prediction, which method would make the most sense to use?

A. Foreshock

B. Radon

C. Fractoluminescence

D. Scientists can only predict when earthquakes can occur, but not where.

4. A major problem with the foreshock method is:

A. It has not been proven to work in predicting past earthquakes.

B. It cannot be used to estimate when an earthquake will occur.

C. It will not work in predicting a large earthquake if there are no foreshocks.

D. It cannot be used to predict large earthquakes.

5. Access to deep mine shafts to gather information about Earth's geological makeup would provide information that would most likely be useful for which of the following methods?

A. Foreshock only

B. Radon only

C. Fractoluminescence only

D. Both radon and fractoluminescence

6. Which is a likely reason that the foreshock method was developed earlier than the radon or fractoluminescence methods?

A. Ease of observation

B. More frequent occurrences of events to be observed

C. Better observation technology at an earlier time

D. Its demonstrated superiority as a prediction method

7. Tsunamis are extremely destructive waves caused by earthquakes that occur in fault lines deep under the ocean. Given that it is extremely difficult to make geological observations deep under the ocean, which of the earthquake prediction methods would provide some useful information about tsunamis?

A. Foreshock

B. Radon

C. Fractoluminescence

D. None of them could provide helpful information.

Answers

1. (A) The last sentence of the Foreshock Method paragraph states that "This method has been successfully employed by the government of China in evacuating a million people before a 1973 earthquake."

2. (H) Fractoluminescence is called an "experimental" method of earthquake predictions, whereas the other methods have been used in actual situations.

3. (B) Radon has a proven track record, and it can be used to predict where an earthquake will occur with precision. Foreshock has a proven track record, but it is imprecise. Fractoluminescence is precise, but it does not have a proven track record.

4. (C) A foreshock can help one predict a coming earthquake, but in the absence of an initial foreshock, there would be no information about a coming earthquake. It is not (A) because it has been proven to be helpful. It is not (B) because it can help predict when another quake could

occur as long as there has been an initial quake. It is not (D) because as long as there is a preceding foreshock, it can predict a coming large earthquake.

5. (D) Access to deep mine shafts would enable the radon method to gather more concrete information about radon gas emissions. Access to the shafts would also help the fractoluminescence method gain access to silica deposits. The foreshock method would not be helped by this since it relies on observations on Earth's surface.

6. (A) Foreshocks are far more easily observed than data for the other methods. One must simply notice that an earthquake is occurring—no specialized scientific equipment is needed. It is not (B) because with adequate technology, one could observe radon emissions or silica deposits with far greater frequency than foreshocks. It is not (C) because scientific technology to observe earthquakes has apparently improved over time. It is not (D) because it is not demonstrably superior to the other methods.

7. (A) The radon and fractoluminescent methods would need access to radon and silica data, respectively. Without access to Earth beneath the water, this would be virtually impossible to achieve. Foreshocks would be quite helpful because although one might be surprised by the first tsunami, one could at least take shelter in preparation for any tsunamis that would follow.

Medium Passage 1

Under the Bohr model, each of an atom's electrons is assigned three quantum numbers based on its probable distribution around the nucleus. Some general properties of quantum numbers are summarized in **Table 1.**

Table 1

Quantum Number	Symbol	Value Range	Maximum Electron Capacity	Character
1st (Principle)	N	Integers 1 through 7	$2N^2$	Energy level
2nd (Angular)	L	Integers 0 through (N-1)	$2(2L + 1)$	Subshell
3rd (Magnetic)	M_L	Integers (-L) through L	N/A	Spatial orientation

Quantum numbers are utilized when establishing an element's electron configuration. **Figure 1** shows a portion of the periodic table of elements modified to highlight the relationship between quantum numbers and the order in which subshells are filled with electrons. **Figure 2** explains the electron configuration of hydrogen, and **Table 2** gives the full electron configuration of three additional elements.

Energy Level

N = 1	1 H	2 He						

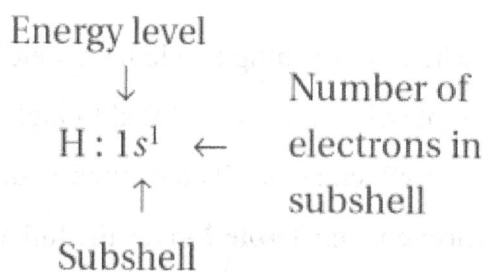

Figure 1

Energy level
↓
H : $1s^1$ ←   Number of electrons in subshell
↑
Subshell

Figure 2

Table 2

Element	Electron Configuration
He	$1s^2$
P	$1s^2 2s^2 2p^6 3s^2 3p^3$
Kr	$1s^2 2s^2 2p^6 3s^2 3p^6 4s2^4 p^6$
Mn	$1s^2 2s^2 2p^6 3s^2 3p^6 4s2^4 p^6 4d^5$

1. According to **Table 1**, which of the following values would NOT have an impact on the maximum electron capacity of a particular atom?

A. L

B. ML

C. N

D. All would have an impact on the atom's maximum electron capacity.

2. Based on Figure 1 or Table 1, what is the maximum electron capacity of energy level 1?

A. 1

B. 2

C. 3

D. 4

3. According to the information in Figure 1 and Table 2, which of the following represents the complete electron configuration of silicon (Si)?

A. [Ne] 3s 2 3p 2

B. 3s 23p 2

C. 1s 22s 22p 63s 23p 3

D. 1s 22s 22p 63s 23p 2

4. Given that electron configuration in an element's valence (final) shell is often indicative of both its physical properties and chemical reactivity, what pair of elements is most likely to demonstrate similar characteristics?

A. Scandium (Sc) and zinc (Zn)

B. Lithium (Li) and potassium (K)

C. Hydrogen (H) and helium (He)

D. Sodium (Na) and copper (Cu)

5. Quantum numbers reflect probable electron distribution around an atom's nucleus when the atom is in its "ground state." Given that electrons can "jump" into higher energy levels by absorbing photons, what character's value is most likely to be altered when an atom enters an excited state?

A. L

B. ML

C. N

D. s

Answers

1. (B) Be sure you notice the NOT in the question. According to Table 1, ML is the only one of these three values that would have no impact on the maximum electron capacity, given that it says "N/A" in the table.

2. (B) According to Table 1, the maximum electron capacity of an energy level is calculated by the formula $2N2$, where N represents the quantum number or energy level. Putting 1 into this equation, we would get 2 as a result. Also, looking at the first energy level in Figure 1, the elements max out at an atomic number of 2.

3. (D) To make things as easy as possible, find an element that is on Table 2 and is as close to Si as possible. P would work, since it is only one more in atomic number than Si. Take the electron configuration for P and subtract 1 electron from the outermost subshell, which would give you (D).

4. (B) Lithium and potassium represent the only pair of elements in the options that have the same number of electrons in their outer shell, since they are in the same column of the periodic table. Having this characteristic would make them share many chemical properties.

5. (C) The symbol "N" corresponds to an atom's energy level, so if an electron jumped from a lower energy level to a higher energy level, this would have to be affected. The other options are not directly associated with an atom's energy level.

Medium Passage 2

Diabetes

Diabetes mellitus affects the body's ability to effectively regulate its blood glucose level. **Figure 1** illustrates the spectrum of fasting blood glucose levels as they relate to pathology.

Fasting Blood Glucose Concentrations

Two hormones are directly responsible for maintaining blood glucose homeostasis—insulin, and glucagon. Insulin causes glucose to be absorbed from the bloodstream, and glucagon causes the body to break down stored glycogen into glucose and release it into the bloodstream. **Figure 2** generalizes the hourly fluctuations in blood glucose and blood insulin for a nondiabetic over the course of a single day. Figure 3 summarizes the changes that occur in a nondiabetic during 24 hours of fasting.

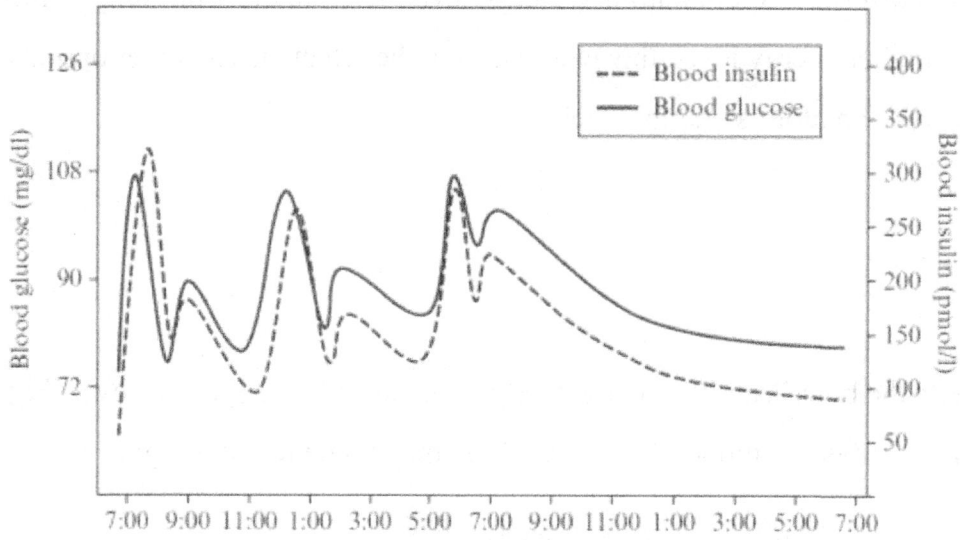

Figure 2

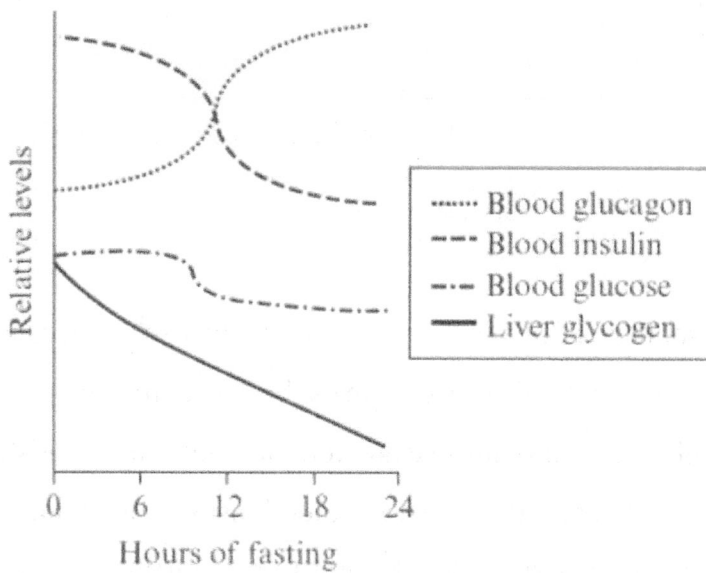

Figure 3

Diabetes mellitus Type I is characterized by low levels of insulin in the bloodstream, and Type II is characterized by insulin resistance at the cellular level. Figure 4 illustrates the daily blood glucose fluctuations for both a Type I and a Type II diabetic.

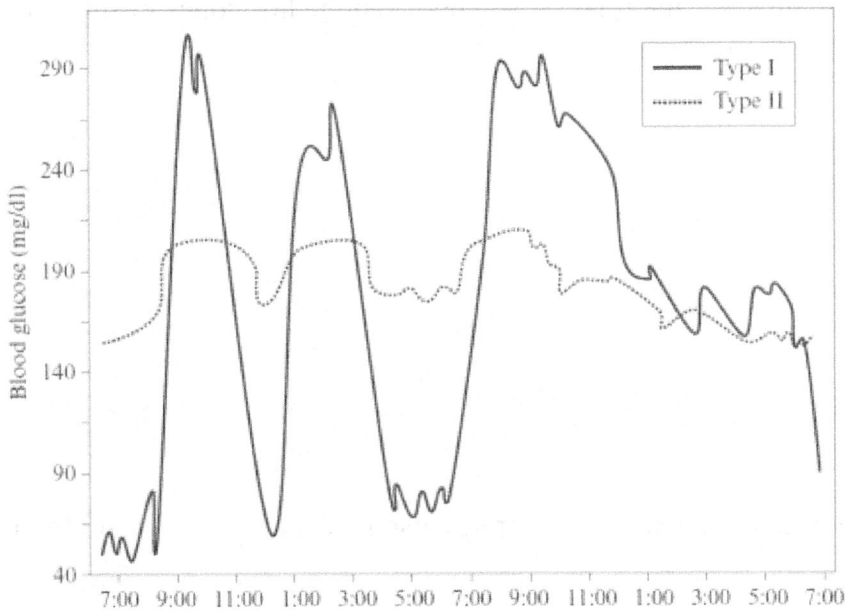

Figure 4

1. Based on Figure 1, an individual with a fasting blood glucose level of 180 mg/dl is best described as:

A. hypoglycemic.

B. healthy.

C. prediabetic.

D. diabetic.

2. Intravenous injection of insulin is a plausible treatment for:

A. Type I diabetes because it is characterized by insulin resistance at the cellular level.

B. Type I diabetes because it is characterized by an inability of the pancreas to produce insulin naturally.

C. Type II diabetes because it is characterized by an inability of the pancreas to produce insulin naturally.

D. Type II diabetes because it is characterized by insulin resistance at the cellular level.

391

3. Based on Figure 3, with respect to glucose, the relationship between the hormones insulin and glucagon is best described as:

A. direct.

B. inverse.

C. constructive.

D. destructive.

4. For a Type II diabetic, secretion of insulin causes cellular glucose levels to _____ and blood glucose levels to _____.

A. increase slightly; decrease slightly

B. increase greatly; decrease slightly

C. increase slightly; decrease greatly

D. increase greatly; decrease greatly

5. In Figure 4, the three large spikes in the Type I diabetic's blood glucose probably correlate with:

A. regular fluctuations in the circadian cycle.

B. regular injections of insulin throughout the day.

C. three meals eaten throughout the day.

D. increased periods of hunger caused by secretion of glucagon from the liver.

Answers

1. (D) Looking at Figure 1, someone with a fasting blood glucose level of 180 mg/dl would fall under the category of "diabetes mellitus," which would correspond to being diabetic.

2. (B) The passage states that "Diabetes mellitus Type I is characterized by low levels of insulin in the bloodstream, and Type II is characterized by insulin resistance at the cellular level." Having regular injections of insulin would be most helpful to someone who could not produce insulin independently.

3. (B) The amount of insulin increases as the amount of glucagon decreases, and vice versa. This makes for an inverse relationship.

4. (A) A Type II diabetic is resistant to insulin when it comes to cellular absorption, making it most likely that it would only slightly increase the cellular glucose levels. The cells absorb glucose from the blood, and since the cells are only absorbing a slight amount, the blood glucose would therefore decrease slightly.

5. (C) The ingestion of food would cause major jumps in blood glucose levels from the digestive process. It is not (A) because this is associated with sleeping and would not account for such large spikes. It is not (B) because we could expect a steadier stream of blood glucose if there were regular injections. It is not (D) because we would expect a more gradual increase in blood glucose if there were increased periods of hunger.

Medium Passage 3

Allergic rhinitis, or "hay fever," results from a hypersensitivity of the immune system to certain types of weed or tree pollen, which results in an acute inflammatory response. The signaling cascade for an allergic rhinitis reaction is illustrated in **Figure 1.**

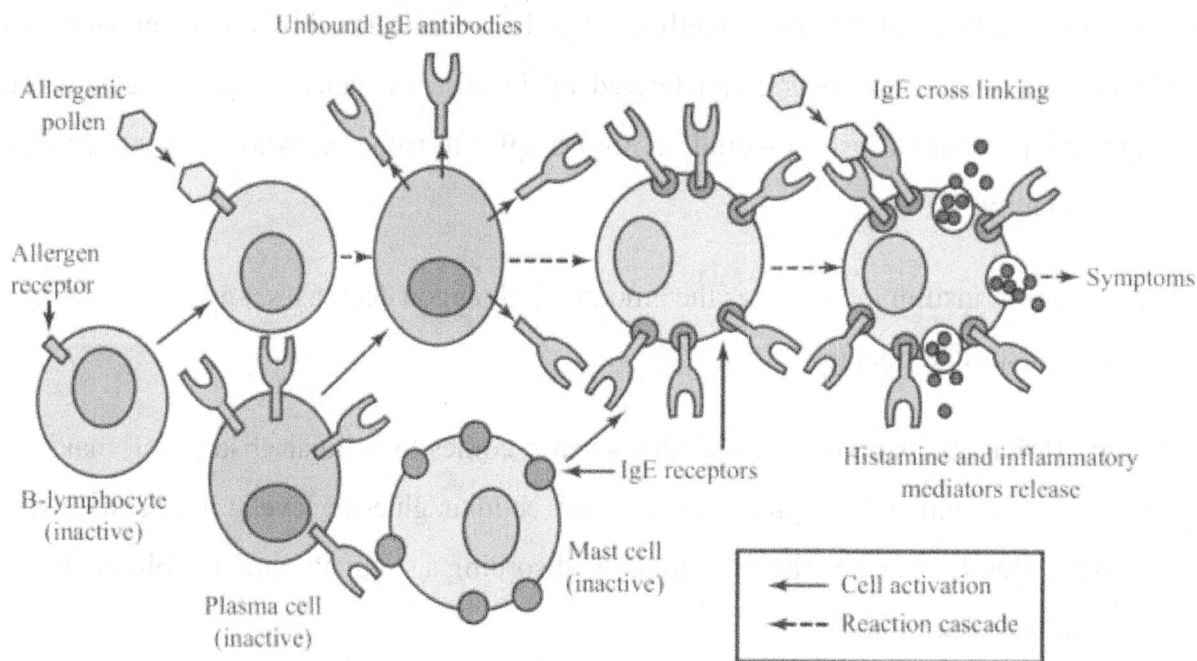

Figure 1

In a condition called "oral allergy syndrome" (OAS), people experience a mild allergic reaction in their mouth while eating many fresh fruits, nuts, and vegetables. However, unlike those with shellfish or peanut allergies, these people do not possess an allergy to the food itself but rather a pollen allergy that undergoes a "cross-reaction," meaning that their pollen antibodies also bind to structurally similar food proteins, causing local inflammation. Table 1 summarizes the most common pollen-food crossreactive patterns. Figure 2 shows an SDS-PAGE plate of the proteins detected in samples of birch pollen, apple, celery, aniseed, and peanut, separating the proteins according to their size. Each of the types of protein in Figure 2 has its lettered name to the right of it, labeled in lane 3.

Table 1

Pollen Type	Family	Cross-Reactive Foods						
Birch	Rosaceae	Apple	Peach	Plum	Pear	Cherry	Apricot	Almond
	Apiaceae	Carrot	Celery	Parsley	Caraway	Fennel	Coriander	Aniseed
	Fabaceae	Soybean			Peanut			
	Betulaceae	Hazelnut						
Ragweed	Cururbitaceae	Cantaloupe	Honeydew	Watermelon		Zucchini	Cucumber	
	Muscaceae	Banana						
Mugwort	Apiaceae	Celery	Carrot	Aniseed	Fennel	Coriander	Caraway	Parsley
	Solanaceae	Bell pepper						
	Liliaceae	Garlic			Onion			
	Piperaceae	Black Pepper						
	Brassicaceae	Mustard		Cauliflower		Cabbage	Broccoli	
Alder	Rosaceae	Almonds	Apples	Cherries	Pears	Strawberry	Raspberry	
	Apiaceae	Celery		Parsley		Aniseed		

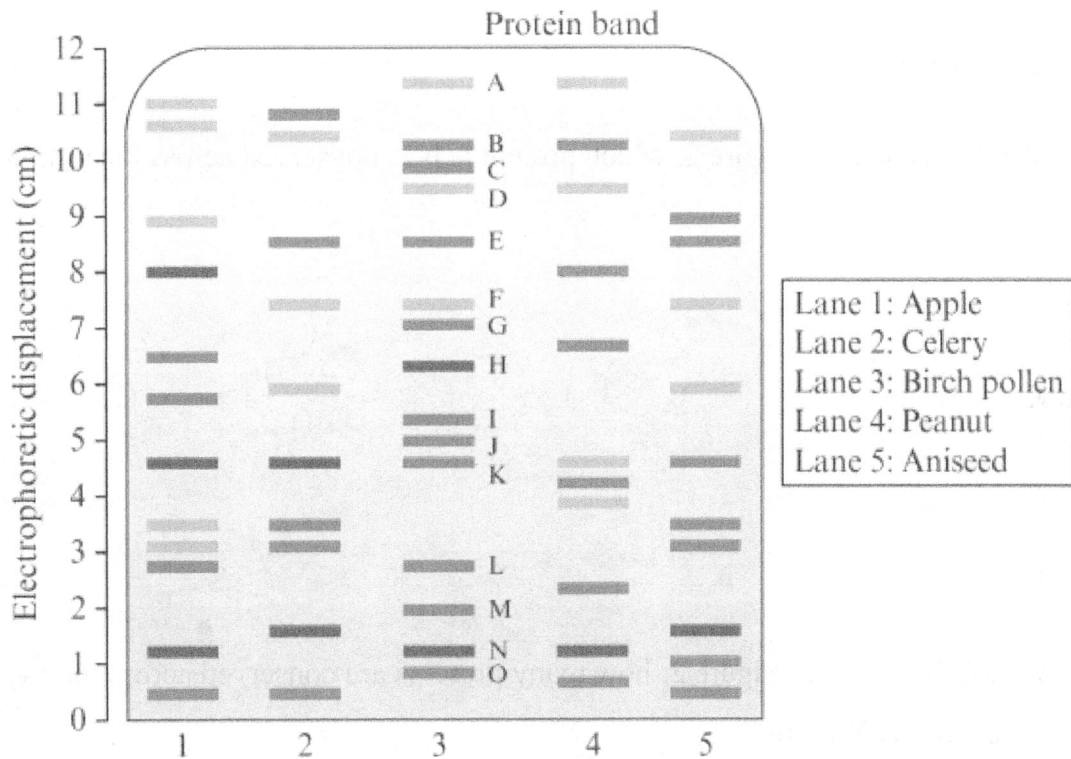

Figure 2

1. If someone were allergic to mugwort, birch, and alder pollens, what would be a food that the person would definitely want to avoid to prevent a possible cross-reaction?

A. Cucumber

B. Watermelon

C. Honeydew

D. Celery

2. What two pollen types shown in Table 1 likely share the most conserved proteins?

A. Birch and alder

B. Ragweed and mugwort

C. Mugwort and birch

D. Alder and ragweed

3. As indicated by its band in Figure 2, which protein is best conserved across the samples tested?

A. Protein E

B. Protein K

C. Protein M

D. Protein N

4. Based on the information in Figure 2, how many proteins are conserved across the two members of the Apiaceae family?

A. 6

B. 8

C. 9

D. 10

5. Allergists have designed immunotherapies that interrupt the reaction cascade at a number of intervals. Which of the following interventions would be LEAST likely to interrupt the cascade?

A. Preventing secretion of IgE

B. Activating mast cells prior to B-lymphocyte-allergen binding

C. Inhibiting release of histamine

D. Chemically inhibiting expression of IgE receptors

Answers

1. (D) Celery is listed as a cross-reactive food for all three of the pollen types, so it would be the one you would want to avoid. The other three options are not present in all three of the pollen types.

2. (A) Birch and alder share the same families—Rosaceae and Apiaceae —so it stands to reason that they would most likely share the most conserved proteins. The other choices do not have the same level of similarity among their families and cross-reactive foods that Rosaceae and Apiaceae do.

3. (B) Protein K is the only option that is present in all five lanes. In other words, Protein K is found at about 4.7 cm along the electrophoretic displacement and is represented in the apple, celery, birch pollen, peanut, and aniseed.

4. (C) According to Table 1, celery and aniseed are both members of the Apiaceae family. Looking at Figure 2, there are a total of nine proteins for which celery (lane 2) shares the same electrophoretic displacement level with aniseed (lane 5).

5. (B) Based on Figure 1, there are other IgE receptors that can be a part of this reaction given the two arrows pointing out of the "IgE receptors" label. So, activating mast cells prior to B-lymphocyteallergen binding would be the LEAST likely of these options to interrupt the cascade since there is an alternative way that this part of the reaction can come about. For all of the other options, there is only one way they can come about so they would all serve to interrupt the reaction cascade.

Medium Passage 4

Researchers compiled statistics on the recent allocation of energy use by the United States. In Figure 1 below is a list of their findings. Petroleum continues to be the greatest source of U.S. energy, with the other fossil fuels of coal and natural gas not far behind. Alternative energy sources include a wide array of technologies, such as wind, tide, solar, and geothermal.

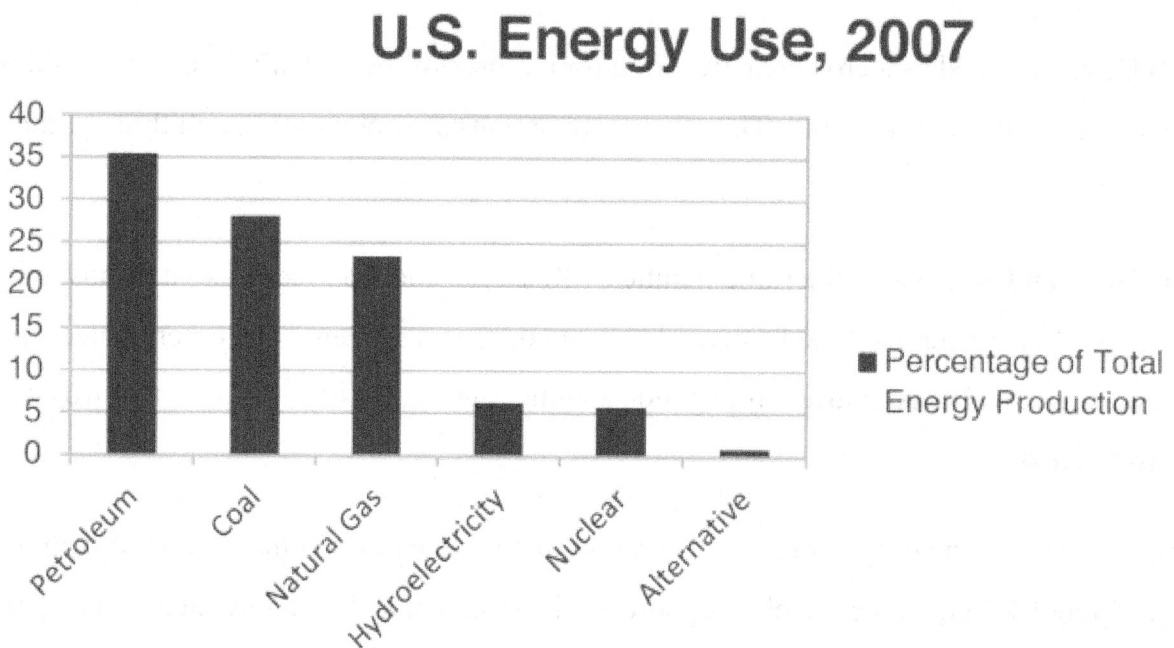

Figure 1

Researchers wanted to determine the extent to which different states choose to embrace different types of energy resources. Statistics on energy use in the states of Texas, New York, and California are provided in Table 1 below.

Table 1

Type of Power Source	State of Texas	State of New York	State of California
% of Total U.S. Electricity Generation	9.2	3.3	5.1
% of Total U.S. Petroleum Use	0.6	3.3	0.3
% of Total U.S. Coal Use	7.4	0.7	0.1
% of Total U.S. Natural Gas Use	17.8	4.7	14.8
% of Total U.S. Hydroelectric Use	0.8	11.8	10.3
% of Total U.S. Nuclear Use	5.7	5.2	3.3
% of Total U.S. Alternative Energy Use	18.5	2.9	14.8

1. According to Figure 1, fossil fuels make up approximately what percent of the total U.S. energy use?

A. 87%

B. 51%

C. 28%

D. 23%

2. According to Figure 1, which of the following correctly lists these energy sources in decreasing percentage of contribution to U.S. energy supplies?

A. Alternative, nuclear, coal, petroleum

B. Natural gas, petroleum, hydroelectricity, coal

C. Coal, natural gas, hydroelectricity, alternative

D. Hydroelectricity, nuclear, alternative, coal

3. Which of the following rationales would best explain the inconsistency between New York's generation of only 3.3% of U.S. electricity and its relatively high use of electricity across virtually every category?

A. New York's use of electricity generated by nearby states

B. New York's relatively low coal usage for electricity

C. New York's lack of capacity for alternative energy caused by geographic factors

D. There is no inconsistency, since the petroleum use and electricity use are both 3.3%

4. Using information from Figure 1 and Figure 2, California's total actual use from which of the following sources of energy is most likely the largest overall?

A. Natural gas

B. Alternative

C. Nuclear

D. Hydroelectric

5. At the time of this study, California's population was approximately 37,000,000, Texas's was approximately 24,000,000, and New York's was approximately 19,000,000. Demographers hypothesized that there would be a direct correlation between the size of a state's population and its percentage of total U.S. electricity generation. Which of the following pieces of data disproves this hypothesis?

A. Texas's percent of total U.S. electricity generation

B. Texas's percent of U.S. petroleum use

C. New York's percent of total U.S. electricity generation

D. New York's percent of U.S. coal use

Answers

1. (A) Include petroleum, coal, and natural gas in your calculation, and the only answer anywhere close would be 87%.

2. (C) Coal is at approximately 28%, followed by natural gas at about 23%, followed by hydroelectricity at about 6%, and alternative at 1%. This is the only choice that puts the amounts in decreasing order of percent of U.S. energy use.

3. (A) Since New York creates only 3.3% of U.S. electricity but uses much more electricity from a variety of other sources, this is the only logical explanation provided. It is not (B) or (C) because New York could have usage and capacity from other sources. (D) is irrelevant.

4. (A) Although California has the same percentages of the total natural gas use and alternative energy use, the total amount of natural gas used in the country is far greater than that of alternative energy. So, 14.8% of the natural gas would be a much larger amount than 14.8% of the alternative energy use.

5. (A) Paraphrasing the hypothesis, population size and electricity generation percentage should go up and down with one another. (A) is the only option to disprove this because Texas produces more electricity than California, yet it has a much smaller population. All of the other choices would serve to support this hypothesis.

Medium Passage 5

Students collected four soil samples from the surrounding region of a nearby river. The samples were enriched in liquid medium containing restricted nutrients that favored the growth of bacteria from the genus Actinomyces. The students conducted three experiments in which they analyzed the environmental isolates under different growth conditions in order to characterize the strains. Experiment 1 The four isolates were plated on petri dishes containing minimal medium with the addition of a specific carbon source. The samples were incubated at 30°C for 24 hours, and growth was observed. The results of Experiment 1 are shown in Table 1

Table 1

	Carbon Source		
	Glucose	Galactose	Pyruvate
Isolate A	–	–	+
Isolate B	+	++	–
Isolate C	+	+	+
Isolate D	–	–	++

Key:
No growth (–)
Moderate growth (+)
High growth (++)

Experiment 2 The four isolates were plated on petri dishes containing enriched LB medium (Lysogeny Broth—a nutritionally rich medium used to grow bacteria). The samples were incubated at different temperatures for 24 hours, and the number of colonies on each plate was counted. The results of Experiment 2 are shown in Table 2.

Table 2

	Temperature		
	4°C	30°C	42°C
Isolate A	0	140	65
Isolate B	0	36	32
Isolate C	0	45	11
Isolate D	0	93	13

Experiment 3 As a population of bacteria grows in liquid medium, the liquid becomes cloudy as more cells accumulate. Bacterial growth can be measured using a spectrophotometer, which uses lasers to measure the optical density (OD) of a liquid. Before each use, the spectrophotometer is calibrated with a sample of distilled water, which is given a value of OD = 0. The isolates were grown in liquid LB medium at 30°C for a period of 24 hours. A small sample was taken each hour and measured using a spectrophotometer. The growth curves of the four isolates were graphed from the data, and the results are shown in Figure 1.

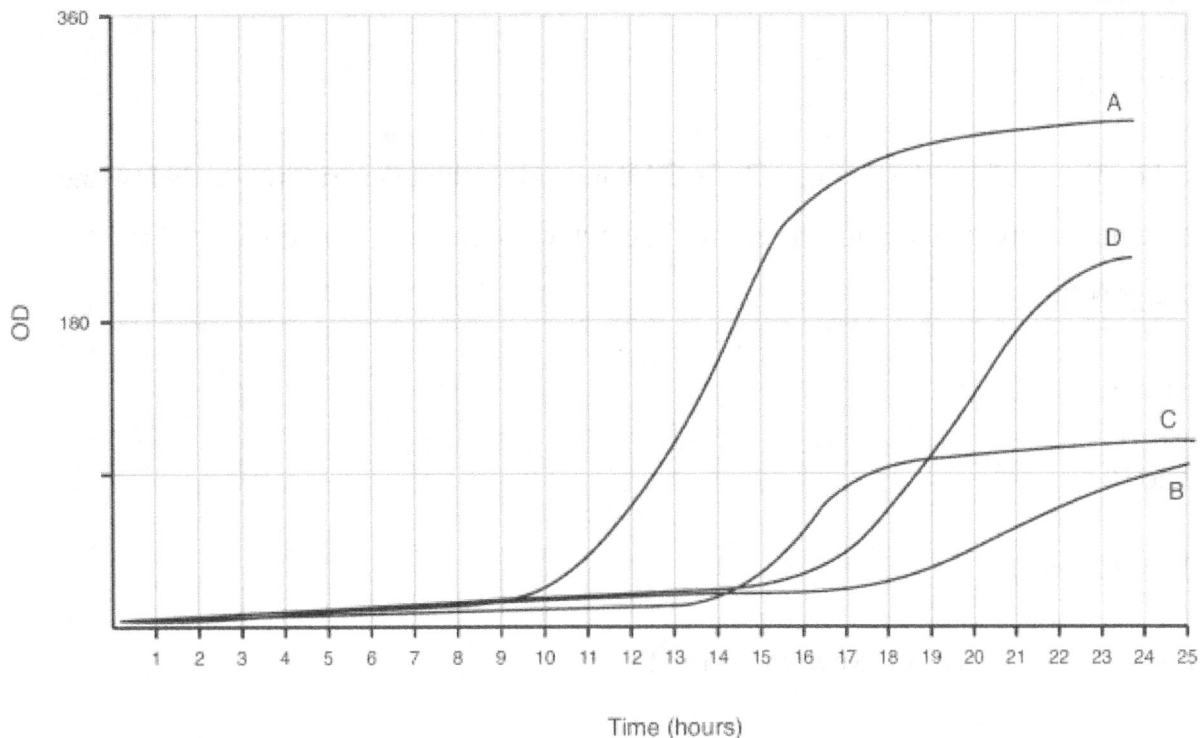

Figure 1

1. According to Experiment 1, which isolate would experience the greatest amount of bacterial growth when given the carbon source galactose?

A. Isolate A

B. Isolate B

C. Isolate C

D. Isolate D

2. Considering each of the values given in Experiment 2, what is the general trend in bacterial growth as temperature decreases?

A. It increases, then decreases.

B. It decreases, then increases.

C. It only increases.

D. It only decreases.

3. Based on the results of Experiment 2, for 24 hours when the temperature was below the freezing temperature of water for the entire time, which bacteria(s) would have the most bacterial growth?

A. Isolate A

B. Isolate B

C. Isolates C and D

D. All would most likely not experience growth.

4. It is reasonable to conclude that if Experiment 3 had been continued up to 34 hours instead of stopping at 24 hours, the final optical density of Isolate C would most likely be closest to:

A. 40.

B. 60.

C. 100.

D. 160.

5. Based on the information in Experiments 1 and 2, what combination of temperature (in degrees Celsius) and carbon source would most likely result in the greatest increase in bacterial growth?

A. 4°, pyruvate

B. 30°, pyruvate

C. 4°, glucose

D. 30°, glucose

6. If the spectrophotometer in Experiment 3 had instead been calibrated with turbid (i.e., cloudy) water, what would most likely happen to the bacterial growth curves? F. There would be no impact. G. Isolates A and B would have lower OD values, while isolates C and D would have higher OD values. H. All isolates would have lower OD values. J. All isolates would have higher OD values. Answers 1. (B) Isolate B is the only isolate to have high bacterial growth with galactose, as indicated on the table with the ++ signs. 2. (F) For each of the isolates in Experiment 2, as the temperature decreases from 42°C to 30°C, the amount of bacteria increases. Then, as the temperature continues to decrease from 30°C to 4°C, the amount of bacteria decreases for each of the isolates. Therefore, the general trend in bacterial growth as temperature decreases is for the growth to increase and then to decrease. 3. (D) None of the isolates experienced growth when they were at a temperature of 4°C. Also, the trend of bacterial growth between 30°C and 4°C is for the bacterial growth to decrease. Generalizing on these trends, if the isolates were below the freezing temperature of water, i.e., 0°C, none of them would experience bacterial growth. 4. (H) According to Figure 1, the slope of the curve of Isolate C begins to level off at around 20 hours. So, if the experiment continued for an additional 10 hours, it is most likely that the optical density would continue to be what it was when 24 hours had passed from the beginning of the experiment. Therefore, the final optical density of Isolate C would be approximately 100. 5. (B) Based on Table 1, pyruvate results in greater overall bacterial growth than glucose since there are more plus signs indicating moderate and high growth in the column. Based on Table 2, when the isolates are at 30°C, they consistently experience the greatest bacterial growth. Therefore, the combination that would result in the greatest bacterial growth would be 30°C and pyruvate. 6. (J) The cloudier the water, the higher its optical density. This can be inferred from the fact that as more bacteria clouds the water in Experiment 3, the optical density increases. If the spectrophotometer had been calibrated with cloudy water instead of distilled water, it would cause all of the isolates to have higher optical density values. Tough Passage #1 A team of biologists set out to study the evolutionary pressure responsible for color change in a set of closely related species of chameleons. At the experiment's outset, the two prevailing hypotheses were natural selection,

whereby color change functioned primarily as camouflage and protection from aerial predation, and social selection, whereby color change functioned primarily as an intermittent conspicuous mating display for conspecifics. As different body sections of a chameleon change color independently, the scientists divided their initial examinations into three general sections, as illustrated in Figure 1.

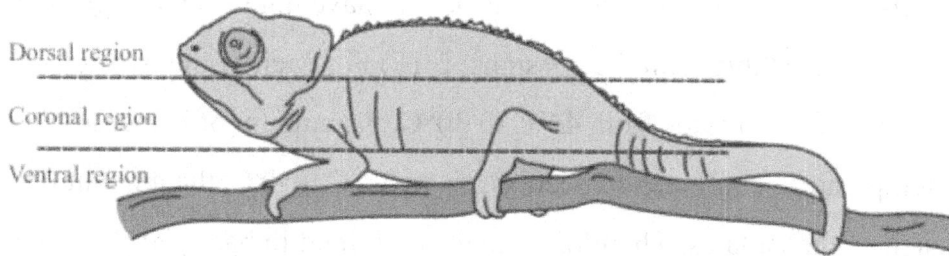

Figure 1

Experiment 1 The scientists studied the reflectance of light from the surface of each chameleon species in two distinct states of courtship and competition. The mean result is given in Figure 2. This data was compared against the relative light absorbance in the visual systems of chameleons, as well as one of their primary avian predators, as shown in Figure 3.

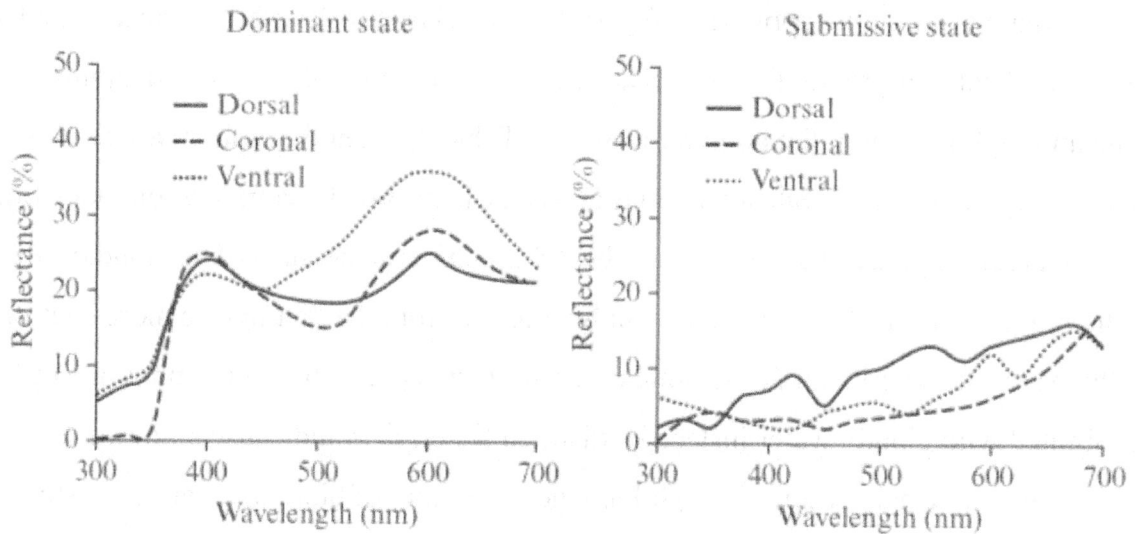

Figure 2

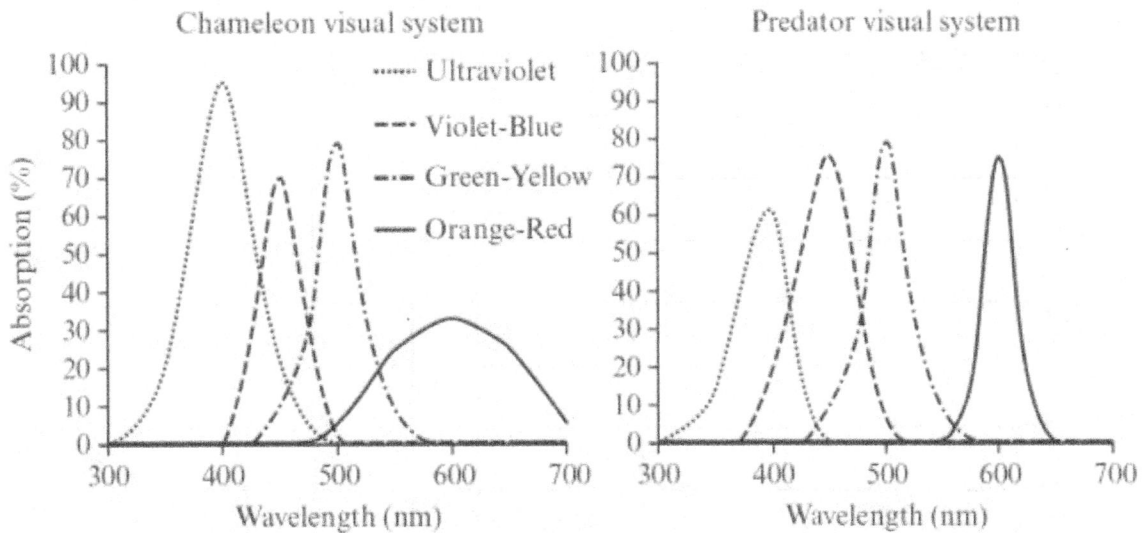

Figure 3

Experiment 2 The scientists then quantified the mean color change for each species entering the dominant state using spectroradiometry and measured this information against final chromatic contrast relative to background vegetation, as shown in Figure 4, and the average density of low branches and perches (fish) in each species' native biotope, as shown in Figure

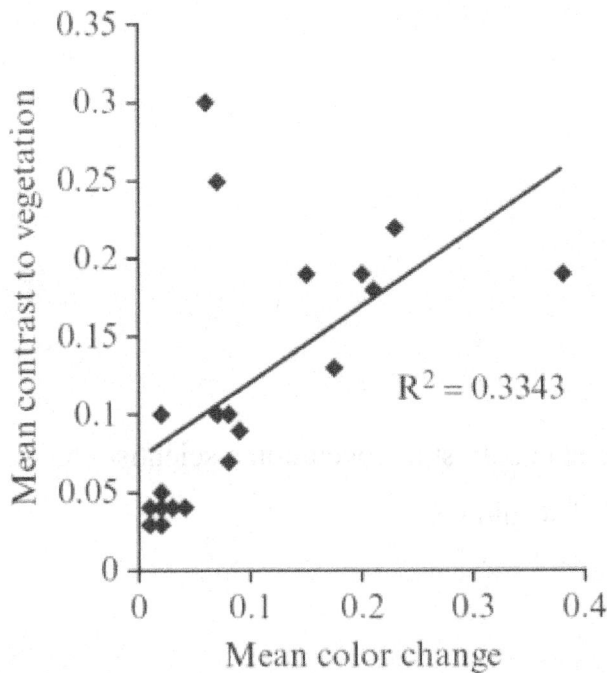

Figure 4

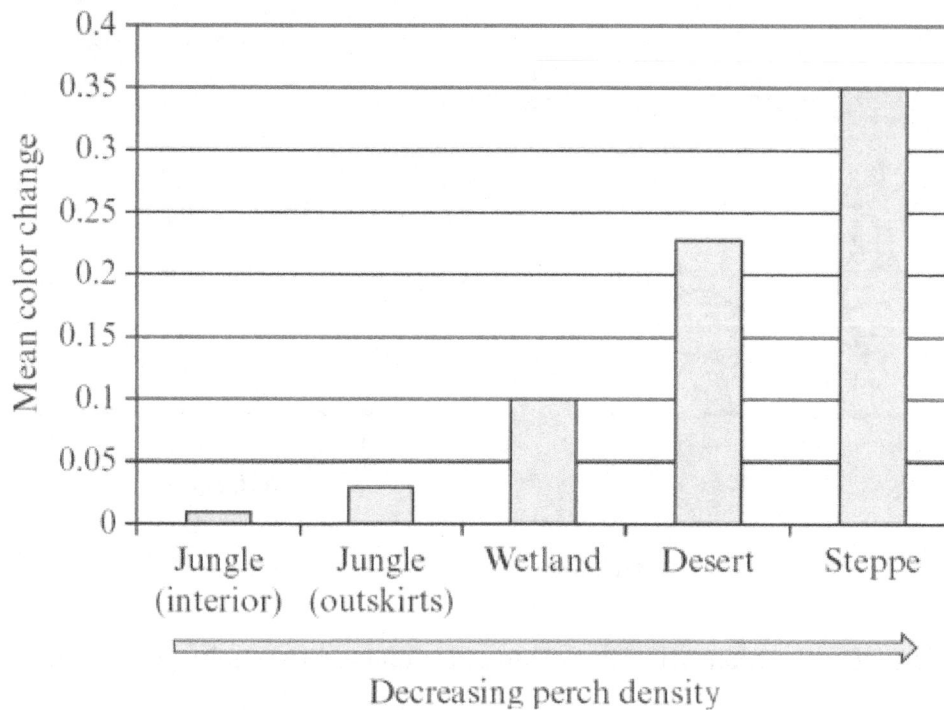

Figure 5

1. The approximate maximum range of wavelengths in Figure 3 in which the absorbance by the chameleon visual system is at least 20% is:

A. 300–750 nm.

B. 350–650 nm.

C. 400–600 nm.

D. 450–550 nm.

2. Based on the information in Figure 4, the mean contrast to vegetation a scientist could most reasonably expect at a mean color change of 0.3 would be:

A. 0.1.

B. 0.15.

C. 0.2.

D. 0.25.

3. According to Figures 1 and 2, the reflectance pattern in which of the following parts of the chameleon most strongly suggests an evolutionary adaptation to help with reproduction?

A. Dorsal

B. Coronal

C. Ventral

D. Dominant

4. Based on Figures 2 and 3, illumination under what color of light and in what reproductive state would most likely pose the least danger to chameleons?

A. Ultraviolet, submissive

B. Ultraviolet, dominant

C. Orange-red, submissive

D. Orange-red, dominant

5. Using evolutionary adaptive considerations, what factors would generally increase the need for more color change ability as demonstrated in Figure 5?

A. More diverse food sources for birds, more plant camouflage

B. More diverse food sources for birds, less plant camouflage

C. Fewer diverse food sources for birds, more plant camouflage

D. Fewer diverse food sources for birds, less plant camouflage

6. In statistics, R^2 indicates the "coefficient of determination," wherein a value of 1 signifies that the model explains all variation and a value of 0 indicates that there is no correlation. If it

is the case that mean color change and mean contrast to vegetation are positively correlated, another scientist who would carefully and accurately replicate Experiment 2 but would have twice as many samples would most likely find an R^2 value for a graph similar to that of Figure 4 of:

A. 0.00.

B. between 0.00 and 0.33.

C. between 0.33 and 1.00.

D. 1.00.

Answers

1. (B) Look at where the value of the curves in Figure 3 are in excess of 20%, and it is roughly between 350 and 650 nm.

2. (H) Match up the value of the mean color change on the x-axis of Figure 4, and see what the corresponding mean contrast would be by looking at the corresponding y value on the best-fit line.

3. (C) The ventral goes from being the most visible in a dominant state to the least visible in a submissive state, indicating that the chameleon has evolved to be much more visible when attempting to reproduce. Having greater reflectance would make the chameleon more visible.

4. (F) The ultraviolet light is the least visible light to the predatory visual system, maxing out at around 60% absorption. The submissive state is least visible to the predators, given its much lower reflectance across all wavelengths.

5. (D) The y-axis of Figure 5 indicates that the chameleons undergo much more substantial color changes in the steppe and the desert. The environment of the steppe is a grassland without forests, and a desert also has little plant life. It would therefore be much easier for a chameleon to be hidden in a heavily forested jungle without having to resort to color changing, and much more difficult to remain hidden in an environment without much vegetation. These

environments would also have fewer food options for birds, given the lack of perch fish, making the chameleon a more appealing food option. In order to avoid being eaten in the steppe and desert, the chameleons would need to remain hidden as well as possible.

6. (C) The ACT has said that it is moving more toward integrating concepts about statistics, so don't be alarmed if you see a question like this. Since the new scientist will have twice as many samples, she would have more data to help estimate the likely relationship between mean color change and mean contrast to vegetation. The question states that these two things are positively correlated, which means that the data gathered under a well-constructed experiment will show that mean color change and mean contrast to vegetation are correlated. This more plentiful data, since it would be gathered under well-designed conditions, should therefore come closer to a "best-fit" line, making the value of the R^2 move higher. As R^2 moves higher in accuracy, it would be most reasonable to put it between 0.33 and 1.00, since it would show more correlation than the current experiment, but would be very unlikely to show 100% of the correlation, as having a 1.00 R^2 would demand. dence against the possibility of a catastrophe.

Tough Passage 3

Two physics students were challenged by their teacher to design a hypothetical experiment that could demonstrate the feasibility of "time travel." Experiment 1 Student 1 conceived an experiment in which a space shuttle leaves Earth in the year 2999 and arrives near the center of the Milky Way galaxy 12 years later. The shuttle orbits a supermassive black hole, traveling at 55% the speed of light for 5 years. According to general relativity, the shuttle must remain outside the black hole's "event horizon"—a boundary beyond which light cannot escape the black hole's gravitational force. The shuttle's orbit is illustrated in Figure 1. Based on the theory of time dilation, which is summarized in Figure 2, the student predicts that when the shuttle returns to Earth, its crew will have traveled roughly six years forward in time.

411

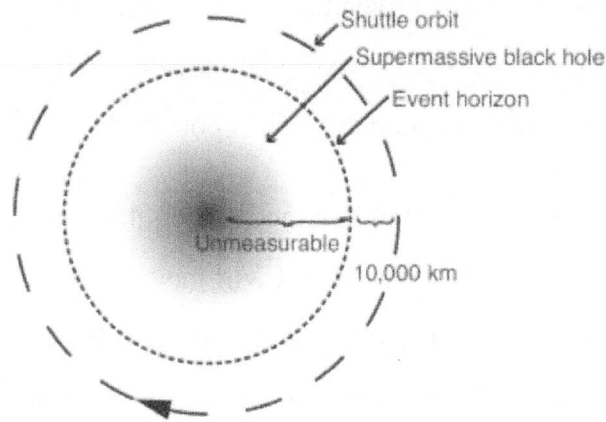

Figure 1

$$t' = \frac{t_0}{\sqrt{1 - \dfrac{v^2}{c^2}}}$$

t' = time observed from external inertial reference frame (Earth)

t_0 = time observed from traveler's reference frame (shuttle)

v = speed of moving object (shuttle and crew)

c = speed of light in a vacuum (approximately 3.00×10^8 m/s)

Figure 2

Experiment 2 The second student conceived of a series of "light cones." A light cone is a way to visualize the potential movement of an object through space and time based on its position in the present. Because nothing can travel faster than the speed of light, an object located in position p at time t0 can only move to locations within c(t1 – t0) in time t1 . All future potential locations of the object are, thus, contained within its light cone, and the actual path it travels is described as its "worldline." A basic light cone and worldline for an object are illustrated in Figure 3. Further, Student 2 noted that general relativity allows both time and space to be bent by gravity. Figure 4 illustrates light cones that curve along a time-like geodesic.

412

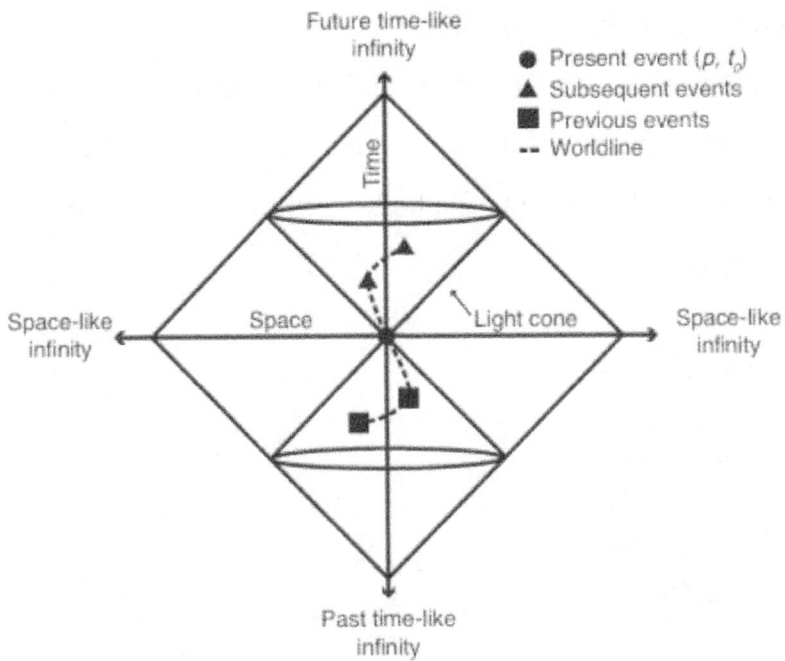

Figure 3

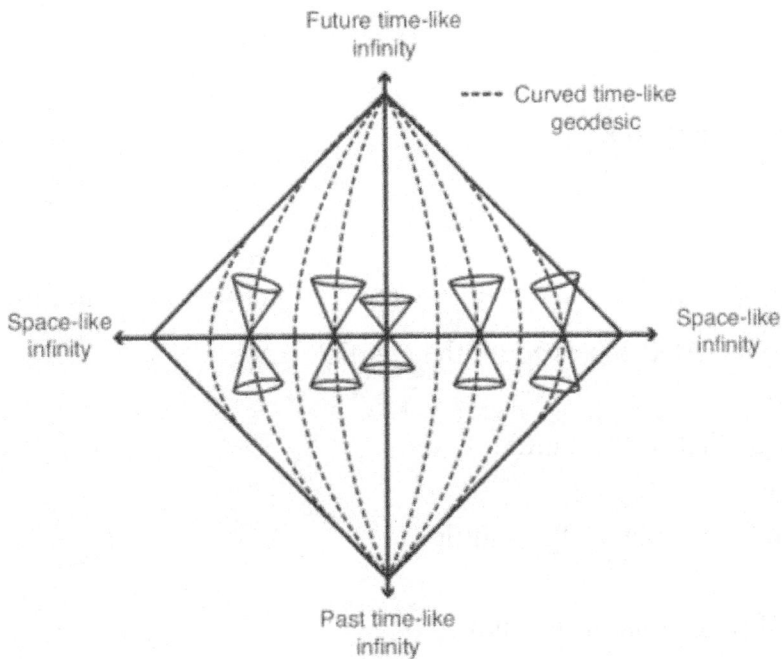

Figure 4

In extreme gravitational conditions, such as those within the event horizon of a black hole, the student theorized that centrifugal force could bend an inertial frame so strongly that its light cone shifts a full 45° in the circumferential direction, producing a "closed time-like curve," with light cones oriented toward every point within the critical orbit. The student posited that, if a shuttle were to begin in the center of orbit and travel outward to the closed time-like curve, the shuttle could then move freely backward or forward in time before returning to the center of orbit. Such a system is illustrated in Figure 5.

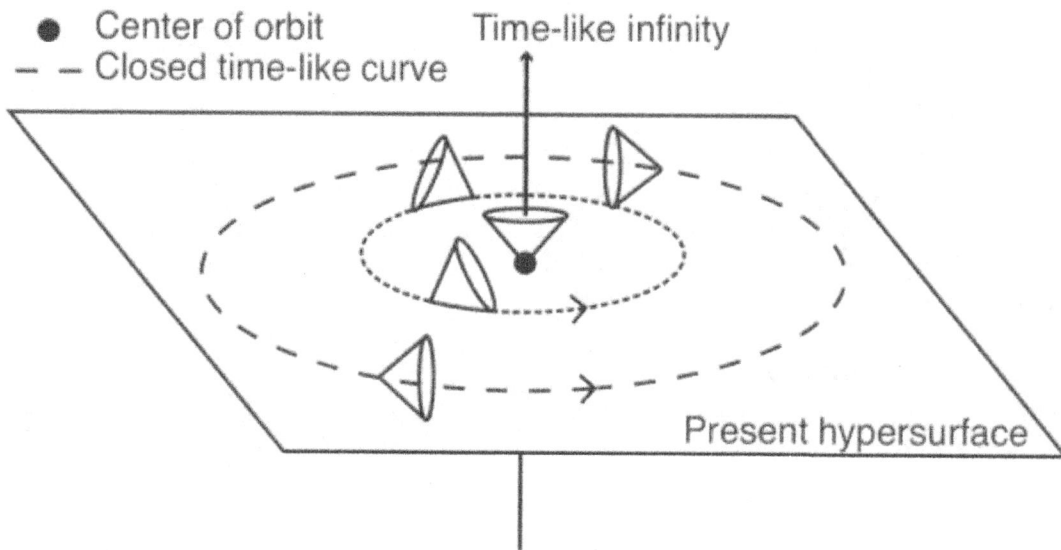

Figure 5

1. Based on the information in Figure 2, if the space shuttle were stationary, how would the time observed on Earth compare to the time observed on the shuttle?

A. The time on Earth would be twice that of the shuttle.

B. The time on Earth would be four times that of the shuttle.

C. The time on Earth would be half times that of the shuttle.

D. The times would be equivalent.

2. In Experiment 1, while orbiting the supermassive black hole, approximately how quickly is the space shuttle traveling?

A. 1.25×108 m/s

B. 1.65×108 m/s

C. 2.35×108 m/s

D. 3.00×108 m/s

3. Based on the assumptions of Experiment 1, in what year should the shuttle's crew arrive back on Earth?

A. 3024

B. 3023

C. 3034

D. There is not enough information provided to make a prediction.

4. In Figure 3, which of the following gives the best reason why the object is prohibited from moving laterally with a zero-slope?

A. The object cannot move through space without also moving through time.

B. The object cannot move through space faster than the speed of light.

C. The object cannot move backward in time.

D. The object cannot deviate from its worldline.

5. In Experiment 2, what does the "light cone" represent?

A. The direction in which light is emitted through space in a vacuum

B. The positional boundary for an object's movement set by the speed of light

C. The maximum curvature along a time-like geodesic

D. The curvature of time as dictated by general relativity

6. What premise makes the measurement of Experiment 2 particularly impractical in comparison to Experiment 1?

A. It requires extreme gravitational conditions.

B. It requires time intervals of space travel significantly longer than a natural human life.

C. It allows that it is possible to travel forward in time.

D. It requires a shuttle to travel within the event horizon of a black hole.

Answers

1. (D) Since the shuttle would be stationary, the value of v in the equation in Figure 2 would be zero. Because of this, the value of t ′ and t0 would be equivalent.

2. (B) According to the second sentence of Experiment 1, the shuttle is traveling at 55% of the speed of light. Figure 2 states that the speed of light is 3.00×108 m/s. 55% of this would be 1.65×108 m/s. Even though you won't have a calculator at your disposal when taking the ACT, you can estimate this by realizing that 55% will be slightly more than half of 3.00×108 m/s. Since half of 3 is 1.5, and 1.65 is slightly more than 1.5, this option makes sense.

3. (C) The journey begins in the year 2999, and it takes 12 years to go to the black hole. The shuttle travels for 5 years around the black hole and travels forward 6 years in time while doing so. Then, the shuttle takes 12 years to travel back to Earth. Therefore, the crew would arrive back on Earth in the year 3034 because $2999 + 12 + 5 + 6 + 12 = 3034$.

4. (A) If the object were to have a lateral (horizontal) slope of zero, then it would be able to move through the dimension of space without also moving through time. (A) directly contradicts this possibility, while the other options are not relevant.

5. (B) The passage directly states that "all future potential locations of the object are thus contained within its light cone." This is best paraphrased by (B), since all future potential

locations of the object would be limited by the physical restraint of the speed of light. The other options do not provide satisfactory and relevant paraphrasing of the information in the passage.

6. (D) Experiment 2 would have the shuttle enter within the event horizon of the black hole, while Experiment 1 would have the shuttle remain outside of it. Since the event horizon is "a boundary beyond which light cannot escape the black hole's gravitational force," being within its bounds would surely result in impractical gravitational conditions. It is not (A) because both experiments would involve extreme gravitation, being in the vicinity of a black hole. It is not (B) because the lengths of time are not longer than a typical human lifespan. (C) is an assumption shared by both experiments.

SCIENCE STRATEGY SUMMARY

- The ACT Science is a 35-minute test with six or seven passages.
- Virtually everything you need to figure out the questions will be right in front of you.
- Spend about 9 minutes for every 10 questions, and guess on the last question of each passage if you need to save time.
- Look at the graphs first, then use the reading as needed (except on the Conflicting Viewpoints).
- Really understand the questions by coasting, pointing, and writing.
- Don't overthink the early questions within a passage and don't underthink the later questions within a passage, since the questions gradually become more difficult within a passage.

Full-Length Practice Test 10 (Writing Test)

The Ethics of Artificial Intelligence

Artificial intelligence (AI) is rapidly transforming our world, permeating various aspects of our lives, from healthcare and education to transportation and entertainment. While AI offers tremendous potential benefits, such as increased efficiency, improved decision-making, and personalized experiences, it also raises ethical concerns that demand careful consideration. Some people argue that AI should be developed and deployed with caution, emphasizing the potential risks to privacy, autonomy, and fairness, while others believe that the benefits of AI outweigh the risks and that its development should be accelerated.

Read and carefully evaluate these points of view. Each puts forth a specific way of thinking about the ethics of AI development and deployment.

Viewpoint 1: AI should be developed and deployed with caution, prioritizing human well-being and ethical considerations.

Viewpoint 2: The benefits of AI outweigh the risks, and its development should be accelerated to maximize its potential for solving global challenges.

Viewpoint 3: AI should be treated as a tool, and its ethical implications depend on how it is used and governed.

ESSAY ASSIGNMENT

Compose a focused essay in which you consider multiple viewpoints on the ethics of artificial intelligence. In your response, be certain to:

- express your own point of view on the topic, and analyze the relationship between your point of view and at least one of the viewpoints provided.
- use reasoning and examples to make your argument.
- write in an organized, logical way.
- communicate effectively using the conventions of standard written English.

Your viewpoint may completely agree, somewhat agree, or not agree at all with any of those presented.

Planning Your Response

Your prewriting notes on this page will not be considered in your score.

Use the following space to brainstorm ideas and map out your response. You may want to think about the following as you analyze the given prompt:

- **Strengths and weaknesses of the three viewpoints**
    - What good points do they make, and what potential objections do they ignore?
    - Why might they be convincing to readers, and why might their perspectives fall short?
- **Your previous experience, background knowledge, and personal values**
    - What is your viewpoint on this topic, and what are the pros and cons of this viewpoint?
    - How will you craft an argument in support of your point of view?

Act Test Day Strategies

The ACT is a crucial step in the college application process, and performing your best on test day requires more than just extensive studying. While thorough preparation is essential, it's equally important to have a well-thought-out plan for managing your time, handling stress, and making the most of the last few minutes before the test. This chapter delves into these crucial test-day strategies, providing you with a comprehensive guide to maximizing your performance on the ACT.

Time Management Tips

Understanding the Importance of Time Management

Time management is critical on the ACT, as you'll need to work efficiently to complete each section within the allotted time. Effective time management not only helps you answer all the questions but also allows you to maintain focus and reduce stress.

Strategies for Managing Time Effectively

1. *Wear a Watch*: Keep track of your pace by wearing a watch that doesn't have any internet connectivity or alarm functions. This allows you to stay aware of the time without getting distracted.

2. *Write Down Key Times at the Beginning of Each Section*: Before starting each section, jot down the times at which you should ideally be finishing specific portions. This helps you maintain a consistent pace and avoid rushing or getting stuck on individual questions.

3. *Skip Questions You Can't Answer Quickly*: If a question seems too time-consuming, skip it and move on to those you can answer more efficiently. Remember, all questions are worth the same number of points, so prioritize those you can solve readily.

4.   *Guess on Questions You Don't Know*: There's no penalty for guessing on the ACT. If you're unsure of an answer, make an educated guess and move on. Don't leave any questions blank.

5.   *Use Your Time Wisely During Breaks*: The ACT includes short breaks between sections. Use this time to relax, have a snack, and use the restroom. Avoid discussing the test with others, as this can increase anxiety.

Section-Specific Time Management

English:

- Pace yourself at approximately nine minutes per passage or fifteen minutes for every twenty-five questions.
- If running short on time, guess on the more time-consuming questions, typically those with a written question at the end of passages.
- If you have ample time, consider reading each passage in its entirety before answering the questions to gain a better understanding of the context.

Mathematics:

- Determine a realistic goal score and focus on completing that number of questions accurately.
- If aiming to complete all questions, spend twenty-five minutes on the first thirty and thirty-five minutes on the last thirty.
- If prone to rushing, start by guessing on some of the last questions, as they tend to be more challenging.
- If prone to getting stuck, plan to have some "throwaway" questions that you'll guess on immediately to avoid wasting time.

Reading:

- For most students, reading the passage before answering the questions is recommended.

- If you're a fast reader, aim for nine minutes per passage, including reading and answering questions.

- If you're a slower reader, consider doing three passages thoroughly and guessing on the fourth.

- If you struggle with reading comprehension, go directly to the questions and spend a little under a minute per question.

Science:

- Aim for approximately nine minutes for every ten questions.

- If you're a slower reader, consider skipping the Conflicting Viewpoints passage, as it requires more reading.

- Look at the graphs first, then read the passage as needed to clarify any confusing information.

Stress Reduction Techniques

Understanding the Impact of Stress

Stress can significantly hinder your performance on the ACT. High levels of stress can lead to a lack of focus, difficulty recalling information, and an increase in careless mistakes. Therefore, it's crucial to have strategies in place to manage stress before and during the test.

Techniques for Reducing Stress

1. *Practice Under Realistic Conditions*: Simulate the test-day environment during your practice sessions. This helps you become accustomed to the time constraints and pressure, reducing anxiety on the actual test day.

2. *Don't Cram*: Avoid last-minute cramming, as this can increase stress and make it harder to recall information. Instead, focus on consistent, long-term preparation.

3. *Get Enough Sleep*: Ensure you get adequate sleep in the nights leading up to the test. A well-rested mind performs better under pressure and is less prone to stress.

4.   *Use Relaxation Techniques*: Practice relaxation techniques such as deep breathing or meditation to calm your mind before and during the test.

5.   *Stay Positive*: Maintain a positive attitude throughout the test. Remind yourself of your preparation and focus on your strengths.

6.   *Don't Compare Yourself to Others*: Avoid comparing your pace or performance to those around you. Focus on your own test and your individual strategies.

7.   *Take Breaks*: Utilize the breaks between sections to relax and clear your mind. Step away from your desk, stretch, and take deep breaths to reduce stress.

Last-Minute Review

The Importance of Targeted Review

While last-minute cramming is discouraged, a targeted review of key concepts can be beneficial. Focus on areas where you feel less confident and review essential formulas or grammar rules.

Strategies for Effective Last-Minute Review

1.   *Review Chapter Summaries*: Skim through the chapter summaries in your study guide to refresh your memory on important concepts and strategies.

2.   *Focus on Weak Areas*: Identify specific areas where you need a confidence boost and review those concepts in more detail.

3.   *Look Over the Diagnostic Test*: Quickly review the diagnostic test to familiarize yourself with the format and types of questions you'll encounter.

4.   *Try a Few Practice Problems*: If time permits, attempt a few practice problems in your weaker areas to reinforce your understanding.

5.   *Avoid New Material*: Don't try to learn new concepts or strategies at the last minute, as this can lead to confusion and anxiety.

Test-day strategies are as crucial as your preparation in determining your ACT performance. By managing your time effectively, reducing stress, and engaging in targeted last-minute review, you can maximize your potential and achieve your desired score. Remember, the ACT is just one step in your academic journey, and your performance doesn't define your worth. Approach the test with confidence, focus on your strengths, and do your best.

Conclusion: Achieving Your ACT Goals

Congratulations on making it to the end of this comprehensive ACT study guide! You've undoubtedly invested a significant amount of time and effort in preparing for this crucial exam, and you're well on your way to achieving your academic goals.

Reflecting on Your Progress

Take a moment to reflect on the journey you've undertaken. You've delved into the intricacies of grammar, explored the complexities of mathematical concepts, honed your reading comprehension skills, and navigated the challenges of scientific reasoning. You've learned valuable strategies, practiced with realistic test questions, and gained a deeper understanding of the ACT format.

Maintaining Momentum

As you approach the final stages of your preparation, it's essential to maintain momentum and stay focused on your goals. Continue practicing with the strategies you've learned, and don't hesitate to revisit challenging concepts or sections.

The Power of Self-Reflection

Self-reflection is a potent tool in maximizing your potential. Take some time to assess your strengths and weaknesses, identify areas where you need further practice, and adjust your study plan accordingly.

Embracing a Growth Mindset

A growth mindset is crucial in achieving your ACT goals. Embrace challenges as opportunities for growth, view setbacks as learning experiences, and believe in your ability to improve.[1]

Seeking Support

Don't hesitate to seek support from teachers, tutors, or peers. They can provide valuable guidance, answer your questions, and offer encouragement.

The Importance of Self-Care

Remember, your well-being is as important as your academic pursuits. Ensure you get adequate sleep, maintain a healthy diet, and engage in activities that help you relax and de-stress.

Visualizing Success

Visualization is a powerful technique in achieving your goals. Imagine yourself performing confidently on the ACT, answering questions with ease, and achieving your desired score.

The Power of Positive Affirmations

Positive affirmations can reinforce your belief in your abilities. Repeat phrases such as, "I am well-prepared for the ACT," or "I am confident in my ability to succeed."

The ACT: A Stepping Stone

Remember, the ACT is just one step in your academic journey. Your score doesn't define your worth or potential. Approach the exam with confidence, focus on your strengths, and do your best.

Looking Ahead

Beyond the ACT, envision the exciting opportunities that await you. Imagine yourself pursuing your passions, contributing to society, and making a positive impact on the world.

The Journey of Learning

Embrace the journey of learning, and never stop seeking knowledge and growth. The skills and strategies you've acquired while preparing for the ACT will serve you well throughout your academic career and beyond.

Believe in Yourself

Believe in yourself, your abilities, and your potential to achieve great things. The ACT is just one milestone in a journey full of exciting possibilities.

As you embark on this next chapter of your academic journey, remember the valuable lessons you've learned, the challenges you've overcome, and the growth you've achieved. The ACT is a stepping stone, and you're well-equipped to navigate the path ahead. Congratulations on your dedication, your hard work, and your commitment to achieving your ACT goals!

ONLINE PRACTICE QUIZ

Scan the QR code below to access the online practice quiz

How to scan the QR code:

1. Open your phone's camera app. Most smartphones have QR code scanning built-in.

2. Point your camera at the QR code. Make sure the entire code is visible in the viewfinder.

3. Hold your phone steady. This helps the camera focus and read the code. You might need to adjust the distance slightly.

4. Wait for the magic! Your phone should automatically recognize the QR code and display a notification or a link.

5. Tap the notification or link. This will take you to the website, app, or information linked to the QR code.